iPhone® 4S

PORTABLE GENIUS

iPhone® 4S
PORTABLE GENIUS

by Paul McFedries

WILEY

John Wiley & Sons, Inc.

iPhone® 4S Portable Genius

Published by
John Wiley & Sons, Inc.
10475 Crosspoint Blvd.
Indianapolis, IN 46256
www.wiley.com

Copyright © 2012 by John Wiley & Sons, Inc., Indianapolis, Indiana

Published simultaneously in Canada

ISBN: 978-1-118-09384-9

Manufactured in the United States of America

10 9 8 7 6 5 4 3 2 1

For general information on our other products and services or to obtain technical support, please contact our Customer Care Department within the U.S. at (877) 762-2974, outside the U.S. at (317) 572-3993 or fax (317) 572-4002.

John Wiley & Sons, Inc. also publishes its books in a variety of electronic formats and by print-on-demand. Some content that appears in standard print versions of this book may not be available in other formats. For more information about Wiley products, visit us at www.wiley.com.

Library of Congress Control Number is available from the publisher.

WILEY

About the Author

Paul McFedries is a full-time technical writer. Paul has been authoring computer books since 1991 and has more than 70 books to his credit. Paul's books have sold more than four million copies worldwide. These books include the Wiley titles *iPad 2 Portable Genius; Macs Portable Genius Second Edition; MacBook Air Portable Genius Third Edition; Switching to a Mac Portable Genius Second Edition; Teach Yourself VISUALLY Macs Second Edition; Twitter Tips, Tricks, and Tweets Second Edition;* and *The Facebook Guide for People Over 50.* Paul is also the proprietor of Word Spy (www.wordspy.com), a website that tracks new words and phrases as they enter the English language. Paul encourages everyone to drop by his personal website at www.mcfedries.com, or to follow him on Twitter at www.twitter.com/paulmcf and www.twitter.com/wordspy.

Credits

Senior Acquisitions Editor
Stephanie McComb

Project Editor
Kristin Vorce

Technical Editor
John Smith

Copy Editor
Marylouise Wiack

Editorial Director
Robyn Siesky

Business Manager
Amy Knies

Senior Marketing Manager
Sandy Smith

Vice President and Executive Group Publisher
Richard Swadley

Vice President and Executive Publisher
Barry Pruett

Project Coordinator
Patrick Redmond

Graphics and Production Specialists
Andrea Hornberger

Quality Control Technician
Melanie Hoffman

Proofreading and Indexing
Laura Bowman
Potomac Indexing, LLC

For Karen.

Acknowledgments

Another year, another iPhone, and another edition of *iPhone Portable Genius*. I enjoy working on this book so much that I almost look forward to writing the new book more than using the new phone (almost!). Why? For starters, it's just pure fun to write about what's new and noteworthy in the new iPhone, particularly the lesser-known features that can make your life easier and more efficient. More than that, however, I get to work with a great bunch of professionals at Wiley. There's a list of all the people who contributed to the making of this book a couple of pages back, and I extend a hearty thanks to all of them for their hard work and competence. A few of those people I had the pleasure of working with directly, including Senior Acquisitions Editor Stephanie McComb, Project Editor Kristin Vorce, and Copy Editor Marylouise Wiack. Many thanks to each of you for the skill, professionalism, sense of humor, and general niceness that made my job infinitely easier and made this a better book.

Contents

chapter 2

How Do I Connect My iPhone to a Network?   42

chapter 3

How Can I Get More Out of the Phone App?   60

chapter 4

How Can I Make the Most of
iPhone Web Surfing?

chapter 5

How Do I Maximize iPhone
E-mail?

How Do I Synchronize My iPhone? 128

chapter 7

How Can I Get More Out of My
iPhone's Audio Features?

chapter 9

How Can I Use My iPhone to Manage
Contacts and Appointments?   224

Introduction

The iPhone is a success not because well over 100 million of them have been sold (or, I should say, not *only* because well over 100 million of them have been sold; that's a lot of phones!), but because the iPhone, in just a few years, has reached the status of a cultural icon. Even people who don't care much for gadgets in general and cell phones in particular know about the iPhone. And for those of us who *do* care about gadgets, the iPhone elicits a kind of technological longing that can only be satisfied in one way: by *buying* one (or, as in my case, by buying five).

Part of the iconic status of the iPhone comes from its gorgeous design and remarkable interface, which makes all the standard tasks — surfing, e-mailing, texting, scheduling, playing — easy and intuitive. But just as an attractive face or an easygoing manner can hide a personality of complexity and depth, so too does the iPhone hide many of its most useful and interesting features.

When you want to get beyond the basics of iPhone and solve some of its riddles, you might consider making an appointment with the Genius Bar at your local Apple Store. More often than not, the on-duty genius gives you good advice on how to get your iPhone to do what you want it to do. The Genius Bar is a great thing, but it isn't always a convenient thing. In some cases, you may even need to leave your iPhone for a while (No!) to get the problem checked out and, hopefully, resolved.

What you really need is a version of the Genius Bar that's easier to access, more convenient, and doesn't require tons of time or leaving your iPhone in the hands of a stranger. What you really need is a *portable* genius that enables you to be more productive and solve problems — wherever you and your iPhone happen to be.

Welcome, therefore, to *iPhone 4S Portable Genius*. This book is like a mini Genius Bar all wrapped up in an easy-to-use, easy-to-access, and eminently portable format. In this book, you learn how to get more out of your iPhone by learning how to access all the really powerful and timesaving features that aren't obvious at a casual glance. In this book, you learn about all of the amazing new things you can do using the iPhone 4S and iOS 5.0, including using Siri, syncing over Wi-Fi, AirPlay mirroring, using the Notification Center, editing photos, creating reminders, integrating Twitter, using iCloud, and much more. In this book, you learn how to prevent iPhone problems from occurring and (just in case your preventative measures are for naught) how to fix many common problems yourself.

This book is for iPhone users who know the basics but want to take their iPhone education to a higher level. It's a book for people who want to be more productive, more efficient, more creative, and more self-sufficient (at least as far as the iPhone goes). It's a book for people who use their iPhone every day, but would like to incorporate it into more of their day-to-day activities. It's a book I had a blast writing, so I think it's a book you'll enjoy reading.

How Do I Configure My iPhone?

The iPhone is justly famous for its stylish, curvaceous design and its slick, effortless touchscreen. However, although good looks and ease of use are important for any smartphone, it's what you do with that phone that's important. The iPhone helps by offering lots of features, but chances are those features aren't set up to suit the way you work. Maybe your most-used Home screen icons aren't at the top of the screen where they should be, or perhaps your iPhone goes to sleep too soon. This chapter shows you how to configure your iPhone to solve these and many other annoyances so the phone works the way you do.

Customizing the Home Screen to Suit Your Style

The Home screen is your starting point for all things iPhone, and what could be simpler? Just tap the icon you want, and the app loads lickety-split. Ah, but things are never so simple, are they? In fact, there are a couple of hairs in the Home screen soup:

- The icons in the top row are a bit easier to find and a bit easier to tap.

- If you have more than 16 icons, they extend onto a second (or third or fourth) Home screen. If the app you want isn't on the main Home screen, you must first flick to the screen that has the app's icon (or tap its dot) and then tap the icon.

- If your icons extend onto multiple Home screens, the four icons in the iPhone Dock appear on every Home screen, so they're always available.

Note

How do you end up with more than 16 icons? Easy: the App Store. This is an online retailer solely devoted to apps designed to work with iPhone technologies: multi-touch, GPS, the accelerometer, wireless, and more. You can download apps via your cellular network or your Wi-Fi connection, so you can always get apps when you need them. I discuss the App Store a bit later in this chapter.

You can make the Home screen more efficient by moving your four most-used icons to the iPhone Dock and by moving four other often-used icons to the top row of the main Home screen. You can do all this by rearranging the Home screen icons as follows:

1. **Display the Home screen.**

2. **Tap and hold any Home screen icon.** When you see the icons wiggling, release your finger.

3. **Tap and drag the icons into the positions you prefer.** To move an icon to a different screen, tap and drag it to the left edge of the current screen if you want to move it to a previous screen, or to the right edge if you want to move it to a later screen. Next, wait for the new screen to appear and then drop the icon where you want it.

4. **Rearrange the existing Dock icons by dragging them left or right to change the order.**

5. **To replace a Dock icon, first tap and drag the icon off the Dock to create some space.** Then, tap and drag any Home screen icon into the Dock.

6. **Press the Home button.** Your iPhone saves the new icon arrangement.

Genius

The icons in the Home screen's menu bar are also fair game. That is, you can drag them left and right to change the order, and you can replace the menu bar icons with any other Home screen icons. For the latter, set the icons jiggling, and then tap and drag an icon off the menu bar to create some space. Now tap and drag any Home screen icon into the menu bar.

Creating an app folder

The best way to make the main Home screen more manageable is to reduce the total number of icons you have to work with. This isn't a problem when you're just starting out with your iPhone, because out of the box it comes with only a limited number of apps. However, the addictive nature of the App Store almost always means that you end up with screen after screen of apps. In fact, the iPhone lets you use a maximum of 11 screens. If you fill each screen to the brim — that's 16 apps per screen — you end up with a total of 180 icons (including the four Dock icons). That's a lot of icons.

Now, when I tell you to reduce the number of icons on the Home screens, I don't mean that you should delete apps. Too drastic! Instead, you can take advantage of a great feature called *app folders*. Just like a folder on your hard drive, which can store multiple files, an app folder can store multiple (up to 16) app icons. This enables you to group related apps together under a single icon, which not only reduces your overall Home screen clutter, but can also make individual apps easier to find.

Here are the steps to follow to create and populate an app folder:

1. **Navigate to the Home screen that contains at least one of the apps you want to include in your folder.**

2. **Tap and hold any icon until you see all the icons wiggling.**

3. **Tap and drag an icon that you want to include in the folder, and drop it on another icon that you want to include in the same folder.** Your iPhone creates the folder and displays a text box so that you can name it. The default name is the underlying category used by the apps, as shown in Figure 1.1. If the apps are in different categories, your iPhone uses the category of the app you dragged and dropped.

1.1 Drop one app icon on another to create an app folder.

4. **Tap inside the text box to edit the name, if you feel like it, and tap Done when you finish.**

5. **Press the Home button.** Your iPhone saves your new icon arrangement.

Use the following techniques to work with your app folders:

● **To add another app to the folder, tap and drag the app icon and drop it on the folder.**

● **To launch an app, tap the folder to open it (see Figure 1.2) and tap the app.**

● **To rename a folder or rearrange the apps within a folder, tap the folder to open it.** Then, tap and hold any app icon within the folder. You can then edit the folder name, or drag and drop the apps within the folder.

● **To remove an app from a folder, tap the folder to open it.** Tap and hold any app icon within the folder, then drag it out of the folder.

1.2 Tap an app folder to reveal its icons.

Adding a Safari web clip to the Home screen

Do you have a web page that you visit all the time? If so, you can set up that page as a bookmark in the iPhone Safari browser, but there's an even faster way to access it: add it to the Home screen as a web clip icon. A *web clip* is a link to a page that preserves that page's scroll position and zoom level. For example, suppose a page has a form at the bottom. To use that form, you have to navigate to the page, scroll to the bottom, and then zoom in to see it better. However, you can perform all three actions — navigate, scroll, and zoom — automatically with a web clip.

Follow these steps to save a page as a web clip icon on the Home screen:

1. **Use the Safari browser on your iPhone to navigate to the page you want to save.**

2. **Scroll to the portion of the page you want to see.**

3. **Pinch and spread your fingers over the area you want to zoom in on until you can comfortably read the text.**

4. **Tap the Actions icon (the arrow) at the bottom of the screen.** iPhone displays a list of actions.

5. **Tap Add to Home Screen.** iPhone prompts you to edit the web clip name, as shown in Figure 1.3.

6. **Edit the name as needed.** Names up to about 10 to 14 characters display on the Home screen without being broken. The fewer uppercase letters you use, the longer the name can be. For longer names, iPhone displays the first and last few characters (depending on the locations of spaces in the name) separated by an ellipsis (...). For example, if the name is My Home Page, it appears in the Home screen as My Ho...Page.

1.3 You can edit the web clip name before adding the icon to the Home screen.

7. **Tap Add.** iPhone adds the web clip to the Home screen and displays the Home screen. If your main Home screen is already filled to the brim with icons, iPhone adds the web clip to the first screen that has space available. Figure 1.4 shows a Home screen with a web clip added.

— Web clip

1.4 The web clip has been added to the Home screen.

Genius

To delete a web clip from the Home screen, tap and hold any Home screen icon until the icon dance begins. Each web clip icon displays an X in the upper-left corner. Tap the X of the web clip you want to remove. When iPhone asks you to confirm, tap Delete, and then press the Home button to save the configuration.

Resetting the default Home screen layout

If you make a bit of a mess of your Home screen, or if someone else is going to be using your iPhone, you can reset the Home screen icons to their default layout. Follow these steps:

1. **On the Home screen, tap Settings.** The Settings app appears.

2. **Tap General.** The General screen appears.

3. **Scroll down and tap Reset.** The Reset screen appears.

4. **Tap Reset Home Screen Layout.** iPhone warns you that the Home screen will be reset to the factory default layout.

5. **Tap Reset Home Screen.** iPhone resets the Home screen to the default layout, but it doesn't delete the icons for any apps you've added.

Working with App Notifications

Lots of apps take advantage of an iOS feature called *notifications,* which enables them to send messages and other data to your iPhone. For example, the Facebook app displays an alert on your iPhone when a friend sends you a message. Similarly, the Foursquare app, which lets you track where your friends are located, sends you a message when a friend checks in at a particular location.

If an app supports notifications, then the first time you start it, your iPhone usually displays a message like the one shown in Figure 1.5, asking if you want to allow push notifications for the app. Tap OK if you're cool with that; if you're not, tap Don't Allow.

There are actually four kinds of push notifications:

- **Sound.** This is a sound effect that plays when some app-related event occurs.

- **Alert.** This is a message that pops up on your iPhone screen. You must then tap a button to dismiss the message before you can continue working with your current app.

- **Banner.** This is a message that appears at the top of the screen, as shown in Figure 1.6. Unlike an alert, a banner allows you to keep using your current app and disappears automatically after a few seconds. If you prefer to switch to the app to view the message, tap the banner. Banners are a new feature in iOS 5.

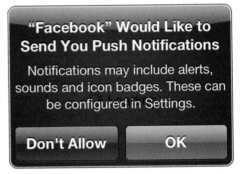

1.5 Your iPhone lets you allow or disallow push notifications for an app.

1.6 iOS 5 can display alert notifications as banners that appear at the top of the screen.

- **Badge.** This is a small, red icon that appears in the upper-right corner of an app icon. The icon usually displays a number, which might be the number of messages you have waiting for you on the server.

Displaying the Notification Center

If you miss an alert or banner, or if you see a banner but ignore it, you can still eyeball your recent notification messages by displaying the Notification Center. This is a new iOS 5 feature that combines all your recent alerts and banners in one handy location. So, not only can you see the most recent alert (as you could in previous versions of iOS), but you can also see the last few so you don't miss anything.

Even better, displaying the Notification Center is a snap — just swipe down from the top of the screen. As you can see in Figure 1.7, the Notification Center displays your recent messages sorted by app. From here, you can either tap an item to switch to that app, or tap elsewhere on the screen to hide the Notification Center.

Customizing notifications

For each app, your iPhone also lets you toggle individual notification types (sounds, alerts, and badges), switch between banner and alert messages, or remove an app from the Notification Center altogether. You can also configure app notifications to appear in the Lock screen, as shown in Figure 1.8. This is handy because you can see your notifications without having to unlock your iPhone.

1.7 Swipe down from the top of the screen to display the Notification Center.

Here's how to configure app notifications:

1. **On the Home screen, tap Settings.** The Settings app appears.

2. **Tap Notifications.** The Notifications screen appears.

3. **Tap the app you want to customize.** The app notification settings appear. Figure 1.9 shows the settings for the Game Center app. Note that not all apps support all possible settings.

4. **To remove the app from the Notification Center, tap the Notification Center switch to Off.**

5. **To set the maximum number of app messages that appear on the Notification Center, tap Show and then tap the number of messages.**

6. **In the Alert Style section, tap the style you prefer for message notifications.** Tap None to turn off alerts, or tap the style you want: Banners or Alerts.

7. **If the app supports badges, use the Badge App Icon switch to toggle this type of notification on or off.**

8. **If the app supports sounds, use the Sounds switch (not shown in Figure 1.9) to toggle this type of notification on or off.**

9. **Use the View in Lock Screen switch (not shown in Figure 1.9) to toggle whether the app's notifications appear in the iPhone Lock screen.**

1.8 App notifications can appear in the iPhone Lock screen.

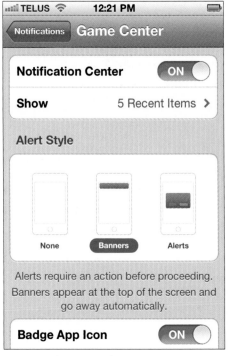

1.9 Use each app's notification settings to control notifications on your iPhone.

10. **Tap Notifications to return to the Notifications screen.**

11. **Repeat Steps 3 to 10 to customize each app.**

More Useful iPhone Configuration Techniques

You've seen quite a few handy iPhone customization tricks so far, but you're not done yet — not by a long shot. The next few sections take you through a few more heart-warmingly useful iPhone customization techniques.

Turning sounds on and off

Your iPhone is often a noisy little thing that makes all manner of rings, beeps, and boops, seemingly at the slightest provocation. Consider a short list of the events that can give the iPhone's lungs a workout:

- Incoming calls
- Incoming e-mail messages
- Outgoing e-mail messages
- Incoming text messages
- New voicemail messages
- Calendar alerts
- Locking and unlocking the phone
- Tapping the keys on the on-screen keyboard

What a racket! None of this may bother you when you're on your own, but if you're in a meeting, at a movie, or anywhere else where extraneous sounds are unwelcome, you might want to turn off some (or all) of the iPhone sound effects.

First, you should know that when a call comes in and you press the Sleep/Wake button once, your iPhone silences the ringer. That's a sweet and useful feature, but the problem is that it may take you one or two rings before you can dig out your iPhone and press Sleep/Wake. By that time, folks nearby are already glaring at you.

To prevent this faux pas, you can switch your iPhone into silent mode, which means it doesn't ring, and it doesn't play any alerts or sound effects. When the sound is turned off, the only alarms that

11

are audible are the ones you've set using the Clock app. The phone still vibrates unless you also turn this feature off. You switch the iPhone between ring and silent modes using the Ring/Silent switch, which is located on the left side panel of the iPhone, near the top. Use the following techniques to switch between silent and ring modes:

- **To put the phone in silent mode, flick the Ring/Silent switch toward the back of the phone.** You see an orange bar on the switch and the iPhone screen displays a bell with a slash through it. Your iPhone is now in silent mode.

- **To resume the normal ring mode, flick the Ring/Silent switch toward the front of the phone.** The iPhone screen displays a bell and your iPhone is now in normal ring mode.

If silent mode is a bit too drastic, you can control exactly which sounds your iPhone utters by following these steps:

1. **On the Home screen, tap Settings.** The Settings app appears.

2. **Tap Sounds.** The Sounds screen appears.

3. **In the Silent section, the Vibrate setting determines whether iPhone vibrates when the phone is in silent mode.** Vibrating is a good idea in silent mode, so On is a good choice here.

4. **In the Ringer and Alerts section, drag the Volume slider to set the volume of the ringtone that plays when a call comes in.**

5. **To lock the ringer volume, tap the Change with Buttons switch to Off.** This means that pressing the Volume buttons on the side of the iPhone will have no effect on the ringer volume.

Genius

Locking the ringer volume is a good idea because it prevents one of the major iPhone frustrations: missing a call because the ringer volume has been muted accidentally (for example, by your iPhone getting jostled in a purse or pocket).

6. **Use the Vibrate setting to determine whether iPhone vibrates when the phone is in ring mode.** Vibrating probably isn't all that important in ring mode, so feel free to change this setting to Off. The exception is if you reduce and/or lock the ringer volume (see Steps 4 and 5), in which case setting Vibrate to On might help you notice an incoming call.

7. **To set a different default ringtone, tap Ringtone to open the Ringtone screen.** Tap the ringtone you want to use (iPhone plays a preview), and then tap Sounds to return to the Sounds screen.

8. **To set a different incoming text message sound, tap Text Tone to open the Text Tone screen.** Tap the sound effect you want to use (iPhone plays a preview), and then tap Sounds to return to the Sounds screen.

9. **For each of the events in the list (from Text Tone to Reminder Alerts), tap the event and then tap the sound you want to hear.** You can also tap None to turn off the event sound.

10. **To turn off the sound that your iPhone makes when you lock and unlock it, tap the Lock Sounds switch to Off.**

11. **To turn off the sound that your iPhone makes each time you tap a key on the virtual keyboard, tap the Keyboard Clicks switch to Off.**

Genius

One of the truly annoying iPhone sound effects is the clicking sound made by each key when using the on-screen keyboard. If it doesn't make you batty after five minutes, it will certainly drive anyone within earshot to thoughts of violence. So I strongly recommend tapping the Keyboard Clicks setting to Off. There, that's better.

Customizing the keyboard

Although you can type on your iPhone, don't expect to pound out the prose as easily as you can on your computer. The on-screen keyboard is a bit too small for rapid and accurate typing, but it's still a far sight better than any other phone out there, mostly because the keyboard was thoughtfully designed by the folks at Apple. It even changes depending on the app you use. For example, the regular keyboard features a spacebar at the bottom. However, if you're surfing the web with the Safari browser, the keyboard that appears when you type in the address bar does away with the spacebar. In its place you find a period (.), a slash (/), and a button that enters the characters *.com*. Web addresses don't use spaces, so Apple replaced the spacebar with three things that commonly appear in a web address. Nice!

Another nice innovation you get with the iPhone keyboard is Auto-Capitalization. If you type a punctuation mark that indicates the end of a sentence — for example, a period (.), a question mark (?), or an exclamation mark (!) — or if you press Return to start a new paragraph, the iPhone automatically activates the Shift key, because it assumes you're starting a new sentence.

On a related note, double-tapping the spacebar activates a keyboard shortcut: Instead of entering two spaces, the iPhone automatically enters a period (.) followed by a space. This is a welcome bit of efficiency because otherwise you'd have to tap the Number key (123) to display the numbers and punctuation marks, tap the period (.), and then tap the spacebar.

Genius

Typing a number or punctuation mark normally requires three taps: tapping Number (123), tapping the number or symbol, and then tapping ABC. Here's a faster way: Press and hold the Number key to open the numeric keyboard, slide the same finger to the number or punctuation symbol you want, and then release the key. This types the number or symbol and returns to the regular keyboard all in one touch.

For many people, one of the keys to quick iPhone typing is to clear the mind and just tap away without worrying about accuracy. In many cases, you'll actually be rather amazed at how accurate this willy-nilly approach can be. Why does it work? The secret is the Auto-Correction feature on your iPhone, which eyeballs what you're typing and automatically corrects any errors. For example, if you tap *hte,* your iPhone automatically corrects this to *the.* Your iPhone displays the suggested correction before you complete the word (say, by tapping a space or a comma), and you can reject the suggestion by tapping it.

If you do end up with spelling errors (for example, by rejecting a proper correction), your iPhone lets you know by displaying the miscreant words underlined with red dots. Tap an underlined term to see a list of suggested corrections, and then tap the correction that works for you.

One thing the iPhone keyboard doesn't seem to have is a Caps Lock feature that, when activated, enables you to type all-uppercase letters. To do this, you need to tap and hold the Shift key, and then use a different finger to tap the uppercase letters. However, the iPhone actually does have a Caps Lock feature; it's just that it's turned off by default.

To turn on Caps Lock, or change the settings for the Auto-Capitalization, spacebar double-tap shortcut, or Auto-Correction features, follow these steps:

1. **On the Home screen, tap Settings.** The Settings app appears.

2. **Tap General.** The General screen appears.

3. **Tap Keyboard.** The Keyboard screen appears, as shown in Figure 1.10.

4. **If you no longer want your iPhone to automatically activate the Shift key at the beginning of sentences, tap the Auto-Capitalization setting to Off.**

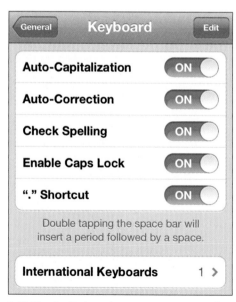

1.10 Use the Keyboard screen to customize a few keyboard settings.

5. **If you no longer want your iPhone to suggest spelling corrections as you type, tap Auto-Correction to Off.**

6. **If you no longer want your iPhone to underline misspelled words in your notes and messages, tap Check Spelling to Off.**

7. **If you want to use the Caps Lock feature, tap the Enable Caps Lock switch to On.**

8. **If you want to use the spacebar double-tap shortcut, tap the "." Shortcut setting to On.**

9. **To add an international keyboard layout, tap International Keyboards to open the Keyboards screen, and then set the keyboard layout you want to add to On.**

Note When you're using two or more keyboard layouts, the keyboard sprouts a new key to the left of the spacebar (it looks like a stylized globe). Tap that key to run through the layouts (the names of which appear briefly in the spacebar).

Configuring Siri

Controlling a computer with just voice commands has been a mainstream dream ever since the first Star Trek series. Mac OS X and Windows come with speech-recognition features, but few people use them because they're difficult to configure and are more often than not frustrating to use. Third-party speech recognition programs are more powerful, but they tend to be expensive and still don't work all that well.

The dream of voice control remains unfulfilled on desktop machines, but on the iPhone 4S, voice control is a reality that comes in the form of the new Siri app. Siri replaces the Voice Control feature from the iPhone 3GS and 4, which was limited to placing phone calls and controlling the Music app with voice commands. Siri is one of the slickest iPhone 4S features because it goes well beyond this by also giving you voice control over web searching, your appointments, your contacts, your reminders, map navigation, text messages, notes, and more.

First, make sure that Siri is activated by tapping Settings in the Home screen, tapping General, tapping Siri, and then tapping the Siri switch to On. While you're here, you should also tell Siri who you are, so that when you use references such as "home" and "work," Siri knows what you're talking about. In the Siri screen, tap My Info and then tap your item in the All Contacts list.

You crank up Siri by using any of the following techniques:

- Pressing and holding the Home button.
- Pressing and holding the Mic button on your iPhone headphones.

- Holding the iPhone up to your ear as though you are on a call.

- Pressing and holding the Mic equivalent on a Bluetooth headset.

In each case, wait until you hear a two-tone beep and you see the Siri screen.

Siri is often easier to use if you define relationships with other people in your Contacts list. So, for example, instead of saying "Call Sandy Evans," you can simply say "Call mom." You can define relationships in two ways:

- **Within the Contacts app.** Open the Contacts app, tap your contact item, tap the Related People field label (it's the one with the default label of "mother"), and then tap the relationship you want to use. Tap the blue More icon to open the All Contacts list and then tap the person you want to add to the field.

- **Within Siri.** Say "*Name* is my *relationship*," where *Name* is the person's name as given in your Contacts list, and *relationship* is the connection, such as wife, husband, spouse, partner, brother, sister, mother, or father. When Siri asks you to confirm, say "Yes."

Creating text shortcuts

The Auto-Correction keyboard feature that I mentioned earlier can speed up your typing chores a tad because it displays suggestions whenever it recognizes the word you're currently typing. When the suggestion appears, tap a word-ending character, such as a space, comma, or period, and your iPhone automatically fills in the rest of the word.

Still, this is only marginally useful for speeding up typing because Auto-Correction plays it safe and usually waits until you have only a character or two left before it displays the suggested word. If you really want to shift your iPhone typing into a higher gear, you need to take advantage of the new text shortcuts feature in iOS 5. If you've ever created a keyboard macro or used the AutoText feature in Microsoft Word, you'll know exactly what's happening here. A *text shortcut* is a short sequence of characters (usually just two or three) that represents a longer phrase. When you type the shortcut characters, your iPhone displays the phrase (much the same way that Auto-Correction does) and you then type a word-ending character to replace the shortcut characters with the entire phrase.

Note

When your iPhone displays the longer phrase, it also includes an X at the end, which you can tap to tell iPhone not to enter the phrase. This is just like Auto-Correction, but remember that the two features aren't the same. If you turn off Auto-Correction, as I describe earlier in this chapter, you can still use text shortcuts.

These phrases can be dozens or even hundreds of characters long, so if you have phrases or boilerplate that you use all the time, your iPhone typing fingers will thank you for saving them a ton of wear and tear. Here are the steps to follow to create a text shortcut:

1. **If you have the phrase you want to use somewhere on your iPhone, copy it.** This saves some time later when you create your shortcut.

2. **On the Home screen, tap Settings.** The Settings app appears.

3. **Tap General.** The General screen appears.

4. **Tap Keyboard.** The Keyboard screen appears.

5. **Tap Add New Shortcut.** The Shortcut screen appears.

6. **If you copied the phrase earlier, paste it into the Phrase text box.** Otherwise, type the phrase.

7. **Use the Shortcut text box to type the characters you want to use to represent the phrase.** The shortcut must be at least two characters long. Figure 1.11 shows an example.

8. **Tap Save.** Your iPhone saves the text shortcut.

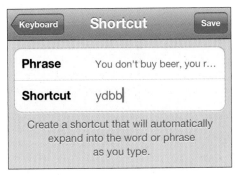

1.11 Type a phrase and two or more characters to represent the phrase.

Note To remove a text shortcut, display the Keyboard screen, tap Edit, tap the red button to the left of the shortcut you want to remove, tap Delete, and then tap Done.

Signing in to your Twitter account

Twitter, that 140-characters-or-less phenomenon, started off by asking you the not-so-musical question, *What are you doing?* It's a question that seems crafted to elicit nothing but the most trivial of replies: I just woke up; I'm having toast for breakfast; I'm in a boring meeting; I just finished dinner; I'm going to bed. But Twitter users took that original question and broadened it into a world of new questions: What are you reading? What great idea did you just come up with? What are you worried about? What interesting person did you just see or hear? What great information did you stumble upon on the web? What hilarious video would you like to share? Which is why, a couple of years ago, Twitter itself changed the original question from *What are you doing?* to *What's happening?*

Of course, what's most likely happening is that you're working or playing with your iPhone, and you've got something to share with your Twitter followers: a link, a photo, a video, or what have you. In the past, sharing such things required jumping through a few too many hoops. However, iOS 5 gets rid of those hoops by baking Twitter right into the system. Once you sign in to your Twitter account using the Settings app, you can tweet stuff directly from apps such as Safari and Photos.

Here's how to sign in:

1. **On the Home screen, tap Settings.** The Settings app appears.
2. **Tap Twitter.** The Twitter screen appears.
3. **Type your Twitter account name in the User Name text box.**
4. **Type your account password in the Password text box.**
5. **Tap Sign In.** Your iPhone connects to your Twitter account. It also prompts you to install the free Twitter iPhone app, so click Later or Install, as you prefer.

Genius If you have multiple Twitter accounts, you can add more by displaying the Twitter screen, tapping Add Account, typing the account username and password, and then tapping Sign In.

Resetting the iPhone

If you've spent quite a bit of time in the Settings app, your iPhone probably doesn't look much like it did fresh out of the box. That's okay, though, because your iPhone should be as individual as you are. However, if you've gone a bit too far with your customizations, your iPhone might feel a bit alien and uncomfortable. That's okay, too, because there's an easy solution to the problem: you can erase all your customizations and revert the iPhone to its default settings.

A similar problem that comes up is when you want to sell or give your iPhone to someone else. Chances are you don't want the new owner to see your data — contacts, appointments, e-mail and text messages, favorite websites, music, and so on — and it's unlikely the other person wants to wade through all that stuff anyway (no offense). To solve this problem, you can erase not only your custom settings, but also all the content you've stored on the iPhone.

Caution If you have any content on your iPhone that isn't synced with iTunes — for example, iTunes music you've recently downloaded or an App Store program that you've recently installed — you lose that content if you choose Reset All Content and Settings. First sync your iPhone with your computer to save your content, and then run the reset.

The Reset app handles these scenarios and a few more to boot. Here's how it works:

1. **On the Home screen, tap Settings.** The Settings app appears.

2. **Tap General.** The General screen appears.

3. **Tap Reset.** The Reset screen appears.

4. **Tap one of the following reset options:**

   - **Reset All Settings.** Tap this option to reset your custom settings to the factory default settings.

   - **Erase All Content and Settings.** Tap this option to reset your custom settings and remove any data you've stored on the iPhone.

   - **Reset Network Settings.** Tap this option to delete your Wi-Fi network settings. This is often an effective way to solve Wi-Fi problems.

   - **Reset Keyboard Dictionary.** Tap this option to reset your keyboard dictionary. This dictionary contains a list of the keyboard suggestions that you've rejected. Tap this option to clear the dictionary and start fresh.

   - **Reset Home Screen Layout.** Tap this option to reset your Home screen icons to their default layout.

   - **Reset Location Warnings.** Tap this option to wipe out the location preferences for your apps. A location warning is the dialog you see when you start a GPS-aware app for the first time. When you start one of these, your iPhone asks if the app can use your current location, and you then tap either OK or Don't Allow.

Note
Remember that the keyboard dictionary contains rejected suggestions. For example, if you type "Viv," iPhone suggests "Bob" instead. If you tap the "Bob" suggestion to reject it and keep "Viv," the word "Bob" is added to the keyboard dictionary.

5. **When the iPhone asks you to confirm, tap the red button.** Note that the name of this button is the same as the reset option. For example, if you tapped the Reset All Settings option in Step 4, the confirm button is called Reset All Settings. iPhone resets the data.

Protecting Your iPhone

These days, an iPhone is much more than just a phone. You use it to surf the web, send and receive e-mail and text messages, manage your contacts and schedules, find your way in the world, and much more. This is handy, for sure, but it also means that your iPhone is jammed with tons of information about you. Even though you might not store the nuclear launch codes on your iPhone, chances are what is on it is pretty important to you. Considering all of this, you should take steps to protect your iPhone, and that's what the next few sections are all about.

Locking your iPhone with a passcode

When your iPhone is asleep, the phone is locked in the sense that tapping the touchscreen or pressing the volume controls does nothing. This sensible arrangement prevents accidental taps when the phone is in your pocket, or rattling around in your backpack or handbag. To unlock the phone, you either press the Home button or the Sleep/Wake button, drag the Slide to Unlock slider, and you're back in business.

Unfortunately, this simple technique means that anyone else who gets his or her mitts on your iPhone can also be quickly back in business — *your* business! If you have sensitive or confidential information on your phone, or if you want to avoid digital joyrides that run up massive roaming or data charges, you need to truly lock your iPhone.

You do that by specifying a passcode that must be entered before anyone can use the iPhone. You can either set a simple four-digit passcode, or you can set one that is longer and more complex, using any combination of numbers, letters, and symbols. Follow these steps to set up your passcode:

1. **On the Home screen, tap Settings.** The Settings app appears.
2. **Tap General.** The General screen appears.
3. **If you prefer to set a complex passcode, tap the Simple Passcode switch to Off.**
4. **Tap Turn Passcode On.** The Set Passcode screen appears.
5. **Tap your passcode.** For security, the characters appear in the passcode box as dots.
6. **If you're entering a complex passcode, tap Next.** Your iPhone prompts you to reenter the passcode.
7. **Tap your passcode again.**
8. **If you're entering a complex passcode, tap Done.**

With your passcode now active, iPhone displays the Passcode Lock screen, as shown in Figure 1.12. You can also get to this screen by tapping Settings in the Home screen, then General, and then Passcode Lock.

This screen offers six settings:

- **Turn Passcode Off.** If you want to stop using your passcode, tap this button and then enter the passcode. This is for security (otherwise an interloper could just shut off the passcode).

- **Change Passcode.** Tap this button to enter a new passcode. Note that you must first enter your old passcode before you can enter the new one.

- **Require Passcode.** This setting determines how much time elapses before the iPhone locks the phone and requests the passcode. The default setting is Immediately, which means you see the Enter Passcode screen as soon as you finish dragging Slide to Unlock. The other options are After 1 minute, After 5 minutes, After 15 minutes, After 1 hour, and After 4 hours. Use one of the latter if you want to be able to work with your

1.12 Use the Passcode Lock screen to configure the passcode security settings on your iPhone.

iPhone for a bit before getting locked out. For example, the After 1 minute option is good if you want to quickly check e-mail without having to enter your passcode.

Caution

You really, really need to remember your iPhone passcode. If you forget it, you're locked out of your own phone. The only way to get back in is to use iTunes to restore the data and settings to your iPhone from an existing backup (as described in Chapter 13).

- **Simple Passcode.** Use this switch to toggle between a simple four-digit passcode and a complex passcode.

- **Siri.** When this setting is On, you can use Siri to dial calls (as explained in Chapter 3), search the web (see Chapter 4), and perform other voice-related tasks, even when your iPhone is locked. If you change this setting to Off, you can no longer use Siri when your iPhone is locked.

● **Erase Data.** When this setting is On, your iPhone will self-destruct — er — I mean erase all of its data when it detects ten incorrect passcode attempts. Ten failed passcodes almost always means that some nasty person has your phone and is trying to guess the passcode. If you have sensitive or private data on your phone, setting it to erase automatically is a good idea.

With the passcode activated, when you bring the iPhone out of standby, you drag the Slide to Unlock slider as usual, and then the Enter Passcode screen appears. Type your passcode (and tap OK if it's a complex passcode) to unlock the iPhone.

Note

If an emergency arises and you need to make a call for help, you probably don't want to mess around with entering a passcode. Similarly, if something happens to you, another person who doesn't know your passcode may need to use your iPhone to call for assistance. In both cases, you can temporarily bypass the passcode by tapping the Emergency Call button on the Enter Passcode screen.

Configuring your iPhone to sleep automatically

You can put your iPhone into standby mode at any time by pressing the Sleep/Wake button once. This drops the power consumption considerably (mostly because it shuts off the screen), but you can still receive incoming calls and text messages, and if you have the Music app running, it continues to play.

However, if your iPhone is on but you're not using it, it automatically goes into standby mode after two minutes. This is called Auto-Lock and it's a handy feature because it saves battery power (and prevents accidental taps) when your iPhone is just sitting there. It's also a crucial feature if you've protected your iPhone with a passcode lock, as I describe earlier, because if your iPhone never sleeps, it never locks, either.

To make sure your iPhone sleeps automatically, or if you're uncomfortable with the default two-minute Auto-Lock interval, you can make it shorter or longer (or turn it off altogether). Here are the steps to follow:

1. **On the Home screen, tap Settings.** The Settings app appears.

2. **Tap General.** The General screen appears.

3. **Tap Auto-Lock.** The Auto-Lock screen appears.

4. **Tap the interval you want to use.** You have six choices: 1 Minute, 2 Minutes, 3 Minutes, 4 Minutes, 5 Minutes, or Never.

Backing up your iPhone

When you sync your iPhone with your computer, iTunes automatically creates a backup of your current iPhone data before performing the sync. Note, however, that iTunes doesn't back up your entire iPhone, which makes sense because most of what's on your phone — music, photos, videos, apps, and so on — is already on your computer. Instead, iTunes only backs up data unique to the iPhone, including your call history, text messages, web clips, network settings, app settings and data, and Safari history and cookies.

However, what if you've configured iTunes not to sync your iPhone automatically? Is there a way to back up your iPhone without performing a sync? You bet there is:

1. **Connect your iPhone to your computer.**

2. **Open iTunes, if it doesn't launch automatically.**

3. **In the Devices section, right-click your iPhone and then click Back Up.** iTunes backs up the iPhone data.

If you have an iCloud account, you can also control where your iPhone gets backed up: to your computer or to iCloud. To configure this, connect your iPhone to your computer and then click your iPhone when it appears in the iTunes Devices list. In the Summary tab's Backup section, select either the Back up to iCloud option or the Back up to this computer option.

If you chose to use iCloud as your backup destination, you can then follow these steps to back up your data to iCloud directly from your iPhone:

1. **Connect your iPhone to a power source and to a Wi-Fi network.** iPhone-to-iCloud backups don't work if your iPhone is running on batteries or is using a cellular network connection.

2. **Tap Settings to launch the Settings app.**

3. **Tap iCloud.**

4. **Tap Storage & Backup.**

5. **Check that the iCloud Backup switch is On.** If not, tap the switch to On and then tap OK when iCloud confirms the setting.

6. **Tap Back Up Now.** Your iPhone backs up its data to your iCloud account.

Configuring parental controls

If your children have access to your iPhone, or if they have iPhones of their own, then you might be a bit worried about some of the content they might be exposed to on the web, on YouTube, or in iTunes. Similarly, you might not want them installing apps or giving away their current location.

For all those and similar parental worries, you can sleep better at night by activating the parental controls on your iPhone. These controls restrict the content and activities that kids can see and do. Here's how to set them up:

1. **On the Home screen, tap Settings.** The Settings app appears.

2. **Tap General.** The General screen appears.

3. **Tap Restrictions.** The Restrictions screen appears.

4. **Tap Enable Restrictions.** iPhone displays the Set Passcode screen, which you use to specify a four-digit code that you can use to override the parental controls. (Note that this passcode is not the same as the passcode lock code I discussed earlier in this chapter.)

5. **Tap the four-digit restrictions passcode and then retype the code.** iPhone returns you to the Restrictions screen and enables all the controls, as shown in Figure 1.13.

6. **In the Allow section, for each app or task, tap the On/Off switch to enable or disable the restriction.**

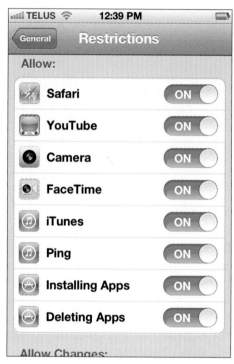

1.13 Use the Restrictions screen to configure the parental controls you want to use.

7. **In the Allow Changes section, use the Location setting to allow or disallow GPS changes.** Use the Accounts setting to allow or disallow changes to mail and calendar accounts.

8. **Tap Ratings For, and then tap the country whose ratings you want to use.**

9. **For each of the content controls — Music & Podcasts, Movies, TV Shows, and Apps — tap the control and then tap the highest rating you want your children to use.**

10. **If you don't want your children to be able to make purchases within apps, tap the In-App Purchases switch to Off.** If you leave this setting on, consider tapping Require Password and then tapping Immediately. This ensures that your children must type a password before they can make in-app purchases. If you leave the Require Password setting at 15 minutes, it means your kids can make in-app purchases without a password for up to 15 minutes after the initial purchase of the app.

11. **In the Game Center section, tap the On/Off switches to enable or disable multi-player games, and to enable or disable adding friends.**

12. **Tap General.** iPhone puts the new settings into effect.

Locating and protecting a lost iPhone

If there's a downside to using a smartphone (particularly one as smart as the iPhone), it's that you end up with a pretty large chunk of your life on that phone. Initially, that may sound like a good thing, but if you happen to lose your phone, you've also lost that chunk of your life. Plus, assuming you haven't configured your iPhone with a passcode lock, as described earlier, you've opened a gaping privacy hole because anyone can now delve into your data.

If you've been syncing your iPhone with your computer regularly, then you can probably recover most, or even all, of that data. However, I'm sure you'd probably rather find your iPhone because it's expensive and there's just something creepy about the thought of some stranger flicking through your stuff.

The old way of finding your missing iPhone consisted of scouring every nook and cranny that you visited before losing it, and calling up various lost-and-found departments to see if anyone turned it in. The new way to find your iPhone is via an app called Find My iPhone. (You can also use this feature through your iCloud account, if you have one.) Find My iPhone uses the GPS sensor embedded inside your iPhone to locate the device. You can also use Find My iPhone to send a message to your iPhone, to remotely lock it, or, in a real pinch, to remotely delete your data. The next few sections provide the details.

Caution The only drawback to Find My iPhone is that if someone else finds your iPhone, that person can easily turn off the feature and disable it. To prevent this, turn on the passcode lock as described earlier in this chapter. If your iPhone is already lost, use Find My iPhone on another iPhone, on an iPad, or on iCloud to remotely lock the iPhone, as described later in this chapter.

Activating Find My iPhone

Find My iPhone works by looking for a particular signal that your iPhone beams out into the ether. This signal is turned off by default, so you need to turn it on if you ever plan to use Find My iPhone. Here are the steps to follow:

1. **Add your iCloud account, if you haven't done so already, as described in Chapter 12.** When you add the account, be sure to tap OK when iCloud asks if it can use your location.

2. **On the Home screen, tap Settings.** The Settings app appears.

3. **Tap iCloud.** Your iCloud account settings appear.

4. **Tap the Find My iPhone switch to On.** Your iPhone asks you to confirm.

5. **Tap Allow.** Your iPhone activates the Find My iPhone feature.

Locating your iPhone on a map

With Find My iPhone now active on your iPhone, you can use the Find My iPhone app or iCloud to locate it at any time. The next two sections show you how to do this.

Locating your iPhone using the Find My iPhone app

Follow these steps to see your lost iPhone on a map using the Find My iPhone app:

1. **On an iPhone, iPad, or iPod touch that has the Find My iPhone app installed, tap the app to launch it.** Find My iPhone prompts you to enter your Apple ID.

2. **Type your Apple e-mail address and password.** Note that you must use the same Apple ID as the one you used to activate the Find My iPhone setting on your iPhone.

3. **Tap Go.** The app signs in to your Apple account.

4. **If you're using Find My iPhone on an iPad, tap My Devices.**

5. **In the list of devices, tap your lost iPhone.** The Find My iPhone app locates the iPhone on a map, as shown in Figure 1.14.

6. **To see if the location has changed, click the Refresh Location button (the circular arrow).** On the iPad version of the app, the Refresh Location button appears to the right of the Devices button; on the iPhone and iPod touch, it appears in the lower-left corner of the screen.

1.14 In the list of devices, tap your iPhone to locate it on a map.

Locating your iPhone using iCloud

Follow these steps to see your lost iPhone on a map using iCloud:

1. **Log in to your iCloud account.**

2. **Click the Switch Apps icon (the cloud) and then click Find My iPhone.** The iCloud Find My iPhone application appears.

3. **Click your iPhone in the My Devices list.** iCloud locates your iPhone on a map.

4. **To see if the location has changed, click the Refresh Location button (the circular arrow in the upper-right corner of the My Devices list).**

Getting an e-mail message when your iPhone comes online

Find My iPhone is only useful if you can, you know, *find* your iPhone. That won't happen if your iPhone is powered off or not connected to the Internet. You could keep refreshing the list of devices, but it could be hours before your iPhone comes online. To avoid a constant vigil, you can tell Find My iPhone to send an e-mail message to your iCloud account as soon as your iPhone comes online:

1. **Tap or click your iPhone in the devices list.** Find My iPhone locates your iPhone on a map.

2. **Tap or click the blue More icon to the right of your iPhone name.** Find My iPhone displays information about your iPhone.

3. **If Find My iPhone has no location data for your iPhone, tap the Email When Found switch to On.** Alternatively, if Find My iPhone has determined that your iPhone is offline, select the Email me when this iPhone is found check box.

Sending a message to your iPhone

If you think another person has your iPhone, you could try calling your number. That might not work, either because you don't have a phone handy or because the person might have already installed a new SIM card. Fortunately, you can still try to contact the person by sending a message to the iPhone using the Find My iPhone app or the iCloud Find My iPhone feature. Here's how it works:

1. **Tap or click your iPhone in the devices list.** Find My iPhone locates your iPhone on a map.

2. **Tap or click the blue More icon to the right of your iPhone name.** Find My iPhone displays information about your iPhone as well as buttons for various actions you can take.

3. **Tap or click Play Sound or Send Message.** Find My iPhone displays the Send Message dialog.

4. **Type your message.** Figure 1.15 shows an example.

1.15 You can send a message to your lost iPhone.

5. **If you want to be sure the other person notices your message, leave the Play Sound switch in the On position.**

6. **Tap or click Send.** iCloud sends the message, which then appears on the iPhone screen, as shown in Figure 1.16.

Remotely locking the data on your iPhone

While you're waiting for the other person to return your iPhone, you probably don't want that person rummaging around in your stuff. To prevent that, you can remotely lock the iPhone. Here's how:

1.16 The sent message appears on the iPhone screen.

1. **Tap or click your iPhone in the devices list.** Find My iPhone locates your iPhone on a map.

2. **Tap or click the blue More icon to the right of your iPhone name.** Find My iPhone displays information about your iPhone as well as buttons for various actions you can take.

3. **Tap or click Remote Lock.** Find My iPhone displays the Remote Lock dialog, as shown in Figure 1.17.

1.17 To prevent anyone from messing with your lost iPhone, you can apply a passcode lock remotely.

4. **Tap or click the numbers in the keypad to enter a four-digit passcode.** Find My iPhone asks you to type the passcode again.

5. **Reenter the four-digit passcode, and then click Lock.** Find My iPhone remotely locks the iPhone.

Remotely deleting the data on your iPhone

If you can't get the other person to return your iPhone and it contains sensitive or confidential data — or just that big chunk of your life I mentioned earlier — you can use the Find My iPhone app or the iCloud Find My iPhone feature to take the drastic step of remotely wiping all of the data from your iPhone. Here's what you do:

1. **Tap or click your iPhone in the devices list.** Find My iPhone locates your iPhone on a map.

2. **Tap or click the blue More icon to the right of the iPhone name.** Find My iPhone displays information about your iPhone, as well as buttons for various actions you can take.

3. **Tap or click Remote Wipe.** Find My iPhone displays the Info dialog shown in Figure 1.18.

4. **Tap or click Wipe iPhone.** Find My iPhone remotely wipes all data from the iPhone.

1.18 If you're certain your lost iPhone is a lost cause, you can remotely erase all of its data.

Enhancing Your iPhone with Apps

Your iPhone is an impressive, eyebrow-raising device right out of the box. It does everything you want it to do — or so you think, until you find out about some previously unknown feature and wonder how you ever lived without it. It's hard to imagine that anyone would, or even could, improve the iPhone. However, as you see in this section, the App Store can make your iPhone more convenient, more productive, and more, well, anything!

Accessing the App Store on your computer

You've seen that your iPhone comes loaded not only with a basketful of terrific technology, but also a decent collection of truly amazing apps, all of which take advantage of the special features on your iPhone. But it probably also won't escape your notice that the iPhone suite of apps is incomplete. Where are the news and sports headlines? Why isn't there an easy way to post a short note to your blog or a link to your Delicious account?

Fortunately, it's possible to fill in these and many other gaping iPhone app holes with the App Store. You browse and purchase apps in the App Store the same way that you browse and purchase music in the iTunes Store — although many apps are free for the downloading. You can even use the familiar iTunes software on your Mac or Windows PC, or you can connect to the App Store directly from your iPhone, which is explained later.

To access the App Store on your computer, follow these steps:

1. **Launch iTunes.**

2. **Click iTunes Store.** The iTunes Store interface appears.

3. **Click App Store.** iTunes loads the main App Store page.

4. **Click the iPhone tab.** iTunes loads the iPhone version of the App Store page, as shown in Figure 1.19.

From here, use the links to browse the apps, or use the iTunes Store search box to look for something specific.

Note Usually you can't tell just by looking whether or not an app is free. However, the App Store does have a Top Charts section on the right-hand side that includes a handy Free Apps list. It's a good place to start if you're looking for free stuff.

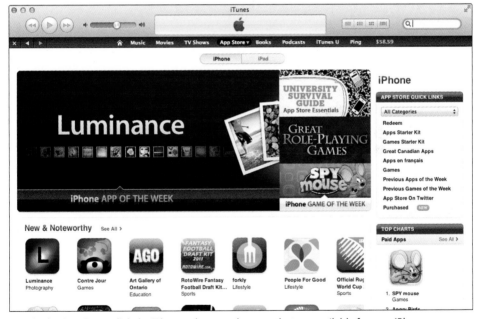

1.19 In the App Store, click the iPhone tab to see the apps that are available for your iPhone.

Accessing the App Store on your iPhone

Getting apps from iTunes is great, but what if you're away from your desk and you hear about an amazing iPhone game, or you realize that you forgot to download an important app using iTunes? This isn't even remotely a problem because your iPhone can establish a wireless connection to the

App Store anywhere you have Wi-Fi access or a cellular signal (ideally 3G for faster downloads). You can browse and search the apps, check for updates, or purchase any app you want (unless it's free, of course). The app then downloads to your iPhone, installs itself on the Home screen, and you're good to go!

To access the App Store on your iPhone, follow these steps:

1. **Tap the Home button to return to the Home screen.**
2. **Tap the App Store icon.**

As you can see in Figure 1.20, your iPhone organizes the App Store similar to the iTunes Store (as well as the Music and YouTube apps). That is, you get five browse buttons in the menu bar: Featured, Categories, Top 25, Search, and Updates. You use these buttons to navigate the App Store.

1.20 Use the browse buttons in the App Store's menu bar to locate and manage apps for your iPhone.

Here's a summary of what each browse button does for you:

- **Featured.** Tap this button to display a list of videos picked by the App Store editors. The list shows each app's name, icon, star rating, number of reviews, and price. Tap New to see the latest apps, tap What's Hot to see the most popular items, and tap Genius to turn on Genius Recommendations for Apps, which shows you apps that are similar to those you currently use.

- **Categories.** Tap this button to see a list of app categories, such as Games and Newsstand. Tap a category to see a list of the apps available.

- **Top 25.** Tap this button to see a list of the 25 most downloaded apps.

- **Search.** Tap this button to display a Search text box. Tap inside the box, enter a search phrase, and then tap Search. The App Store sends back a list of apps that match your search term.

- **Updates.** Tap this button to install updated versions of your apps.

Syncing apps

After you download an app or two into iTunes, they won't do you much good just sitting there. To actually use the apps, you need to get them on your iPhone. Here's how:

1. **Connect your iPhone to your computer.** iTunes opens and accesses the iPhone.

2. **In iTunes, click your iPhone in the Devices list.**

3. **Click the Apps tab.**

4. **Select the Sync Apps check box.**

5. **In the app list, select the check box beside each app that you want to sync, as shown in Figure 1.21.**

6. **Click Apply.** iTunes syncs the iPhone using your new app settings.

Genius

By default, any new apps you add to your computer are automatically synced to your iPhone. If you'd rather not have all your new apps synced without your say so, deselect the Automatically sync new apps check box (not shown in Figure 1.21, but it appears just below the app list).

1.21 You can sync selected apps with your iPhone.

Viewing and updating your apps

When you click Apps in the iTunes Library, you see a list of icons that represent all the apps that you've downloaded from the App Store, as shown in Figure 1.22.

1.22 In the iTunes Library, click the Apps category to see your downloaded apps.

To check for updates to your apps, click *X* Updates Available (where *X* is the number of updates you have waiting for you). When the developer releases a new version of an app, the App Store compares the new version with what you have. If you have an earlier version, it offers to update the app for you (usually without charge).

When you access the App Store with your iPhone, take a look at the Updates browse button in the menu bar. If you see a red dot with a white number inside it superimposed over the Updates button (see Figure 1.20), it means some of your installed apps have updated versions available. The number inside the dot tells you how many updates are waiting for you. It's a good idea to update your apps whenever a new version becomes available. The new version usually fixes bugs, but it might also supply more features, give better performance, or beef up the app's security.

Follow these steps to install an update:

1. **On the Home screen, tap App Store.** Your iPhone connects to the App Store.

2. **Tap the Updates button.** Remember that you are only able to tap this button if you see the red dot with a number that indicates the available updates. You then see the Updates screen, as shown in Figure 1.23.

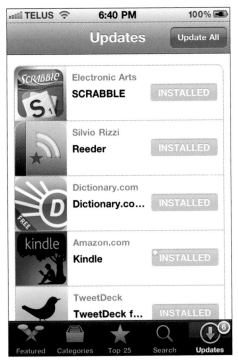

1.23 Use the Updates screen to choose the app you want to update.

3. **Tap an update.** The App Store displays a description of the update.

4. **Tap Update.** Your iPhone downloads and installs the app update.

Multitasking apps

Your iPhone is capable of multitasking, which enables you to run multiple apps at the same time. This is useful if, say, you're playing a game and an e-mail message comes in. You can switch to the message, read it, respond to it, and then resume your game right where you left off.

At its most basic, multitasking on the iPhone means that whenever you run an app and then switch to another app, your iPhone keeps the first app running in the background. In most cases, the first app does nothing while it's in the background — it doesn't take any processor time away from your current app and it doesn't use battery power. This means that you're free to open as many apps as you like. However, if the first app is performing some task and you switch to another app, the first app will continue to perform the task in the background.

To get a firm grip on how iPhone multitasking works, you need to understand the three modes an app can have on the iPhone:

- **Closed State.** This mode means the app is completely shut down. If you reboot your iPhone (by turning it off and then back on), all of your apps are then in the Closed State.

- **Suspended State.** If you launch an app, then press the Home button to return to the Home screen, usually your iPhone places the running app into the Suspended State. This means the app remains loaded into memory, but it's not running, it's not using up processor time, and it's not draining the battery. However, the app still maintains its current conditions, so that when you return to it, the app resumes where you left off.

- **Background State.** If you launch an app, start some process such as playing music, and then press the Home button to return to the Home screen, your iPhone puts the app into the Background State, which means it keeps the app's process running in the background. When you return to the app, either you see the process still running, or it has been completed.

I should note, as well, that the vast majority of apps go into the Suspended State when you switch to another app. However, if you launch an app and your iPhone doesn't have enough free memory available, the iPhone starts putting suspended apps into the Closed State to free up memory.

So how do you switch from one app to another? Double-tap the Home button to reveal the multi-tasking bar, which displays the running apps, as shown in Figure 1.24. Flick left or right to bring the app icon into view and then tap the app to switch to it.

As an added bonus, the multitasking bar also includes a few useful iPhone tools. Flick the multi-tasking bar to the right until you see the controls shown in Figure 1.25. Tap the Rotation Lock icon to prevent the iPhone from rotating between portrait and landscape modes, and use the audio icons to control the playback of the most recently used audio app (which, in Figure 1.25, is the Music app icon).

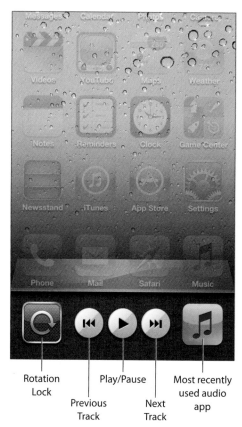

1.24 Double-tap the Home button to see the running apps.

Rotation Lock   Play/Pause   Most recently used audio app

Previous Track   Next Track

1.25 Double-tap the Home button and then flick right to see these audio controls.

Flick to the right one more time to display the playback volume control, as well as the Output icon, which you use to send the iPhone audio output to another device, such as a Bluetooth headset or an Apple TV.

Genius

To help you navigate the list of running apps, shut down any apps you won't be using for a while. Double-tap the Home button to display the multitasking bar, and press and hold any app to put the icons into edit mode. Then, tap the red Delete icon in the upper-left corner of any app you want to shut down. When you finish, press the Home button to exit edit mode.

Pairing Your iPhone to Bluetooth Devices

Your iPhone is configured to use a wireless technology called Bluetooth, which enables you to make wireless connections to other Bluetooth-friendly devices. Most Macs come with Bluetooth built in, and they use it to connect to a wide range of devices, including mice, keyboards, cell phones, printers, digital cameras, and even other Macs. Your iPhone can, at the very least, connect to a Bluetooth headset on which you can listen to phone conversations, music, and movies without wires and without disturbing your neighbors.

In theory, connecting Bluetooth devices should be criminally easy: you bring them within 33 feet of each other (the maximum Bluetooth range), and they connect without further ado. In practice, however, there's usually at least a bit of further ado (and sometimes plenty of it). This usually takes one or both of the following forms:

- **Making the devices discoverable.** Unlike Wi-Fi devices that broadcast their signals constantly, most Bluetooth devices only broadcast their availability — that is, they make themselves *discoverable* — when you say so. This makes sense in many cases because you usually only want to connect a Bluetooth component such as a headset with a single device. By controlling when the device is discoverable, you ensure that it works only with the device you want it to.

- **Pairing the iPhone and the device.** As a security precaution, many Bluetooth devices need to be *paired* with another device before the connection is established. Usually, the pairing is accomplished by entering a multidigit *passkey* — your iPhone calls it a PIN — that you must then enter into the Bluetooth device (assuming, of course, that it has some kind of keypad). In the case of a headset, the device comes with a default passkey that you must enter into your iPhone to set up the pairing.

Making your iPhone discoverable

So your first order of Bluetooth business is to ensure that your iPhone is discoverable by activating the Bluetooth feature. Follow these steps to turn on Bluetooth and make your iPhone discoverable:

1. **On the Home screen, tap Settings.** The Settings app appears.

2. **Tap General.** The General screen appears.

3. **Tap Bluetooth.** The Bluetooth screen appears.

4. **Tap the Bluetooth switch to change the setting to On, as shown in Figure 1.26.**

Bluetooth icon

1.26 Use the Bluetooth screen to make your iPhone discoverable.

In Figure 1.26, notice, too, that the status bar now shows the Bluetooth logo to the left of the Battery Status icon, which tells you that Bluetooth is up and running on your phone.

Pairing your iPhone with a Bluetooth keyboard

The iPhone virtual keyboard is an ingenious invention, but it's not always a convenient one, particularly when you need to type fast or type a lot. Fortunately, iOS supports connections to a Bluetooth keyboard that, while paired, disables the on-screen keyboard. Follow these steps to pair your iPhone with a Bluetooth keyboard:

1. **On the Home screen, tap Settings.** The Settings app appears.

2. **Tap General.** The General screen appears.

3. **Tap Bluetooth.** The Bluetooth screen appears.

4. **If the keyboard has a separate switch or button that makes the device discoverable, turn on that switch or press that button.** Wait until you see the device appear in the Bluetooth screen, as shown earlier in Figure 1.26.

5. **Tap the name of the Bluetooth keyboard.** Your iPhone displays a passkey, as shown in Figure 1.27.

6. **On the Bluetooth keyboard, type the passkey and press Return or Enter.** Your iPhone pairs with the keyboard and returns you to the Bluetooth screen, where you now see Connected beside the keyboard.

Pairing your iPhone with a Bluetooth headset

If you want to listen to music, headphones are a great way to go because the sound is often better than with the built-in iPhone speakers

"Microsoft Bluetooth Mobile Keyboard 6000" would like to pair with your iPhone.

Enter the PIN code "8164" on "Microsoft Bluetooth Mobile Keyboard 6000", followed by the return or enter key.

Cancel

1.27 Your iPhone displays a passkey, which you then type on the Bluetooth keyboard.

(and no one else around is subjected to Weezer at top volume). Similarly, if you want to conduct a hands-free call, a headset (a combination of headphones for listening and a microphone for talking) makes life easier because you can put the phone down and make all the hand gestures you want (provided you aren't driving, of course). Add Bluetooth into the mix, and you've got an easy and wireless audio solution for your iPhone.

Follow these general steps to pair your iPhone with a Bluetooth headset:

1. **On the Home screen, tap Settings.** The Settings app appears.

2. **Tap General.** The General screen appears.

3. **Tap Bluetooth.** The Bluetooth screen appears.

4. **If the headset has a separate switch or button that makes the device discoverable, turn on that switch or press that button.** Wait until you see the correct headset name appear in the Bluetooth screen.

5. **Tap the name of the Bluetooth headset.** Your iPhone should pair with the headset automatically and you should see Connected in the Bluetooth screen. If you see this, you can skip the rest of these steps. Otherwise you see the Enter PIN screen.

6. **Enter the headset's passkey in the PIN box.** See the headset documentation to get the passkey (it's often 0000).

7. **Tap Done.** Your iPhone pairs with the headset and returns you to the Bluetooth screen, where you now see Connected beside the headset name.

Selecting a paired headset as the audio output device

After you pair a Bluetooth headset, you usually need to configure your iPhone to blast your tunes through the headset rather than the phone's built-in speaker. Here's what you do:

1. **On the Home screen, tap Music.** The Music app loads.

2. **Tap a song to start the playback.**

3. **Tap the Output icon that appears to the right of the playback controls.** The Output dialog appears, as shown in Figure 1.28. You can also display the Output dialog by double-clicking the Home button to display the multitasking bar, flicking the bar to the right two times, and then tapping the Output icon.

1.28 Use the Output dialog to select your paired Bluetooth headset.

4. **Tap your paired Bluetooth headset.** Your iPhone starts playing the song through the headset.

Unpairing your iPhone from a Bluetooth device

If you no longer plan to use a Bluetooth device, you should unpair it from your iPhone. Follow these steps:

1. **On the Home screen, tap Settings.** The Settings app appears.

2. **Tap General.** The General screen appears.

3. **Tap Bluetooth.** The Bluetooth screen appears.

4. **Tap the name of the Bluetooth device.**

5. **Tap Forget this Device.** Your iPhone unpairs the device.

How Do I Connect My iPhone to a Network?

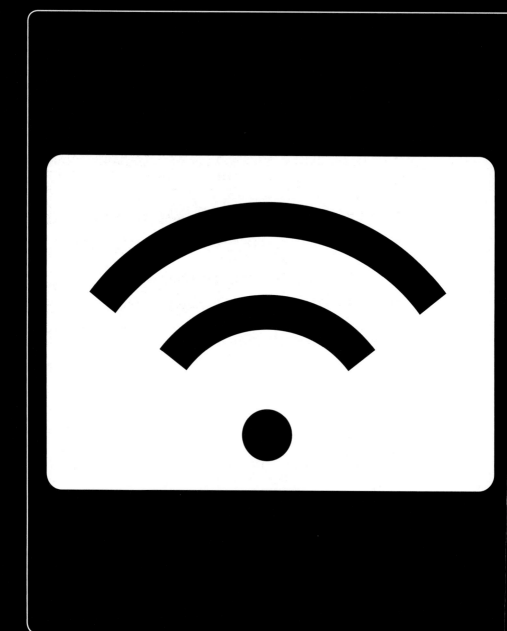

As a stand-alone device, your iPhone works just fine, thank you, because you can make calls, listen to music, take pictures, record and edit video, work with your contacts and calendars, take notes, play games, and much more. But your iPhone was made to connect: to surf the web, exchange e-mail and text messages, watch YouTube videos, navigate with maps, and on and on. To do all that, your iPhone must first connect to a network, and that's what this chapter is all about. I show you how to make, monitor, and control network connections, set up your iPhone as an Internet hub, and more.

Connecting to a Wi-Fi Network

Connections to a cellular network are automatic and occur behind the scenes. As soon as you switch on your iPhone, it checks for a 3G signal. If it finds one, it connects to the network and displays the 3G icon in the status bar, as well as the connection strength (the more bars, the better). If your current area doesn't do the 3G thing, your iPhone tries to connect to a slower EDGE network instead. If that works, you see the E icon in the status bar (plus the usual signal strength bars). If none of that works, you see No Signal, so you might as well go home.

Making your first connection

Things aren't automatic when it comes to Wi-Fi connections, at least not at first. As soon as you try to access something on the Internet — a website, your e-mail, a Google Map, or whatever — your iPhone scours the surrounding airwaves for Wi-Fi network signals. If you've never connected to a Wi-Fi network, or if you're in an area that doesn't have any Wi-Fi networks that you've used in the past, you see the Select a Wireless Network dialog, as shown in Figure 2.1. If you don't see the Select a Wireless Network dialog, you can still connect to a wireless network; see the section about how to stop Wi-Fi network prompts later in this chapter.

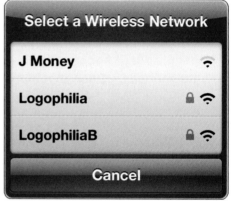

2.1 If you're just starting out on the Wi-Fi trail, your iPhone displays a list of nearby networks.

This dialog displays a list of the Wi-Fi networks that are within range. For each network, you get three tidbits of data:

- **Network name.** This is the name that the administrator has assigned to the network. If you're in a coffee shop or similar public hot spot and you want to use that network, look for the name of the shop (or a variation on the name).

- **Password-protection.** If a Wi-Fi network displays a lock icon, it means that it's protected by a password, and you need that password to make the connection.

- **Signal strength.** The Signal Strength icon gives you a rough idea of how strong the wireless signals are. The stronger the signal (the more bars you see, the better the signal), the more likely you are to get a fast and reliable connection.

Follow these steps to connect to a Wi-Fi network:

1. **Tap the network you want to use.** If the network is protected by a password, your iPhone prompts you to enter it, as shown in Figure 2.2.

2. **Use the keyboard to type the password.**

3. **Tap Join.** The iPhone connects to the network and adds the Wi-Fi Network Signal Strength icon to the status bar.

2.2 If the Wi-Fi network is secured with a password, use this screen to enter it.

Caution Because the password box shows dots instead of the actual text for added security, this is no place to demonstrate your iPhone speed-typing prowess. Slow and steady wins the password-typing race (or something).

To connect to a commercial Wi-Fi operation — such as those you find in airports, hotels, and convention centers — you almost always have to take one more step. Usually, the network prompts you for your name and credit card data so you can be charged for accessing the network. If you're not prompted right away, you will be as soon as you try to access a website or check your e-mail. Enter your information and then enjoy the Internet in all its Wi-Fi glory.

Note If you're not close enough to a Wi-Fi hot spot, you can still access the Internet via the cellular connection. Your iPhone tries to use the 3G network, but if that's a no-go, it uses the dreaded EDGE network.

Connecting to known networks

Your iPhone remembers any Wi-Fi network to which you connect. So, if the network is one that you use all the time — for example, your home or office — your iPhone makes the connection without so much as a peep as soon as that network comes within range.

Stopping incessant Wi-Fi network prompts

The Select a Wireless Network dialog is a handy convenience if you're not sure whether a Wi-Fi network is available. However, as you move around town, you may find that dialog popping up all over the place as new Wi-Fi networks come within range. This constant tapping of the Cancel button can wear down your finger to the bone. However, you can just tell your iPhone to shut up already with the Wi-Fi prompting. Here's how:

1. **On the Home screen, tap Settings.** The Settings app appears.

2. **Tap Wi-Fi.** iPhone opens the Wi-Fi Networks screen.

3. **Tap the Ask to Join Networks switch to Off, as shown in Figure 2.3.** Your iPhone no longer prompts you with nearby networks. Whew!

2.3 Toggle the Ask to Join Networks switch to Off to put a gag on the network prompts.

Okay, I hear you ask, if I'm no longer seeing the prompts, how do I connect to a Wi-Fi network if I don't even know it's there? That's a good question, and here's a good answer:

1. **On the Home screen, tap Settings.** Your iPhone displays the Settings app.

2. **Tap Wi-Fi.** The Wi-Fi Networks screen appears, and the Choose a Network list shows you the available Wi-Fi networks.

3. **Tap the network you want to use.** If the network is protected by a password, your iPhone prompts you to enter it.

4. **Use the keyboard to tap the password.**

5. **Tap Join.** The iPhone connects to the network and adds the Wi-Fi Network Signal Strength icon to the status bar.

Connecting to a hidden Wi-Fi network

Each Wi-Fi network has a network name — often called the Service Set Identifier, or SSID — that identifies the network to Wi-Fi–friendly devices, such as your iPhone. By default, most Wi-Fi networks broadcast the network name so that you can see it and connect to it. However, some Wi-Fi networks disable network name broadcasting as a security precaution. The idea here is that if an unauthorized user can't see the network, he or she can't attempt to connect to it. (However, some devices can still pick up the network name when authorized computers connect to it, so this is not a foolproof security measure.)

You can still connect to a hidden Wi-Fi network by entering the connection settings by hand. You need to know the network name, its security and encryption types, and the network password. Here are the steps to follow:

1. **On the Home screen, tap Settings to open the Settings app.**

2. **Tap Wi-Fi.** You see the Wi-Fi Networks screen.

3. **Tap Other.** Your iPhone displays the Other Network screen, as shown in Figure 2.4.

4. **Type the network name in the Name text box.**

5. **Tap Security to open the Security screen.**

6. **Tap the type of security used by the Wi-Fi network: WEP, WPA, WPA2, WPA Enterprise, WPA2 Enterprise, or None.**

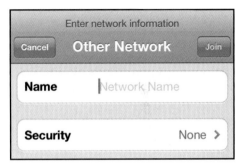

2.4 Use the Other Network screen to connect to a hidden Wi-Fi network.

7. **Tap Other Network to return to the Other Network screen.** If you chose WEP, WPA, WPA2, WPA Enterprise, or WPA2 Enterprise, your iPhone prompts you to type the password.

8. **Type the password in the Password text box.**

9. **Tap Join.** The iPhone connects to the network and adds the Wi-Fi Network Signal Strength icon to the status bar.

Forgetting a Wi-Fi network

Having the iPhone remember networks you've joined is certainly convenient, except of course when it's not. For example, if you have a couple of networks nearby that you can join, you might connect to one and then realize that the other is better in some way (for example, it's faster or cheaper). Unfortunately, there's a good chance your iPhone will continue to connect to the network you don't want every time it comes within range, which can be a real hassle. Rather than threatening to throw your iPhone in the nearest trash can, you can tell it to forget the network you don't want to use. Here's how it's done:

1. **On the Home screen, tap Settings.** The Settings app appears.

2. **Tap Wi-Fi.** The iPhone opens the Wi-Fi Networks screen.

3. **If you're not currently connected to the network you want your iPhone to forget, connect to that network.**

4. **Tap the blue More Info icon to the right of the network.** Your iPhone displays the network's settings screen.

5. **Tap Forget this Network.** Your iPhone asks you to confirm.

6. **Tap Forget.** Your iPhone discards the login data for the network and no longer connects to the network automatically.

Turning off the Wi-Fi antenna

Your iPhone's Wi-Fi antenna is constantly on the lookout for nearby Wi-Fi networks. That's useful because it means you always have an up-to-date list of networks to check out, but it also takes its toll on the iPhone battery. If you know you won't be using Wi-Fi for a while, you can save some battery juice for more important pursuits by turning off your iPhone's Wi-Fi antenna. Here's how:

1. **On the Home screen, tap Settings.** The Settings app appears.

2. **Tap Wi-Fi.** The Wi-Fi Networks screen appears.

3. **Tap the Wi-Fi switch to Off.** Your iPhone disconnects from your current network and hides the Choose a Network list.

When you're ready to resume your Wi-Fi duties, return to the Wi-Fi Networks screen and tap the Wi-Fi switch to On.

Setting Up Your iPhone as an Internet Hub

Here's a scenario you've probably tripped over a time or two when roaming around with both your iPhone and your notebook computer along for the ride. You end up somewhere where you have access to just a cellular network, with no Wi-Fi in sight. This means that your iPhone can access the Internet (using the cellular network), but your notebook can't. That's a real pain if you want to do some work involving Internet access on the computer. To work around this problem, you can use a nifty feature called Personal Hotspot, which enables you to configure your iPhone as a kind of Internet hub or gateway device — something like the hot spots that are available in coffee shops and other public areas. To do this, you connect your iPhone to your notebook (either directly via a USB cable or wirelessly via Wi-Fi or Bluetooth), and your notebook can then use the iPhone's cellular Internet connection to get online. This is often called Internet tethering. Even better, you can connect up to five devices to your iPhone, so you can also share your iPhone's Internet connection with desktop computers, tablets, other cell phones, and pretty much anything else that can connect to the Internet.

This sounds too good to be true, but it's real, I swear. The downside (you just knew there had to be a downside) is that additional usage charges will apply. In the United States, for example, AT&T offers a Smartphone Tethering plan that costs $45 per month, which is $20 more than the next lowest price plan (although you also get an extra 2GB of data). Similarly, Sprint's tethering plan costs an extra $29.99 per month for 5GB of tethering data, while Verizon's tethering option costs an extra $30 per month, but includes unlimited tethering data.

Activating the Personal Hotspot

Your first step down the Personal Hotspot road is to activate the feature. Here's how it's done:

1. **On the Home screen, tap Settings.** The Settings app appears.

2. **Tap Personal Hotspot.** iPhone opens the Personal Hotspot screen.

3. **Tap the Personal Hotspot switch to On.** If you don't have the Bluetooth antenna turned on so it is discoverable, as I describe in Chapter 1, your iPhone asks if you want to turn it on, as shown in Figure 2.5.

4. **If you'll be connecting Bluetooth devices to a Personal Hotspot, tap Turn on Bluetooth.** Otherwise, tap Wi-Fi and USB Only.

2.5 When you activate Personal Hotspot, your iPhone might ask if you want to enable Bluetooth.

5. **Personal Hotspot generates a Wi-Fi password automatically, but you can set your own by tapping Wi-Fi Password, typing the new password, and then tapping Done.**

Connecting to the Personal Hotspot using Wi-Fi

With Personal Hotspot enabled, follow these steps to connect a device to it via Wi-Fi:

1. **On the device, display the list of nearby wireless networks.**

2. **In the network list, click the one that has the same name as your iPhone, as shown in Figure 2.6.** Your device prompts you for the Wi-Fi password.

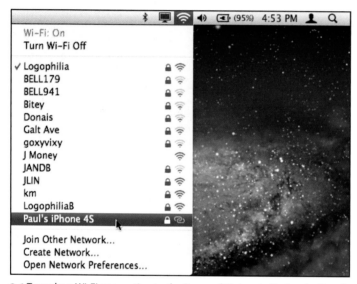

2.6 To make a Wi-Fi connection to the Personal Hotspot, display the list of wireless networks and then select your iPhone.

3. **Type the Personal Hotspot Wi-Fi password and then click OK.** Under the status bar, your iPhone displays Personal Hotspot: 1 Connection, as shown in Figure 2.7.

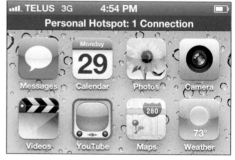

Connecting to the Personal Hotspot using Bluetooth

To connect a Bluetooth device to a Personal Hotspot, first pair the device with your iPhone, and then use the device interface to connect it

2.7 When you successfully set up a connection to the Personal Hotspot, the iPhone displays a banner showing you how many current connections you have.

to the Bluetooth network. To give you an idea how this works, follow these steps to connect a Mac to the Personal Hotspot via Bluetooth:

1. **Click System Preferences in the Dock.** Your Mac opens the System Preferences window.

2. **Click Bluetooth.** The Bluetooth window appears.

3. **Beneath the list of Bluetooth devices, click Add (+).** Your Mac launches the Bluetooth Setup Assistant.

4. **Click your iPhone in the list of nearby Bluetooth devices, and then click Continue.**

5. **On your iPhone, tap Pair.**

6. **On your Mac, click Quit.**

7. **When your Mac tells you a new network interface has been detected, click Network Preferences.** If you don't see this message, click Show All in the Preferences window, and then click Network.

8. **In the Network window, click Bluetooth PAN.** Make sure your iPhone is displayed in the Device list (see Figure 2.8) and then click Connect. Your Mac connects to your iPhone's Personal Hotspot.

2.8 To make a Bluetooth connection to a Personal Hotspot, use the Bluetooth PAN network interface to connect to your iPhone.

Genius

If you're using a Bluetooth-enabled Windows PC, first make sure Bluetooth is on (how you do this depends on the version of Windows) and then pair it with your iPhone. Use the Bluetooth menu to select your iPhone and then click Connect.

Connecting to the Personal Hotspot using USB

To connect a USB device to a Personal Hotspot, first connect your iPhone to the device with the USB cable. Then, use the device interface to connect it to the USB network. To give you an idea how this works, follow these steps to connect a Mac to the Personal Hotspot via USB:

1. **When your Mac tells you a new network interface has been detected, click Network Preferences.**

2. **In the Network window, click iPhone USB.**

3. **Click Apply.** Your Mac connects to your iPhone's Personal Hotspot, as shown in Figure 2.9.

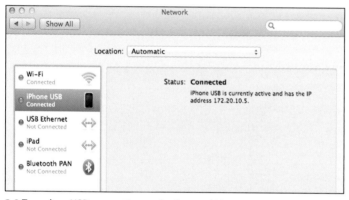

2.9 To make a USB connection to the Personal Hotspot using a Mac, use the iPhone USB network interface to connect to your iPhone.

Genius

If you're using a Windows PC, as soon as you connect the iPhone to the PC using the USB cable, Windows should automatically connect to the Personal Hotspot and start using the Internet connection. If not, open the Network Connections window (how you do this depends on the version of Windows) and make sure the Apple Mobile Device Ethernet connection is enabled.

Keeping an Eye on Your Data Usage

If you're using your iPhone with a plan that comes with a maximum amount of monthly data and you exceed that monthly cap, you'll almost certainly pay big bucks for the privilege. To avoid that, most cellular providers are kind enough to send you a message when you approach your cap. However, if you don't trust that process, or if you're just paranoid about these things (justly, in my view), then you can keep an eye on your data usage yourself. Your iPhone keeps track of the cellular network data it has sent or received, as well as the Internet tethering data it has sent or received using Personal Hotspot.

First, take a look at your most recent bill from your cellular provider and, in particular, look for the dates the bill covers. For example, the bill might run from the 24th of one month to the 23rd of the next month. This is important because it tells you when you need to reset the usage data on your iPhone.

Now follow these steps to check your cellular data usage:

1. **On the Home screen, tap Settings.** The Settings app appears.

2. **Tap General to open the General screen.**

3. **Tap Usage.** The Usage screen opens.

4. **Tap Cellular Usage.** The Cellular Usage screen opens.

5. **In the Cellular Network Data section, read the Sent and Received values, as shown in Figure 2.10.**

6. **If you've been using the Personal Hotspot, also read the Sent and Received values in the Tether Data section.**

7. **If you're at the end of your data period, tap Reset Statistics to start with fresh values for the new period.**

Usage	Cellular Usage	
Call Time		
Current Period		2 Minutes
Lifetime		2 Minutes
Cellular Network Data		
Sent		1.2 MB
Received		21.5 MB
Tether Data		
Sent		4.4 MB
Received		16.6 MB

2.10 In the Cellular Usage screen, use the values in the Cellular Network Data and Tether Data sections to track your total data usage.

Controlling Network Data

Your iPhone gives you fairly precise control over your network data. For example, you can toggle just the 3G data, all cellular data, data roaming, or all your iPhone antennas. The next few sections provide the details.

Turning off 3G

Using the 3G cellular network is a real pleasure because it's so much faster than a molasses-in-January EDGE connection. If 3G has a downside, it's that it uses up a lot of battery power. That's true even if you're currently connected to a Wi-Fi network, because the 3G antenna is constantly looking for a 3G signal. If you'll be on your Wi-Fi network for a while, or if your battery is running low and you don't need a 3G cellular connection, you should turn off the 3G antenna to reduce the load on your iPhone's battery. Here's how:

1. **On the Home screen, tap Settings.** The Settings app appears.
2. **Tap General to open the General screen.**
3. **Tap Network.** The Network screen opens.
4. **Tap the Enable 3G switch to Off, as shown in Figure 2.11.**

Turning off cellular data

If you've reached the limit of your cellular data plan, you almost certainly want to avoid going over the cap because the charges are usually prohibitively expensive. As long as you have a Wi-Fi network in range, or you're disciplined enough not to surf the web or cruise YouTube when there's no Wi-Fi in sight, you'll be okay. Still, accidents can happen. For example, you might accidentally tap a link in an e-mail message or text message, or someone in your household might use your phone without knowing about your restrictions.

2.11 Use the Network screen to change the Enable 3G setting to Off.

To prevent these sorts of accidents (or if you simply don't trust yourself when it comes to YouTube), you can turn off cellular data altogether, which means your iPhone only accesses Internet data if it has a Wi-Fi signal. Follow these steps to turn off cellular data on your iPhone:

1. **On the Home screen, tap Settings.** The Settings app appears.
2. **Tap General to open the General screen.**

3. **Tap Network.** The Network screen opens.

4. **Tap the Cellular Data switch (see Figure 2.11, shown earlier) to Off.**

Now, if you try to access the Internet without a Wi-Fi connection, you see the dialog shown in Figure 2.12. If you really must connect, you can tap Settings to jump directly to the Network screen.

Turning off data roaming

Data roaming is an often-convenient cell phone feature that enables you to make calls — and, with your iPhone, surf the web, check and send e-mail, and exchange text messages — when you're outside of your normal coverage area. The downside is that roaming charges are almost always eye-poppingly expensive. You're often talking several dollars per minute, depending on where you are and what type of service you're using. Not good!

2.12 With cellular data turned off, you see this dialog when you try to access Internet data without being connected to a Wi-Fi network.

Unfortunately, if you have your iPhone's Data Roaming feature turned on, you may incur massive roaming charges even if you never use your phone! That's because your iPhone still performs background checks for things like incoming e-mail messages and text messages, so a week in some far-off land could cost you hundreds of dollars without even using your phone.

To avoid this insanity, turn off your iPhone's Data Roaming feature when you don't need it. Follow these steps:

1. **On the Home screen, tap Settings.** The Settings app appears.

2. **Tap General.** The General screen appears.

3. **Tap Network.** The Network screen appears.

4. **Tap the Data Roaming switch (see Figure 2.11, shown earlier) to Off.**

Switching your iPhone to Airplane mode

When you board a flight, aviation regulations in most countries are super strict about cell phones — no calls in and no calls out. In fact, most of those regulations ban wireless signals of any kind. This means your iPhone is a real hazard to sensitive airline equipment because it transmits Wi-Fi and Bluetooth signals, even if there are no Wi-Fi receivers or Bluetooth devices within 30,000 feet of your current position.

Your pilot or friendly flight attendant will suggest that passengers simply turn off their phones. Sure, that does the job, but darn it, you've got an iPhone, which means there are plenty of things you can do outside of its wireless capabilities, such as listen to music or an audiobook, watch a show, view photos, and much more.

So how do you reconcile the no-wireless-and-that-means-you regulations with the iPhone's multitude of no-wireless-required apps? You put your iPhone into a special state called Airplane mode. This mode turns off the transceivers — the internal components that transmit and receive wireless signals — for the phone, Wi-Fi, and Bluetooth features. With your iPhone now safely in compliance of federal aviation regulations, you're free to use any app that doesn't rely on wireless transmissions.

Follow these steps to activate Airplane mode:

1. **On the Home screen, tap Settings.** The Settings app appears.

2. **Tap the Airplane Mode switch to turn this setting On, as shown in Figure 2.13.** Your iPhone disconnects your cellular network and your wireless network (if you have a current connection). Notice, as well, that while Airplane mode is on, the Airplane icon appears in the status bar in place of the Signal Strength and Network icons.

2.13 When your iPhone is in Airplane mode, the Airplane icon appears in the status bar.

Note

If a flight attendant sees you playing around with your iPhone, he or she may ask you to confirm that the phone is off. (One obviously iPhone-savvy attendant even asked me if my phone was in Airplane mode.) Showing the Airplane icon should be sufficient.

Creating a VPN Connection

What do you do if you want to transfer secure data, such as financial information or personal files, between your network and your iPhone? With most connections, that's a problem. A malicious hacker might not be able to access your system directly, but he certainly can use a packet sniffer (or similar technology) to access your incoming and outgoing data. Because that data isn't encrypted, the hacker can easily read the contents of the packets.

The solution is a tried-and-true technology called virtual private networking (VPN), which offers secure access to a private network over a public connection, such as the Internet. VPN is secure because it uses a technique called tunneling, which establishes a connection between two computers — a VPN server and a VPN client — using a specific port (such as port 1723). Control-connection packets are sent back and forth to maintain the connection between the two computers (to, in a sense, keep the tunnel open).

When it comes to sending the actual network data — sometimes called the payload — each network packet is encrypted and then encapsulated within a regular IP packet, which is then routed through the tunnel. Any hacker can see this IP packet traveling across the Internet, but even if he intercepts and examines it, no harm is done because the content of the packet — the actual data — is encrypted. When the IP packet arrives at the other end of the tunnel, VPN decapsulates the network packet and then decrypts it to reveal the payload (which is part of the reason why VPN connections tend to be quite slow).

Your iPhone supports VPN and it can use any of the following three tunneling protocols:

- **Point-to-Point Tunneling Protocol (PPTP).** This protocol is the most widely used in VPN setups. It was developed by Microsoft and is related to the Point-to-Point Protocol (PPP) that's commonly used to transport IP packets over the Internet. PPTP sets up the tunnel and encapsulates the encrypted network packets in an IP packet for transport across the tunnel.

- **IP Security (IPSec).** This protocol encrypts the payload (IP packets only), sets up the tunnel, and encapsulates the encrypted network packets in an IP packet for transport across the tunnel.

- **Layer 2 Tunneling Protocol (L2TP).** This protocol goes beyond PPTP by allowing VPN connections over networks other than just the Internet (such as networks based on X.25, ATM, or Frame Relay). L2TP uses the encryption portion of IPSec to encrypt the network packets.

If you have a VPN server set up at work, your administrator can supply you with the necessary data for the connection: the type of protocol, the server name or address, your account username and password, and so on. With all that in hand, follow these steps to set up a VPN connection on your iPhone:

1. **On the Home screen, tap Settings.** The Settings app appears.

2. **Tap General.** The General screen appears.

3. **Tap Network.** The Network screen appears.

4. **Tap VPN.** The VPN screen appears.

5. **Tap Add VPN Configuration.** The Add Configuration screen appears.

6. **Tap the protocol you want to use.** Figure 2.14 shows the PPTP tab.

7. **Type the connection data provided by your administrator.**

8. **Tap Save.** Your iPhone adds the connection to the VPN screen.

9. **Tap the VPN switch to On.** Your iPhone connects to the VPN server.

2.14 Tap the VPN protocol used by your network and then enter the connection details.

How Can I Get More Out of the Phone App?

The iPhone is chock-full of great apps that enable you to surf the web, send and receive e-mail messages, listen to music, take photos, organize your contacts, schedule appointments, and much, much more. These features put the *smart* in iPhone's status as a *smartphone,* but let's not forget the *phone* part! So, while you're probably familiar with the basic steps required to make and answer calls, iPhone's powerful phone component is loaded with amazing features that can make the cell phone portion of your life easier, more convenient, and more efficient. This chapter takes you through these features.

Working with Outgoing Calls

You can do much more with your iPhone than just make a call the old-fashioned way — by dialing the phone number. There are speedy shortcuts you can take, and even settings to alter the way your outgoing calls look on the receiver's phone.

Making calls quickly

The iPhone has a seemingly endless number of methods you can use to make a call. It's nice to have the variety, but in this have-your-people-call-my-people world, the big question is not how many ways can you make a call, but how *fast* can you make a call? Here are my favorite iPhone speed-calling techniques:

- **Favorites list.** This list acts as a kind of speed dial for the iPhone because you use it to store the phone numbers you call most often, and you have space to add your top 20 numbers. To call someone in your Favorites list, tap the Phone icon on the Home screen, tap Favorites, and then tap the number you want to call. I show you how to manage your Favorites later in this chapter.

- **Visual Voicemail.** If you're checking your voicemail messages (from the Home screen, tap Phone, and then tap Voicemail) and you want to return someone's call, tap the message and then tap Call Back.

- **Text message.** If someone includes a phone number in a text message, your iPhone handily converts it into a link. The number appears in blue, underlined text, much like a link on a web page, as shown in Figure 3.1. Tap the phone number to call it. You can also use a similar technique to call numbers embedded in web pages (see Chapter 4) and e-mail messages (see Chapter 5).

3.1 Your iPhone is kind enough to convert a phone number in a text message into a link that you can tap to call.

Note You can do a lot more than just call a number in a text message. Tap the blue Info icon (the arrow) that appears to the right of the message and you see a menu of actions you can take with the phone number, including texting, initiating a FaceTime call, creating a new contact, and adding the number to an existing contact.

- **Recent numbers.** The Recent Calls list (from the Home screen, tap Phone, and then tap Recents) shows your recent phone activity: calls you've made, calls you've received, and calls you've missed. Recent Calls is great because it enables you to quickly redial someone with whom you've had recent contact. To call the person using a different phone number, tap the Info icon (the arrow to the right of the name or number), and then tap the phone number you want to use to make the call. If you want to return a missed call, tap Missed and then tap the call.

Genius If your Recent Calls list is populated with names or numbers that you know you won't ever call back, you should clear the list and start fresh. In the Recent Calls screen, tap Edit, tap Clear, and then tap Clear All Recents.

Voice dialing a call with Siri

Tapping a favorite number, a recent number, or a text message phone number link are all pretty easy methods to launch a phone call, but there's an even easier way that doesn't require a single tap on your part. I speak, of course, of voice dialing, which is part of the Siri app.

To get started, tap and hold the Home button (or press and hold the Mic button of the iPhone headphones, or the equivalent button on a Bluetooth headset). The Siri screen appears. You have six ways to tell Siri to initiate a call:

- **To call a person in your Contacts list.** Say "Call *first last,*" where *first* and *last* are the person's first and last names as given in your Contacts list. If the contact is a business, say "Call *company,*" where *company* is the business name as given in your Contacts list.

Note Besides the verb "Call," Siri also initiates a call if you say "Telephone," "Phone," or "Dial."

● **To call a person who has a relationship with you that you've defined with Siri.** Say "Call *relationship*," where *relationship* is the connection you've defined (such as brother or mother).

● **To call a person in your Contacts list with a unique first name.** Say "Call *first*," where *first* is the person's first name as given in your Contacts list. If the name isn't unique, Siri displays a list of matching contacts and asks you to say the one you want to call.

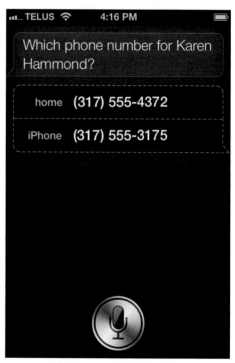

● **To call a person in your Contacts list who has multiple numbers.** Say "Call *first last label*," where *first* and *last* are the person's first and last names as given in your Contacts list, and *label* is the label you assigned to that number (such as "mobile" or "home"). If you're not sure of the correct label, skip that part and Siri will display the screen shown in Figure 3.2 and will let you know which labels are available. You then say the label of the number you want to call.

● **To call one of your own numbers.** Say "Call *label*," where label is the label of the number in your Contacts data that you want to call.

3.2 You see this screen if the person you're calling has multiple numbers and you don't specify a label.

● **You only have a phone number.** Say "Call *number*," where number is the full phone number you want to dial.

Genius You can be fairly casual about the syntax you use when specifying a label. For example, you can say something like "Call Belinda Gray at home" or "Call my sister on her mobile phone."

That's it. For a contact, Siri responds with "Calling *name label*" (where *name* is the person's name and *label* is the label assigned to the phone number). For a phone number, Siri responds with "Calling *number*" (where *number* is the phone number you specified).

Configuring your iPhone not to show your caller ID

When you use your iPhone to call someone, and the called phone supports Caller ID, your number and often your name appear. If you'd rather hide your identity for some reason, you can configure your iPhone not to show your caller ID:

1. **On the Home screen, tap Settings.** The Settings app appears.

2. **Tap Phone.** The Phone screen appears.

3. **Tap Show My Caller ID.** The Show My Caller ID screen appears.

4. **Tap the Show My Caller ID switch to Off.** Your iPhone disables Caller ID.

Handling Incoming Calls

When a call comes into your iPhone, you answer it, right? What could be simpler? You'd be surprised. Your iPhone gives you quite a few options for dealing with that call, aside from just answering it. After all, you don't want to talk to everyone all the time, do you?

Note If you have a Verizon or Sprint cellular plan, remember that these providers use the CDMA cellular protocol, which is a monotasking system. This means, for example, that if you're on the phone, you can't surf the web or perform any data-related activities. Similarly, if you're surfing the web, you can't send calls, and if a call comes in, your iPhone stops your web session to receive it.

Silencing an incoming call

When you're in a situation where the ringing of a cell phone is inappropriate, bothersome, or just plain rude, you, of course, practice *celliquette* (that is, cell etiquette) and turn off your ringer. (On your iPhone, position the phone in portrait mode with the Home button at the bottom and then flick the Silent/Ring switch on the left side panel to the silent position.) However, we're merely human and we all forget to turn off our phone's ringer once in a while.

Your job in that situation is to grab your phone and answer it as quickly as possible. However, what if you're in a situation where answering the call is bad form? Or what if you'd prefer to delay answering the call until you can leave the room or get out of earshot? That's a stickier situation, for sure, but the iPhone designers have been there and they've come up with a simple solution: press either the Sleep/Wake button on the phone's top panel (again, assuming you have the phone in portrait mode with the Home button at the bottom) or one of the Volume buttons on the left side panel. Either of these actions stops your iPhone from ringing (or vibrating). The ringing is still going on (your caller hears it on her end), so you've still got the usual four rings to answer the call should you decide to.

Sending an incoming call directly to voicemail

Sometimes you just don't want to talk to someone. Whether this person is your significant other calling to complain, a friend who never seems to have anything to say and just talks in circles for ten minutes, or someone who calls while you're indisposed, you might prefer to ignore the call.

That's not a problem on your iPhone:

- If the phone isn't locked, tap the red Decline button on the touchscreen.
- If you're using the earbuds, you just need to squeeze and hold the microphone/clicker for two seconds.
- Press the Sleep/Wake button twice in quick succession.

Any of these methods sends the call directly to voicemail.

Note

If you ignore a call, as with any phone, the caller will know that you've ignored the call when voicemail kicks in before the normal four rings. If you don't want someone to know you are ignoring his or her call, just silence the ring. The caller will still hear the standard four rings before the voicemail and be none the wiser that you just didn't pick up your phone.

Turning off Call Waiting

If you're already on a call and another one comes in, your iPhone springs into action and displays the person's name or number, as well as three options: Ignore, Hold Call + Answer, and End Call + Answer. (See the section about handling multiple calls later in this chapter for more info on these options.) This is part of your iPhone's Call Waiting feature, and it's great if you're expecting an important call or if you want to add the caller to a conference call that you've set up.

However, the rest of the time you might just find it annoying and intrusive (and anyone you put on hold or hang up on to take the new call probably finds it rude and insulting). In that case, you can turn off Call Waiting by following these steps:

1. **On the Home screen, tap Settings.** The Settings app appears.
2. **Tap Phone.** The Phone screen appears.

3. **Tap Call Waiting.** The Call Waiting screen appears.

4. **Tap the Call Waiting switch to Off.** Your iPhone disables Call Waiting.

Forwarding calls to another number

What do you do about incoming calls if you can't use your iPhone for a while? For example, if you're going on a flight, you must either turn off your iPhone or put it in Airplane mode (as described in Chapter 2) so incoming calls won't go through. Similarly, if you have to return your iPhone to Apple for repairs or battery replacement, the phone won't be available if anyone tries to call you.

For these and other situations where your iPhone can't accept incoming calls, you can work around the problem by having your calls forwarded to another number, such as your work or home number. Here's how it's done:

1. **On the Home screen, tap Settings.** The Settings app appears.

2. **Tap Phone.** The Phone screen appears.

3. **Tap Call Forwarding.** The Call Forwarding screen appears.

4. **Tap the Call Forwarding switch to On.** Your iPhone displays the Forwarding To screen.

5. **Tap the phone number to use for the forwarded calls.**

6. **Tap Call Forwarding to return to the Call Forwarding screen.** Figure 3.3 shows the Call Forwarding screen set up to forward calls. In the status bar at the top of the screen, note the little phone icon with an arrow that appears to the right of the time to let you know that Call Forwarding is on.

Call Forwarding icon

3.3 Activate Call Forwarding to have your iPhone calls forwarded to another number.

Juggling Multiple Calls and Conference Calls

We all juggle multiple tasks and duties these days, so it's not surprising that sometimes this involves juggling multiple phone calls:

- You might need to call two separate people on a related issue, and then switch back and forth between the callers as the negotiations (or whatever) progress.

● You might already be on a call and another call comes in from a person you need to speak to. So, you put the initial person on hold, deal with the new caller, and then return to the first person.

● You might need to speak to two separate people at the same time on the same phone call — in other words, a conference call.

In the real world, juggling multiple calls or setting up conference calls often requires a special phone or a fancy phone system. In the iPhone world, however, these things are a snap. In fact, the way the iPhone juggles multiple calls really is something spectacular. Jumping back and forth between calls is simple, putting someone on hold to answer an incoming call is a piece of cake, and creating a conference call from incoming or outgoing calls is criminally easy.

When you're on an initial call, your iPhone displays the Call Options screen, as shown in Figure 3.4. To make another call, tap add call and then use the Phone app to place your second call.

Once the second call goes through, the Call Options screen changes: The top of the screen shows the first caller's name (or number) with HOLD beside it, and below that you see the

3.4 When you're on a call, your iPhone displays these call options.

name (or number) of the second caller and the duration of that call. Figure 3.5 shows the new screen layout. To switch to the person on hold, tap the swap button. iPhone puts the second caller on hold and returns you to the first caller. Congratulations! You now have two calls going at once.

Genius

You may be wondering how you put a phone call on hold. For reasons that remain mysterious, your iPhone hides this useful feature. To see it, you have to turn off the FaceTime video calling feature, as described later in this chapter. When you do that, your iPhone replaces the FaceTime icon shown in Figure 3.4 with a Hold icon. To put the current caller on hold, tap that icon.

If you're already on the phone and another call comes in, your iPhone displays the number (and the name, if the caller is in your Contacts list) and gives you three ways to handle the call, as shown in Figure 3.6:

- **Ignore.** Tap this option to send the incoming call directly to voicemail.

- **Hold Call + Answer.** Tap this option to put the first call on hold and answer the incoming call. You're working with two calls again in this scenario, so you can tap swap to switch between the callers.

- **End Call + Answer.** Tap this option to drop the first call and answer the incoming call.

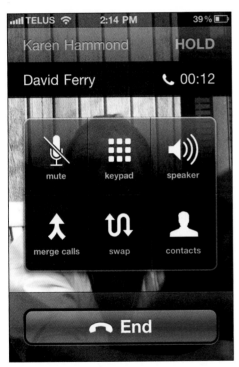

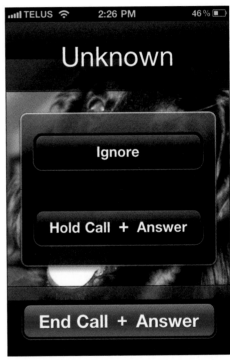

3.5 The iPhone Call Options screen with two phone calls on the go.

3.6 The iPhone displays this screen if a new call comes in while you're on another.

If you have two calls going, you might prefer that all three of you be able to talk to each other in a conference call. Easier done than said — just tap merge calls. iPhone combines everyone into a single conference call and displays Conference at the top of the Call Options screen. Click the Info arrow and iPhone displays the participants' names (or numbers) in the Conference screen, as shown in Figure 3.7.

From here, there are a few methods you can use to manage your conference call:

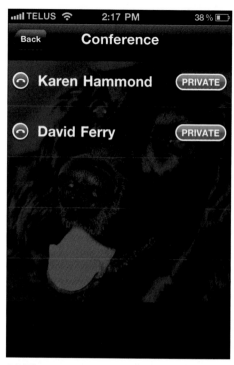

- **To speak with one of the callers privately, tap the green Private key next to that person's name or number.** This places you in a one-on-one call with that person and places the other caller on hold.

- **To drop someone from the conference call, tap the red Phone icon to the left of that person's name or number, and then tap End Call to confirm.** iPhone drops that caller and you resume a private call with the other party.

- **To add someone else to the conference call, tap Back to return to the Call Options screen.** Tap add call and then make the call. Once the call goes through, tap merge calls.

- **To add an incoming caller to the conference call, tap Hold Call + Answer.** Once you're connected, tap merge calls.

3.7 When you merge two phone calls, the participants' names or numbers appear in the Conference screen.

Clearly, juggling multiple calls on a phone has never been easier. The iPhone does a remarkable job of organizing calls and giving you an admirably easy process to swap, add, drop, or combine calls in conference.

Caution You can hold a conference call with up to five people at once by repeating the steps outlined for conference calls. However, remember that conference calls use up your minutes faster — two callers use them up twice as fast, three callers use them up three times as fast, and so on — so you may want to be judicious when using this feature.

Managing Your Favorites List

The iPhone's Favorites list is great for making quick calls because you can often get someone on the horn in just three finger gestures (from the Home screen, tap Phone, tap Favorites, and then tap the number). Of course, this only works if the numbers you call most often appear on your Favorites list. Fortunately, your iPhone gives you lots of different ways to populate the list. Here are the easiest methods to use:

- **In the Favorites list, tap + to open the All Contacts screen and then tap the person you want to add.** If that person has multiple phone numbers, tap the number you want to use as a favorite. When the iPhone asks how you want to call the person, tap either Voice Call or FaceTime.

Note

This is a good place to remind you that the Favorites list isn't a list of people, it's a list of numbers. That's why the list shows both the person's name and the type of phone number (work, home, mobile, and so on).

- **In the Recent Calls list, tap the More Info icon to the right of the call from (or to) the person you want to add and then tap Add to Favorites.** If the person has multiple phone numbers, tap the number you want to use as the favorite, and then tap either Voice Call or FaceTime. iPhone adds a star beside the phone number to remind you that it's a favorite.

- **In Visual Voicemail, tap the More Info icon beside a message, tap Add to Favorites, and then tap either Voice Call or FaceTime.**

- **In the Contacts list, tap the person you want to add and then tap Add to Favorites.** If the person has multiple phone numbers, tap the number you want to use as the favorite, and then tap either Voice Call or FaceTime. iPhone adds a star beside the phone number to remind you that it's a favorite.

You can add up to 20 numbers in the Favorites list, but the iPhone screen only shows eight at a time. This means that if you want to call someone who doesn't appear in the initial screen, you need to scroll down to bring that number into view. Therefore, your Favorites list is most efficient when the people you call most often appear in the first eight numbers. Your iPhone adds each new number to the bottom of the Favorites list, so chances are that at least some of your favorite numbers aren't showing up in the top eight. Follow these steps to fix that:

1. **In the Favorites list, tap Edit.** iPhone displays Delete icons to the left of each favorite and Drag icons to the right, as shown in Figure 3.8.

2. **If you want to get rid of a favorite, tap its Delete icon, tap Remove, and then tap Edit to return to Edit mode.**

3. **To move a favorite to a new location, tap and drag the icon up or down until the favorite is where you want it, and then release the icon.**

4. **Tap Done.**

Converting a Phone Number into a Contact

Your iPhone is at its most efficient when the numbers you call are part of your Contacts list. Then, not only can you add contacts to the Favorites list for quick, speed-dial-like access, but you can also use the index (the letters A, B, C, and so on that run down the right side of the Contacts list). Then, it just takes a few finger flicks to rapidly find and tap the person with whom you want to chin-wag.

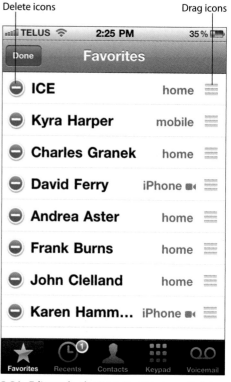

Delete icons   Drag icons

3.8 In Edit mode, the Favorites list shows Delete icons on the left and Drag icons on the right.

Genius

You can also convert a phone number on your Recent Calls list to a contact. On the Home screen, tap Phone, and then tap Recents to open the Recent Calls list. Locate the name or phone number you want to convert to a contact and then tap the blue More Info icon. Tap Create New Contact, fill in the other contact info, and then tap Save.

I talk about ways to add contacts in Chapter 9. For now, here's a quick way to add a contact right from the Phone app keypad:

1. **In the Home screen, tap Phone.** The Phone app appears.

2. **In the menu bar, tap Keypad.** The Keypad screen appears.

3. **Type the phone number of a person you want to add as a contact.**

4. **Tap the Add Contact icon, to the left of the Call button, as shown in Figure 3.9.**

5. **Tap Create New Contact.** The New Contact screen appears.

6. **Fill in the other contact info as needed.**

7. **Tap Save.** Your iPhone adds the new contact and returns you to the Keypad screen.

8. **Tap Call to proceed with the phone call.**

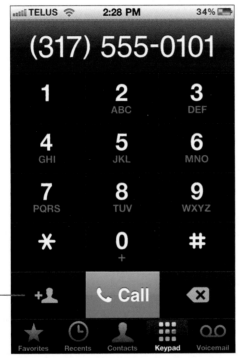

Add Contact

3.9 After you type a phone number using the keypad, tap the Add Contact icon to create a contact for the number.

Note The phone number you're dialing might be an alternative number of an existing contact. For example, you may already have set up the contact with a home number, but now you're dialing that person's cell number. In that case, tap the Add Contact icon and then tap Add to Existing Contact. Use the Contacts list to tap the contact, choose the phone type (such as mobile), and then tap Save.

Video Calling with FaceTime

One of the most welcome features in the iPhone is a front-mounted camera, which means you can finally take pictures of yourself without guessing where the Shutter button is! Fortunately, that's not all the front camera is good for. With the Apple FaceTime feature, you can use your iPhone to make video calls where you can actually see the other person face to face. It's an awesome feature, but to use it, the other person must be using an iPhone 4 or 4S, an iPad 2 or later, a fourth-generation (or later) iPod touch, or a Mac with a video camera and the FaceTime application installed.

Note

In previous versions of iOS, both of you also needed to be on a Wi-Fi connection. That restriction has been dropped in iOS 5. You can now conduct FaceTime calls over a 3G connection.

The good news about FaceTime (besides how cool it is), is that it's a complete no-brainer to use. You don't have to activate any options, configure any settings, download any software, or connect to any servers.

Initiating a FaceTime call

To initiate a FaceTime call, you have a wide variety of choices:

- Call the other person normally, and once you're connected, tap the FaceTime icon, shown in Figure 3.10.

- If the other person is in your Contacts list, open the contact and tap the FaceTime button, shown in Figure 3.11.

- In the Messages app, start a new conversation with the person — or open an existing one — scroll to the top of the window, and then tap FaceTime.

- Press and hold the Home button (or the Mic button on your iPhone headphones) until you see the Siri app. Then, say "FaceTime *name*" (where *name* is the name of the other person).

- If you've recently made a FaceTime call to someone, tap the Phone app's Recents icon, and then tap the FaceTime call (which the Phone app indicates with a FaceTime icon).

3.10 To convert the current call to a FaceTime video call, tap the FaceTime icon.

If another FaceTime user calls you, you see the message "*Name* would like FaceTime" (where *Name* is the caller's name if he is in your Contacts list), as shown in Figure 3.12.

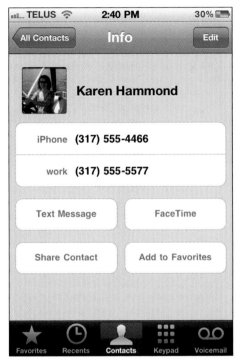

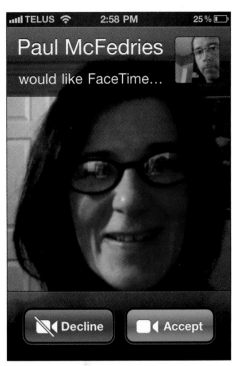

3.11 To call a contact using FaceTime, open the contact and tap the FaceTime button.

3.12 When a FaceTime user calls you, tap Accept to initiate a FaceTime video call.

Tap Accept and your video call connects, just like that. You see your caller's (hopefully) smiling face in the full iPhone screen, and your own mug in a picture-in-picture (PIP) window, as shown in Figure 3.13.

Genius

Your PIP window appears by default in the upper-right corner. If you prefer a different position, tap and drag the PIP window to any corner of the screen.

The FaceTime calling screen includes three buttons in the menu bar:

- **Mute.** Tap this icon (it's the one on the left) to mute the sound from your end of the conversation (you can still hear sound from the other person's end).

- **End.** Tap this button (it's the one in the middle) to end the call.

Caution Mute is the FaceTime equivalent of hold. Note, however, that there's no way to put a FaceTime caller on hold while you answer another call. If a new call comes in while you're on FaceTime and you accept the call, your iPhone disconnects the FaceTime call.

● **Switch Cameras.** Tap this button to switch your video output to the rear camera (for example, to show your caller something in front of you).

Disabling FaceTime

There will certainly be times when you simply don't want a face-to-face conversation, no matter who's calling. Perhaps you're in a secret location or you just don't look your best that day. Whatever the reason, you can follow these steps to turn off FaceTime:

1. **In the Home screen, tap Settings.** The Settings app appears.

2. **Tap FaceTime.** The FaceTime screen appears.

3. **Tap the FaceTime switch to Off.**

Now, when people try to call you using FaceTime, they see a message saying that you're "not available for FaceTime."

3.13 Face-to-face calling on the iPhone: the future is finally here!

How Can I Make the Most of iPhone Web Surfing?

One of the most popular modern pastimes is web surfing, and now you can surf even when you're out and about thanks to the large screen on your iPhone and support for speedy networks, such as 3G and Wi-Fi. You perform these surfin' safaris using, appropriately enough, the Safari web browser app, which is easy to use and intuitive. However, the Safari app offers quite a few options and features, many of which are hidden in obscure nooks and crannies of the iPhone interface. If you think your surfing activities could be faster, more efficient, more productive, or more secure, this chapter can help.

Touchscreen Tips for Websites

The touchscreen operates much the same way in Safari as it does in the other iPhone apps. You can use it to scroll pages, zoom in and out, click links, fill in forms, enter addresses, and more. The screen is remarkably fluid in its motion, and its response to your touch is neither hyperactive nor sluggish. It actually makes surfing the web a pleasure, which isn't something you can say about most smartphones.

Here's a little collection of touchscreen tips that ought to make your web excursions even easier:

- **Precision zooming.** Zooming on the iPhone is straightforward. To zoom in, spread two fingers apart; to zoom out, pinch two fingers together. However, when you zoom in on a web page, it's almost always because you want to zoom in on something. It might be an image, a link, a text box, or just a section of text. To ensure that your target ends up in the middle of the zoomed page, place your thumb and forefinger together on the section of the screen you want to zoom, and then spread your thumb and forefinger apart to zoom in.

- **The old pan-and-zoom.** Another useful technique for getting a target in the middle of a zoomed page is to zoom and pan at the same time. That is, as you spread (or pinch) your fingers, you also move them up, down, left, or right to pan the page at the same time. This takes a bit of practice, and often the iPhone only allows you to pan either horizontally or vertically (not both), but it's still a useful trick.

- **Double-tap.** A quick way to zoom in on a page that has various sections is to double-tap on the specific section — it could be an image, a paragraph, a table, or a column of text — that you want magnified. Your iPhone zooms the section to fill the width of the screen. Double-tap again to return the page to the regular view.

Note

The double-tap-to-zoom trick only works on pages that have identifiable sections. If a page is just a wall of text, you can double-tap until the cows come home (that's a long time) and nothing much happens.

- **One tap to the top.** If you're reading a particularly long-winded web page and you're near the bottom, you may have quite a long way to scroll if you need to head back to the top to get at the address bar or tap the Search icon. Save the wear and tear on your flicking finger! Instead, tap the status bar at the top of the screen; Safari immediately transports you to the top of the page.

● **Tap and hold to see where a link takes you.** You "click" a link in a web page by tapping it with your finger. In a regular web browser, you can see where a link takes you (that is, the URL) by hovering the mouse pointer over the link and checking out the link address in the status bar. That doesn't work on your iPhone, but you can still find out the address of a link before tapping it. Hold your finger on the link for a few seconds. Safari then displays a pop-up screen showing the link text and, more importantly, the URL, as shown in Figure 4.1. If the link looks legit, either tap Open to surf there in the current browser page,

4.1 Hold your finger on a link to see the URL and several link options.

or tap Open in New Page to start a fresh page (see the section about opening and managing multiple browser pages later in this chapter for more info). If you decide not to follow the link, tap Cancel.

● **Tap and hold to make a copy of a link address.** If you want to include a link address in another app, such as a note or an e-mail message, you can copy it. Tap and hold your finger on the link for a few seconds and Safari displays the pop-up screen shown in Figure 4.1. Tap Copy to place the link address into memory, switch to the other app, tap the cursor, and then tap Paste.

● **Use the portrait view to navigate a long page.** When you rotate your iPhone 90 degrees, the touchscreen switches to landscape view, which gives you a wider view of the page. Return the iPhone to its upright position, and you return to portrait view. If you have a long way to scroll in a page, first use the portrait view to scroll down, and then switch to the landscape view to increase the text size. I find that scrolling in the portrait view goes much faster than in landscape.

● **Two-fingered frame scrolling.** Some websites are organized using a technique called frames, where the overall site takes up the browser window, but some of the site's pages appear in a separate rectangular area — called a frame — usually with its own scroll bar. In such sites, you may find that the usual one-fingered scroll technique only scrolls the entire browser window, not the content within the frame. To scroll the frame stuff, you must use two fingers to do the scrolling. Weird!

● **Getting a larger keyboard.** The on-screen keyboard appears when you tap into a box that allows typing. However, the keyboard you get in landscape view uses noticeably larger keys than the one you see in portrait view. For the fumble-fingered among us, larger keys are a must, so always rotate the iPhone into landscape mode to enter text.

Note Remember that rotating the iPhone only changes the view if your iPhone is upright. The iPhone uses gravity to sense the change in orientation, so if it's lying flat on a table, rotating the iPhone won't do anything. So rotate it first before you put it on the table.

● **Quick access to common top-level domains.** A top-level domain (TLD) is the part of the domain name that comes after the last dot. For example, in wiley.com, the *.com* part is the TLD. The most common TLD is *.com,* so your iPhone thoughtfully includes a .com key on the Safari keyboard. If you regularly use any of the other TLDs, you might think you have to type them the old-fashioned way. Nope! Tap and hold the .com key, and a pop-up appears with keys for .net, .edu, and .org, as well as .us. Just tap the one you want.

Browsing Tips for Faster Surfing

If you're like me, the biggest problem you have with the web is that it's just so darned huge. We spend great big chunks of our day visiting sites and still never seem to get to everything on that day's To Surf list. The iPhone helps lessen (but, alas, not eliminate) this problem by allowing you to surf wherever Wi-Fi can be found (or just wherever if you only have a 3G connection). Even so, the faster and more efficient your iPhone surfing sessions are, the more sites you see. The touchscreen tips I covered earlier can help, and in this section I take you through a few more useful tips for speedier surfing.

Opening and managing multiple browser pages

When you're perusing web pages, what happens when you're on a page that you want to keep reading, but you also need to leap over to another page for something? On your computer's web browser, you probably open another tab, use that tab to open the other page, and then switch back to the first page when you finish. It's an essential web-browsing technique, but can it be done with the Safari browser on your iPhone?

Well, the Safari app may not have tabs, but it has the next best thing: pages. With this feature, you can open a second browser window and load a different page into it. Then, it's just a quick tap and flick to switch between them. You're not restricted to a meager two pages either. Your iPhone lets you open up to eight — count 'em, *eight* — pages, so you can throw some wild web page parties.

Note

Some web page links are configured to automatically open the page in a new window, so you might see a new page being created when you tap a link. Also, if you add a web clip to your Home screen (as described in Chapter 1), tapping the icon opens the web clip in a new Safari page.

Here are the steps to follow to open and load multiple pages:

1. **In Safari, tap the Pages icon in the menu bar (see Figure 4.2).** Safari displays a thumbnail version of the current page.

Pages

4.2 Check the Pages icon to see how many web pages you have open, or tap it to open a new one.

2. **Tap New Page.** Safari opens a blank page using the full screen.

3. **Load a website into the new page.** You can do this by selecting a bookmark, entering an address, or whatever.

4. **Repeat Steps 1 to 3 to load as many pages as you need.** As you add pages, Safari keeps track of how many are open and displays the number in the Pages icon, as shown in Figure 4.2.

Once you have two or more pages fired up, here are a couple of techniques you can use to impress your friends:

- **Switch to another page.** Tap the Pages icon to get to the thumbnail view (see Figure 4.3). Flick right or left to bring the page into view, and then tap the page.

- **When you no longer need a page.** Tap the Pages icon, and flick right or left to bring the page into view. Then, tap the X in the upper-left corner. Safari trashes the page without a whimper of protest.

Note

Below the page thumbnails you see several dots, one for each open page, with the current page shown as a white dot. Rather than flicking through the pages, tap to the right of the current dot to navigate to the next page, or tap to the left of the current dot to see the previous page.

Opening a page in the background

When you tap and hold a link and then tap Open in New Page, Safari immediately switches to the new page and loads the link while you wait. That's often the behavior you want because it lets you view the new web page as soon as it loads. However, you might find that most of the time you prefer to stay on the current web page and check out the new page later. In those situations, having to perform those extra taps to get back to the current page gets old in a hurry. The solution is to configure Safari to always open new tabs in the background. Here's how:

1. **On the Home screen, tap Settings.** The Settings app slides in.

2. **Tap Safari.** Your iPhone displays the Safari screen.

3. **Tap Open Links.** Your iPhone displays the Open Links screen.

4. **Tap In Background.**

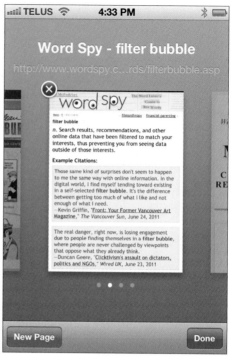

4.3 Tap the Pages icon to see thumbnail versions of your open pages.

Viewing a page without distractions

It seems like only a few years ago that purse-lipped pundits and furrow-browed futurologists were lamenting that the Internet signaled the imminent demise of reading. With pursuits such as viral videos and online gaming a mere click or two away, who would ever sit down and actually read things? Well, a funny thing happened on the way to the future: people read more now than they ever did. Sure, there's some concern that we're no longer reading long articles and challenging books, but most of us spend much of the day reading online.

On the one hand, this isn't all that surprising because there's just so much text out there, most of it available free, and much of it professionally written and edited. On the other hand, this is actually quite surprising, because reading an article or essay online is no picnic. The problem is the sheer amount of distraction on almost any page: background colors or images that clash with the text; ads above, to the side of, and within the text; site features such as search boxes, feed links, and content lists; and those ubiquitous icons for sharing the article with your friends on Facebook, Twitter, Digg, and on and on. Figure 4.4 shows a typical example.

Fortunately, Safari for iOS 5 can help solve this problem by offering the Reader feature. Reader removes all those extraneous page distractions that just get in the way of your reading pleasure. So, instead of a cacophony of text, icons, and images, you see pure, simple, large-enough-to-be-easily-read text. How do you arrive at this blissful state? By tapping the Reader icon, which appears on the right side of the address bar, as pointed out in Figure 4.4. Safari instantly transforms the page, and you see something similar to the page shown in Figure 4.5 (which is the Reader version of the page shown in Figure 4.4).

Reader icon

4.4 Today's web pages are all too often festooned with ads, icons, and other bric-a-brac.

4.5 The Reader version of a web page is a simple and easy-to-read text affair.

Adding bookmarks manually

Although you've seen that the Safari browser on your iPhone offers a few tricks to ease the pain of typing web page addresses, it's still slower and quite a bit more cumbersome than a full-size, physical keyboard (which lets even inexpert typists rattle off addresses lickety-split). All the more reason that you should embrace bookmarks with all your heart. After all, a bookmark lets you jump to a web page with precisely no typing — just a tap or three and you're there.

You probably want to get your iPhone bookmarks off to a flying start by copying a bunch of existing bookmarks from your Mac or Windows PC. That's a good idea, and I show you how to do it in Chapter 6.

Note Syncing bookmarks is a two-way street, which means that any site you bookmark in your iPhone is added to your desktop version of Safari (or Internet Explorer) the next time you sync.

But even if you've done the sync and now have a large collection of bookmarks at your beck and call, it doesn't mean your iPhone bookmark collection is complete. After all, you might find something interesting while you're surfing with the iPhone. If you think you'll want to pay that site another visit down the road, you can create a new bookmark right on the iPhone. Here are the steps to follow:

1. **On the iPhone, use Safari to navigate to the site you want to save.**

2. **Tap the Actions icon in the menu bar.** This is the icon with the arrow in the middle of the Safari menu bar, as shown later in Figure 4.7.

3. **Tap Add Bookmark.** This opens the Add Bookmark screen, as shown in Figure 4.6.

4. **Tap in the top box and enter a name for the site that helps you remember it.** This name is what you see when you scroll through your bookmarks.

5. **Tap Bookmarks.** This displays a list of your bookmark folders.

4.6 Use the Add Bookmark screen to specify the bookmark name and location.

6. **Tap the folder you want to use to store the bookmark.** Safari returns you to the Add Bookmark screen.

7. **Tap Save.** Safari saves the bookmark.

Managing your bookmarks

Once you have a few bookmarks stashed away in the bookmarks list, you may need to perform a few housekeeping chores from time to time, including changing a bookmark's name, address, or folder; reordering bookmarks or folders; or getting rid of bookmarks that have worn out their welcome.

Before you can do any of this, you need to get the Bookmarks list into Edit mode by following these steps:

1. **In Safari, tap the Bookmarks icon in the menu bar, as shown in Figure 4.7.** Safari opens the Bookmarks list.

2. **If the bookmark you want to mess with is located in a particular folder, tap to open that folder.** For example, if you've synced with Safari, then you should have a folder named Bookmarks Bar, which includes all the bookmarks and folders that you've added to the Bookmarks Bar in your desktop version of Safari.

3. **Tap Edit.** Your iPhone switches the Bookmarks list to Edit mode, as shown in Figure 4.8. With Edit mode on the go, you're free to toil away at your bookmarks. Here are the techniques to master:

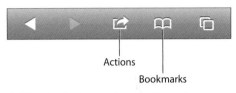

Actions

Bookmarks

4.7 Tap the Bookmarks icon to display the Bookmarks list.

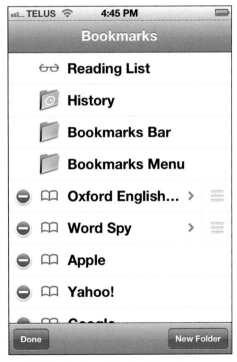

4.8 With the Bookmark list in Edit mode, you can edit, rearrange, and delete bookmarks to your heart's content.

87

- **Edit bookmark info.** Tap the bookmark to fire up the Edit Bookmark screen. From here, you can edit the bookmark name, address, or its folder. When you're done, tap the name of the current bookmark folder in the top-left corner of the screen.

- **Change the bookmark order.** Use the Drag icon on the right to tap and drag a bookmark to a new position in the list. Ideally, you should move your favorite bookmarks near the top of the list for easiest access.

- **Add a bookmark folder.** Tap New Folder to launch the Edit Folder screen, then tap a folder title and select a location. Feel free to use bookmark folders at will because they're a great way to keep your bookmarks neat and tidy (if you're into that kind of thing).

- **Delete a bookmark.** No use for a particular bookmark? No problem. Tap the Delete icon — the minus (–) sign to the left of the bookmark — and then tap the Delete button that appears.

When the dust settles and your bookmark chores are done for the day, tap Done to get out of Edit mode.

Saving a page to read later

In your web travels, you'll often come upon a page with fascinating content that you can't wait to read. Unfortunately, a quick look at the length of the article tells you that you're going to need more time than what you currently have available. So what's a body to do? Quickly scan the article and move on with your life? No, when you come across good web content, you need to savor it. So, should you bookmark the article for future reference? That's not bad, but bookmarks are really for things you want to revisit often, not for pages that you might only read once.

The best solution is a new Safari 5 feature called the Reading List. As the name implies, this is a simple list of things to read. When you don't have time to read something now, add it to your Reading List and you can read it at your leisure.

There are a couple of techniques you can use to add a page to your Reading List:

- Use Safari to navigate to the page that you want to read later, tap the Actions icon, and then tap Add to Reading List.

- Tap and hold a link for the page that you want to read later and then tap Add to Reading List.

When you're settled into your favorite easy chair and have the time (finally!) to read, open Safari, tap the Bookmarks icon, and then tap Reading List. Safari displays the Unread list (see Figure 4.9) and you just tap the article you want to read. Safari immediately removes the page from the Unread list, but if you need to see it again, tap All in the Reading List.

Retracing your steps with the handy History list

Bookmarking a website is a good idea if that site contains interesting or fun content that you want to revisit in the future. However, sometimes you may not realize that a site had useful data until a day or two later. Similarly, you might like a site's stuff, but decide against bookmarking it, only to regret that decision down the road. You could waste a big chunk of your day trying to track down the site. Unfortunately, you may have run into Murphy's Web Browsing Law: a cool site that you forget to bookmark is never found again.

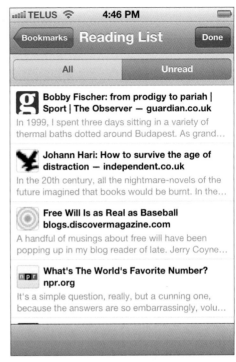

4.9 Load up the Reading List with your recent web finds for easy reading when it's convenient for you.

Fortunately, your iPhone has your back. As you navigate the nooks and crannies of the web, iPhone keeps track of where you go, storing the name and address of each page in the History list. The limited memory on iPhone means that it can't store tons of sites, but it might have the one you're looking for. Here's how to use it:

1. **In Safari, tap the Bookmarks icon in the menu bar.** Safari opens the Bookmarks list.

2. **If you see the Bookmarks screen (shown earlier in Figure 4.8), skip to Step 3.**
   Otherwise, tap the folder names that appear in the upper-left corner of the screen until you get to the Bookmarks screen.

3. **Tap History.** Safari opens the History screen, as shown in Figure 4.10. It shows the sites you've visited today at the top, followed by a list of previous surfing dates.

4. **If you visited the site you're looking for on a previous day, tap that day.** Safari displays a list of only the sites you visited on that day.

5. **Tap the site you want to revisit.** Safari loads it.

Filling in Online Forms

Many web pages include forms where you fill in some data and submit it, which sends the data off to some server for processing. Filling in these forms in your Safari browser is mostly straightforward:

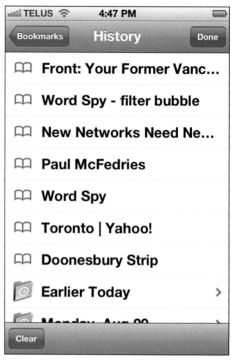

4.10 Safari stores your recent browsing past in the History list.

- **Text box.** Tap inside the text box to display the touchscreen keyboard, tap out your text, and then tap Done.

- **Text area.** Tap inside the text area, and then use the keyboard to tap your text. Most text areas allow multiline entries, so you can tap Return to start a new line. When you finish, tap Done.

- **Check box.** Tap the check box to toggle the check mark on and off.

- **Radio button.** Tap the radio button to activate it.

- **Command button.** Tap the button to make it do its thing (usually submit the form).

Many online forms consist of a bunch of text boxes. If the idea of performing the tap-type-Done cycle over and over isn't appealing to you, fear not. The Safari browser on your iPhone offers an easier method:

1. **Tap inside the first text box.** The keyboard appears.

2. **Tap to type the text you want to submit.** Above the keyboard, notice the Previous and Next buttons, as shown in Figure 4.11.

3. **Tap Next to move to the next text box.** If you need to return to a text box, tap Previous instead.

4. **Repeat Steps 2 and 3 to fill in the text boxes.**

5. **Tap Done.** Safari returns you to the page.

I haven't yet talked about selection lists, and that's because the browser on your iPhone handles them in an interesting way. When you tap a list, Safari displays the list items in a separate box, as shown in Figure 4.12. Tap the item you want to select. As with text boxes, if the form has multiple lists, you see the Previous and Next buttons, which you can tap to navigate from one list to another. After you make all your selections, tap Done to return to the page.

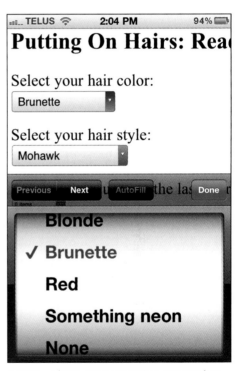

4.11 If the form contains multiple text boxes, you can use the Previous and Next buttons to navigate them.

4.12 Tap a list to see its items in a separate box for easier selection.

Turning on AutoFill for faster form input

The Safari browser on your iPhone makes it relatively easy to fill in online forms, but it can still be slow going, particularly if you have to do lots of typing. To help make forms less of a chore, Safari supports a welcome feature called AutoFill. Just as with the desktop version of Safari (or just about any other mainstream browser), AutoFill remembers the data you enter into forms and then enables you to fill in similar forms with a simple tap of a button. You can also configure AutoFill to remember usernames and passwords.

To take advantage of this nifty feature, you first have to turn it on by following these steps:

1. **In the Home screen, tap Settings.** Your iPhone opens the Settings app.

2. **Tap Safari.** The Safari screen appears.

3. **Tap AutoFill to open the AutoFill screen.**

4. **Tap the Use Contact Info switch to On.** This tells Safari to use your item in the Contacts app to grab data for a form. For example, if a form requires your name, Safari uses your contact name. Safari displays the All Contacts screen.

5. **Tap your name in the All Contacts list.**

6. **If you want Safari to remember the usernames and passwords you use to log in to sites, tap the Names and Passwords switch to On.** A completed AutoFill screen appears in Figure 4.13.

Now when you visit an online form and access any text field in the form, the AutoFill button becomes enabled. Tap AutoFill to fill in those portions of the form that correspond with your contact data, as shown in Figure 4.14. Notice that the fields Safari was able to automatically fill in display with a colored background.

4.13 Fill in the AutoFill screen to make online forms less of a chore.

Saving website login passwords

If you enabled the Names & Passwords option in the AutoFill screen, each time you fill in a username and password to log in to a site, Safari displays the dialog shown in Figure 4.15. It asks if you want to remember the login data, and gives you three choices:

- **Yes.** Tap this button to have Safari remember your username and password.

- **Never for this Website.** Tap this button to tell Safari not to remember the username and password, and to never again prompt you to save the login data.

- **Not Now.** Tap this button to tell Safari not to remember the username and password this time, but to prompt you again next time you log in to this site.

4.14 Tap the AutoFill button to fill in form fields with your contact data.

Note

Your iPhone is cautious about this password stuff, so it doesn't offer to save all the passwords you enter. In particular, if the login form is part of a secure site, then your iPhone doesn't ask if you want to save the password. This means you won't be tempted to store the password for your online bank, corporate website, or any other site where you save your credit card data (such as Amazon and similar shopping sites).

4.15 If you configured Safari to remember usernames and passwords, you see this dialog when you log in to a site.

Getting More Out of Safari on Your iPhone

You've seen lots of great Safari tips and techniques so far in this chapter, but I hope you're up for even more, because you've got a ways to go. In the rest of this chapter, you learn such useful techniques as maintaining your privacy, tweeting a web page, changing the default search engine, configuring the Safari security options, and searching a web page.

Maintaining your privacy by deleting the History list

The History list of sites you've recently surfed on your iPhone is a great feature when you need it, and it's an innocuous feature when you don't. However, there are times when the History list is just plain uncool. For example, suppose you shop online to get a nice gift for your spouse's birthday. If he or she also uses your iPhone, your surprise may be ruined if the purchase page accidentally shows up in the History list. Similarly, if you visit a private corporate site, a financial site, or any other site you wouldn't want others to see, the History list might betray you.

And sometimes unsavory sites can end up in your History list by accident. For example, you might tap a legitimate-looking link in a web page or e-mail message, only to end up in some dark, dank Net neighborhood. Of course, you high-tail it out of there right away with a quick tap of the Safari Back button, but that nasty site is now lurking in your History.

Whether you've got sites on the History list that you wouldn't want anyone to see, or if you just find the idea of your iPhone tracking your movements on the web to be a bit sinister, follow these steps to wipe out the History list:

1. **In Safari, tap the Bookmarks icon in the menu bar.** Safari opens the Bookmarks list.
2. **Tap the folder names that appear in the upper-left corner of the screen until you get to the Bookmarks screen.**
3. **Tap History.** Safari opens the History screen.
4. **Tap Clear.** Safari prompts you to confirm.
5. **Tap Clear History.** Safari deletes every site from the History list.

Genius Here's another way to clear the History, and it might be faster if you're not currently working in Safari. In the Home screen, tap Settings, tap Safari, and then tap Clear History. When your iPhone asks you to confirm, tap Clear History.

Deleting website data

As you wander around the web, Safari gathers and saves bits of information for each site. For example, it stores some site text and images so that it can display the page faster if you revisit the site in the near future. Similarly, if you activated AutoFill for names and passwords, Safari stores that data on your iPhone. Finally, most major sites store small text files called cookies on your iPhone that save information for things like site preferences and shopping carts.

Storing all this data on your iPhone is generally a good thing because it can speed up your surfing. However, it's not always a safe or private thing. For example, if you elect to have Safari save a site password, you might change your mind later on, particularly if you share your iPhone with other people. Similarly, cookies can sometimes be used to track your activities online, so they're not always benign.

In previous versions of iOS, you could use the Settings app to clear all of your stored cookies, saved passwords, or stored web page text and images (this is called the *cache*). However, those were awfully blunt instruments, particularly if you were only concerned about a site or two. Fortunately, iOS 5 introduces a more finely honed tool that enables you to delete the data for an individual website. Here's how it works:

1. **On the Home screen, tap Settings.** Your iPhone opens the Settings app.

2. **Tap Safari.** The Safari screen appears.

3. **Tap Advanced.** The Advanced screen appears.

4. **Tap Website Data.** Safari displays a list of the recent sites for which it has stored data, as well as the size of that data, as shown in Figure 4.16.

5. **If you don't see the site you want to remove, tap Show All Sites at the bottom of the list.**

6. **Tap Edit.**

.ııll TELUS 🔶	4:53 PM

| Advanced | Website Data | Edit |

Website Data	1.1 MB
www.google.ca	1.1 MB
doonesbury.com	1.2 KB
google.ca	0.7 KB
m.spectrum.ieee.org	0.5 KB
yahoo.com	0.3 KB
a1502.phobos.apple.com	0.3 KB
a1033.phobos.apple.com	0.3 KB
a1484.phobos.apple.com	0.3 KB

4.16 The Website Data screen shows you which sites have saved data on your iPhone.

7. **Tap the red Delete icon to the left of the site you want to clear.**

8. **Tap the Delete icon that appears to the right of the site's data size value.** Safari removes the site's data.

Browsing privately

If you find yourself constantly deleting your browsing history or website data, you can save yourself a bit of time by configuring Safari to do this automatically. This is called *private browsing* and it means that Safari doesn't save any data as you browse. Specifically, it doesn't save the following:

- Sites aren't added to the history (although the Back and Forward buttons still work for navigating sites that you've visited in the current session).
- Web page text and images aren't saved.
- Search text isn't saved with the search box.
- AutoFill passwords aren't saved.

To activate private browsing, follow these steps:

1. **On the Home screen, tap Settings.** The Settings app appears.

2. **Tap Safari.** The Safari screen appears.

3. **Tap the Private Browsing switch to On.** The Settings app asks if you want to close your existing Safari tabs.

4. **To close the tabs, tap Close All.** If you prefer to keep the tabs open, tap Keep All, instead.

Tweeting a web page

If you have a Twitter account, there's a good chance that one of your favorite 140-characters-or-less pastimes is sharing interesting, useful, or funny websites with your followers. Using a client such as the official Twitter app or TweetDeck is fine for this, but it means you have to copy the site address, switch to the app, and then paste the address. For quick tweets, it's easier and faster just to stay in Safari, which now lets you send a tweet directly from a web page. Here's what you do:

1. **Use Safari to navigate to the page that you want to tweet.**

2. **Tap the Actions icon.**

3. **Tap Tweet.** Safari displays the Tweet dialog.

4. **If you added more than one account to the iPhone Twitter settings, tap the user-name in the From section and then tap the name of the account you want to use to send the tweet.**

5. **Type your tweet text in the large text box.** As you can see in Figure 4.17, the Tweet dialog displays a number in the lower-right corner telling you how many characters you have left.

6. **If you want to include your present whereabouts as part of the tweet, tap Add Location.**

7. **Tap Send.** Your iPhone posts the tweet.

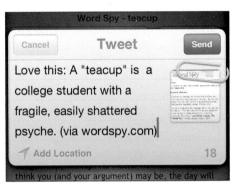

4.17 iOS 5 lets you tweet about a website directly from Safari.

Changing the default search engine

When you tap the Search icon at the top of the Safari screen, your iPhone loads the Address Bar screen and places the cursor inside the Search box so that you can type. The button you tap to launch the search is named Google, which is appropriate as Google is the default search engine on your iPhone. Almost everyone uses Google, of course, but if you have something against it, you can switch and use either Yahoo! or Bing as your search engine. Here's how:

1. **In the Home screen, tap Settings.** Your iPhone opens the Settings app.

2. **Tap Safari.** The Safari screen appears.

3. **Tap Search Engine.** Your iPhone opens the Search Engine screen.

4. **Tap the search engine you want to use.** You have three choices: Google, Yahoo!, or Bing.

Dialing a phone number from a web page

Your iPhone's membership in the smartphone club is fully confirmed with this next feature. A common chore when you surf business or retail sites is hunting down the phone number for a person, a department, customer service, technical support, or whatever. In a regular browser, you note the phone number, head for the nearest phone, and then dial. Hah! The iPhone laughs at all that extra work. Why? Because when the iPhone Safari browser comes upon a phone number in a web page, Safari conveniently converts it into a link, as shown in Figure 4.18. Tap the number, tap Call in the dialog that pops up, and you're immediately switched to the Phone app, which dials the number for you. Sweet!

Setting the web browser security options

It's a jungle out there in cyberspace, with nasty things lurking in the digital weeds. The folks at Apple are well aware of these dangers, of course, so they've clothed your iPhone in protective gear to help keep the bad guys at bay. Safari, in particular, has four layers of security:

Customer Service

Apple Store Customer Service
To view the most up-to-date status and make changes to your Apple Online Store order, visit online Order Status. You can contact Apple Store Customer Service at 1-800-676-2775 or online Help for more information.

North American Corporate Contacts

United States

1 (800) 676-2775

Apple Enterprise Sales

Cancel   Call

4.18 Your iPhone smartly converts a web page phone number into a link that you can tap to call the number.

- **Phishing protection.** A *phishing* site is a website that, on the surface, appears to belong to a reputable company, such as an online bank or major corporation. In reality, some dark-side hackers have cobbled the site together to fool you into providing your precious login or credit card data, Social Security number, or other private information. Many of these sites either are well known or sport telltale signs that mark them as fraudulent. The Safari app comes with a Fraud Warning setting that, when activated, displays a warning about such sites.

- **JavaScript.** This is a programming language that website developers commonly use to add features to their pages. However, programmers who have succumbed to the dark side of The Force can use JavaScript for nefarious ends. Your iPhone comes with JavaScript support turned on, but you can turn it off if you're heading into an area of the web where you don't feel safe. However, many sites won't work without JavaScript, so I don't recommend turning it off full time.

- **Pop-up blocking.** Pop-up ads (and their sneakier cousins, pop-under ads) are annoying at the best of times, but they really get in the way on the iPhone because the pop-up not only creates a new Safari page, but it immediately switches to that page. So now you have to tap the Pages icon, delete the pop-up page, and then (if you already had two or more pages running) tap the page that generated the pop-up. Boo! So you can thank your preferred deity that not only does your iPhone come with a pop-up blocker that stops these pop-up pests, but it's turned on by default, to boot. However, there are sites that use pop-ups for legitimate reasons, such as media players, login pages, and important site announcements. For those sites to work properly you may need to temporarily turn off the pop-up blocker.

⊙ **Cookies.** These are small text files that many sites store on the iPhone; these sites then use those files to store information about your browsing session. The most common example is a shopping cart, where your selections and amounts are stored in a cookie. However, for every benign cookie, there's at least one not-so-nice cookie used by a third-party advertiser to track your movements and display ads supposedly targeted to your tastes. Yuck. By default, your iPhone doesn't accept third-party cookies, so that's a good thing. However, you can configure Safari to accept every cookie that comes its way or no cookies at all (neither of which I recommend).

Follow these steps to customize your web security options on your iPhone:

1. **In the Home screen, tap Settings.** The Settings app slides in.

2. **Tap Safari.** Your iPhone displays the Safari screen.

3. **To configure the cookies that Safari allows, tap Accept Cookies.** Tap the setting you want — None, From visited, or Always — and then tap Safari. The From visited setting (the default) means that Safari accepts cookies directly only from the sites you visit and spits out any from third-party sites, such as advertisers.

4. **Tap the Fraud Warning setting to toggle phishing protection On and Off.**

5. **Tap the JavaScript setting to toggle JavaScript support On and Off.**

6. **Tap the Block Pop-ups setting to toggle pop-up blocking On and Off.**

Searching web page text

When you're perusing a page on the web, it's not unusual to be looking for specific information. In those situations, rather than reading through the entire page to find the info you seek, it would be a lot easier to search for the data. You can easily do this in the desktop version of Safari or any other computer browser, but, at first glance, the Safari app doesn't seem to have a Find feature anywhere. It's there all right, but you need to know where to look:

1. **Use the Safari app to navigate to the web page that contains the information you seek.**

2. **Tap inside the Search box in the top-right corner of the Safari window.**

3. **Tap the search text you want to use.** Safari displays the usual web page matches, but it also displays "On This Page (*X* matches)," where *X* is the number of times your search text appears on the web page.

4. **Flick the search results up to hide the keyboard.** The On This Page message now appears at the bottom of the results screen, as shown in Figure 4.19.

5. **Tap Find *search* (where *search* is the search text you entered).** Safari highlights the first instance of the search term, as shown in Figure 4.20.

6. **Tap the right arrow to cycle forward through the instances of the search term that appear on the page.** Note that you can also cycle backward through the results by tapping the left arrow.

7. **When you're finished with the search, tap Done.**

4.19 The On This Page message tells you the number of matches that appear on the current web page.

4.20 Safari highlights the first instance of the search term that appears on the current web page.

Printing a web page with AirPrint

If you have a printer that supports the AirPrint standard for wireless printing, then you can send documents, such as web pages, directly to your printer.

Note As I write this, only a selected number of Hewlett-Packard printers support the AirPrint standard. To find out more, and to see a list of AirPrint-ready printers, visit www.hp.com/sbso/printing/mac/hp-airprint.html.

Here's how it works:

1. **Use the Safari app to navigate to the web page you want to print.**

2. **Tap the Actions icon.** A menu of web page actions appears.

3. **Tap Print.** The Printer Options screen appears.

4. **Tap Printer.** If the Printer field already shows the printer you want to use, you can skip to Step 6. Your iPhone looks for wireless printers on your network and then displays a list of the available printers.

5. **Tap the printer you want to use.** Your iPhone adds the printer to the Printer Options screen and then enables the other controls on the screen, as shown in Figure 4.21.

6. **In the Copy field, tap + to set the number of copies you want to print.**

7. **Configure the other printer options as needed.** Note that the options you see will vary from printer to printer.

8. **Tap Print.** Your iPhone sends the web page to the printer.

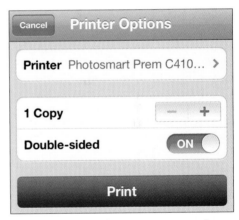

4.21 Use the Printer Options screen to configure the print job and then print the web page.

Searching the web with Siri voice commands

You can use Safari to type search queries either directly into the Search box or by navigating to a search engine. However, if you have an iPhone 4S, typing suddenly seems like such a quaint pastime thanks to the voice recognition prowess of the Siri app. So why type a search query when you can just tell Siri what you're looking for?

Launch Siri by tapping and holding the Home button (or pressing and holding the Mic button of the iPhone headphones, or the equivalent button on a Bluetooth headset). Here are some general tips for web searching with Siri:

- **Searching the entire web.** Say "Search the web for *topic*," where *topic* is your search criteria.

- **Searching Wikipedia.** Say "Search Wikipedia for *topic*," where *topic* is the subject you want to look up.

- **Searching with a particular search engine.** Say "*engine topic*," where *engine* is the name of the search engine, such as Google or Bing, and *topic* is your search criteria.

Siri also understands commands related to searching for businesses and restaurants through its partnership with Yelp. To look for businesses and restaurants using Siri, the general syntax to use is the following (although, as usual with Siri, you don't have to be too rigid about this):

"Find (or Look for) *something somewhere*."

Here, the *something* part can be the name of a business (such as "Starbucks"), a type of business (such as "gas station"), a type of restaurant (such as "Thai restaurants"), or a generic product (such as "coffee"). The *somewhere* part can be something relative to your current location (such as "around here" or "near me" or "within walking distance") or a specific location (such as "in Indianapolis" or "in Broad Ripple"). Here are some examples:

- "Find a gas station within walking distance."

- "Look for pizza restaurants in Indianapolis."

- "Find coffee around here."

- "Look for a grocery store near me."

Note, too, that if you add a qualifier such as "good" or "best" before the *something* portion of the command, Siri returns the results organized by their Yelp rating.

Siri also partners with Wolfram Alpha, the "computational knowledge engine," so you can search for specific tidbits of information, such as "What was the Best Picture of 1959?" or "What is the population of Scotland?"

Note

Wolfram Alpha is a massive knowledge base that allows you to query information on dozens of topics. To learn the kinds of data it can provide (and, therefore, the kinds of questions you can ask Siri), see the Examples by Topic page at www.wolfram alpha.com/examples.

How Do I Maximize iPhone E-mail?

E-mail has been called the "killer app" of the Internet, and it certainly deserves that title. Yes, chat and instant messaging are popular; social networks such as Facebook, Twitter, and LinkedIn get lots of press; and blogging sites appeal to a certain type of person. However, while not everyone uses these services, it's safe to say that almost everyone uses e-mail. You probably use e-mail all day, particularly when you're on the go with your iPhone in tow, so learning a few useful and efficient e-mail techniques can make your day a bit easier and save you time for more important pursuits.

Managing Your iPhone E-mail Accounts

Your iPhone comes with the Mail app, which is a radically slimmed-down version of the Mail application that's the default e-mail program on Mac machines. Mail on the iPhone may be a pale shadow of its OS X cousin, but that doesn't mean it's a lightweight — far from it. It has a few features and settings that make it ideal for your traveling e-mail show. First, however, you have to set up your iPhone with one or more e-mail accounts.

Adding an account by hand

The Mail application on your iPhone is most useful when it's set up to use an e-mail account that you also use on your computer. That way, when you're on the road or out on the town, you can check your messages and rest assured that you won't miss anything important (or even anything unimportant, for that matter). This is most easily done by syncing an existing e-mail account between your computer and your iPhone, and I show you how that's done in Chapter 6.

Caution For some accounts, you need to be careful that your iPhone doesn't delete incoming messages from the server before you have a chance to download them to your computer. I show you how to set this up later in this chapter.

However, you might also prefer to have an e-mail account that's for iPhone only. For example, if you join an iPhone mailing list, you might prefer to have those messages sent to only your iPhone. That's a darn good idea, but it means that you have to set up the account on the iPhone itself, which, as you'll soon see, requires a fair amount of tapping.

How you create an account on your iPhone with the sweat of your own brow depends on the type of account you have. First, there are the six e-mail services that your iPhone recognizes:

- **iCloud.** This is the Apple web-based e-mail service (that also comes with applications for calendars, contacts, and more).
- **Microsoft Exchange.** Your iPhone supports accounts on Exchange servers, which are common in large organizations like corporations or schools. Exchange uses a central server to store messages, and you usually work with your messages on the server, not your iPhone. However, one of the great features in the iPhone is support for Exchange ActiveSync, which automatically keeps your phone and your account on the server synchronized. I discuss the ActiveSync settings later in this chapter.

- **Gmail.** This is a web-based e-mail service run by Google.

- **Yahoo!** This is a web-based e-mail service run by Yahoo!.

- **AOL.** This is a web-based e-mail service run by AOL.

- **Windows Live Hotmail.** This is a web-based e-mail service run by Microsoft.

Genius You might think you can avoid the often excessive tapping required to enter a new e-mail account into your iPhone by creating the account in your computer's e-mail program and then syncing with your iPhone. That works, but there's a hitch: You must leave the new account in your e-mail program. If you delete it or disable it, iTunes also deletes the account from the iPhone.

Your iPhone knows how to connect to these services, so to set up any of these e-mail accounts you only need to know the address and the account password.

Otherwise, your iPhone Mail app supports the following e-mail account types:

- **POP (Post Office Protocol).** This is the most popular type of account. Its main character-istic for your purposes is that incoming messages are only stored temporarily on the pro-vider's mail server. When you connect to the server, the messages are downloaded to your iPhone and removed from the server. In other words, your messages (including copies of messages you send) are stored locally on your iPhone. The advantage here is that you don't need to be online to read your e-mail. Once it's downloaded to your iPhone, you can read it or delete it at your leisure.

- **IMAP (Internet Message Access Protocol).** This type of account is most often used with web-based e-mail services. It's the opposite of POP (sort of) because all your incoming messages, as well as copies of messages you send, remain on the server. In this case, when Mail works with an IMAP account, it connects to the server and works with the messages on the server, not on your iPhone (although it looks like you're working with the messages locally). The advantage here is that you can access the messages from mul-tiple devices and multiple locations, but you must be connected to the Internet to work with your messages.

Your network administrator or your e-mail service provider can let you know what type of e-mail account you have. Your administrator or provider can also give you the information you need to set up the account. This includes your e-mail address; the username and password you use to check for new messages (and perhaps also the security information you need to specify to send messages); the host name of the incoming mail server (typically something like mail.*provider*.com, where *provider*.com is the domain name of the provider); and the host name of the outgoing mail server (typically either mail.*provider*.com or smtp.*provider*.com).

With your account information ready, follow these steps to forge a brand-new account:

1. **On the Home screen, tap Settings.** Your iPhone opens the Settings app.

2. **Tap Mail, Contacts, Calendars.** The Mail, Contacts, Calendars screen appears.

3. **Tap Add Account.** This opens the Add Account screen, as shown in Figure 5.1.

4. **You have two ways to proceed:**

   - **If you're adding an account for iCloud, Microsoft Exchange, Gmail, Yahoo!, AOL, or Windows Live Hotmail, tap the corresponding logo.** In the account information screen that appears, enter your name, e-mail address, password, and an account description. Tap Next, make sure the Mail switch is set to On, tap Save, and you're done!

   - **If you're adding another account type, tap Other and continue with Step 5.**

5. **Tap Add Mail Account to open the New Account screen.**

6. **Use the Name, Address, and Description text boxes to enter the corresponding account information, and then tap Next.**

7. **Tap the type of account you're adding: IMAP or POP.**

8. **In the Incoming Mail Server section, use the Host Name text box to enter the host name of your provider's incoming mail server, as well as your username and password.**

5.1 Use the Add Account screen to choose the type of e-mail account you want to add.

108

9. **In the Outgoing Mail Server (SMTP) section, use the Host Name text box to enter the host name of your provider's outgoing (SMTP) mail server.** If your provider requires a username and password to send messages, enter those as well.

10. **Tap Save.** Your iPhone verifies the account info and then returns you to the Mail settings screen with the account added to the Accounts list.

Specifying the default account

If you've added two or more e-mail accounts to your iPhone, Mail specifies one of them as the default account. This means that Mail uses this account when you send a new message, when you reply to a message, and when you forward a message. The default account is usually the first account you add to your iPhone. However, you can change this by following these steps:

1. **On the Home screen, tap Settings.** The Settings app appears.

2. **Tap Mail, Contacts, Calendars.** Your iPhone displays the Mail, Contacts, Calendars screen.

3. **At the bottom of the Mail section, tap Default Account.** This opens the Default Account screen, which displays a list of your accounts. The current default account is shown with a check mark beside it, as shown in Figure 5.2.

4. **Tap the account you want to use as the default.** Your iPhone places a check mark beside the account.

5. **Tap Mail to return to the Mail settings screen.**

5.2 Use the Default Account screen to set the default account that you want Mail to use when sending messages.

Temporarily disabling an account

The Mail app checks for new messages at a regular interval. (I show you how to configure this interval in Chapter 13.) If you have several accounts configured in Mail, this incessant checking can put quite a strain on your iPhone battery. To ease up on the juice, you can disable an account temporarily to prevent Mail from checking it for new messages. Here's how:

109

1. **On the Home screen, tap Settings.** Your iPhone displays the Settings app.

2. **Tap Mail, Contacts, Calendars.** The Mail settings screen appears.

3. **Tap the account you want to disable.** Your iPhone displays the account's settings.

4. **Depending on the type of account, use one of the following techniques to temporarily disable the account:**

   - **For an iCloud, Exchange, Gmail, Yahoo!, AOL, or Windows Live Hotmail account, tap the Mail switch to Off, as shown in Figure 5.3.** If the account syncs other types of data, such as contacts and calendars, you can also turn off those switches, if you want.

   - **For a POP or IMAP account, tap the Account switch to Off.**

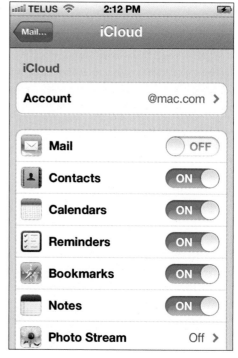

When you're ready to work with the account again, repeat these steps to turn the Mail switch or the Account switch back to On.

Deleting an account

If an e-mail account has grown tiresome and boring (or you just don't use it anymore), you should delete it to save storage space, speed up sync times, and save battery power. Follow these steps:

5.3 For an iCloud, Exchange, Gmail, Yahoo!, AOL, or Windows Live Hotmail account, tap the Mail switch to Off.

1. **On the Home screen, tap Settings.** The Settings app appears.

2. **Tap Mail, Contacts, Calendars.** The Mail settings screen appears.

3. **Tap the account you want to delete.** This opens the account's settings.

4. **At the bottom of the screen, tap Delete Account.** Your iPhone asks you to confirm.

5. **Tap Delete Account.** Your iPhone returns you to the Mail settings screen, and the account no longer graces the Accounts list.

Switching to another account

When you open the Mail app, you usually see the Inbox folder of your default account. If you have multiple accounts set up on your iPhone and you want to see what's going on with a different account, follow these steps to make the switch:

1. **On the Home screen, tap Mail to open the Mail app.**

2. **Tap the Back button (the left-pointing arrow) that appears in the top-left corner of the screen (but below the status bar).** The Mailboxes screen appears, as shown in Figure 5.4.

3. **Tap the account with which you want to work:**

   - **If you only want to see the account's Inbox folder, tap the account name in the Inboxes section of the Mailboxes screen.**

   - **If you want to see all the account's available folders, tap the account name in the Accounts section of the Mailboxes screen.** Mail displays a list of the account's folders, and you then tap the folder with which you want to work.

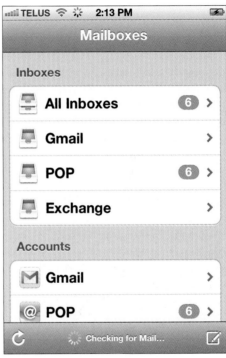

5.4 Use the Mailboxes screen to choose another e-mail account.

Configuring E-mail Accounts

Setting up an e-mail account on your iPhone is one thing, but making that account do useful things — or sometimes, anything at all — is quite another. The next few sections take you through a few useful settings that help you to get more out of e-mail and to troubleshoot e-mail problems.

Managing multiple devices by leaving messages on the server

In today's increasingly mobile world, it's not unusual to find you need to check the same e-mail account from multiple devices. For example, you might want to check your business account not only using your work computer, but also using your home computer, or using your iPhone while commuting or traveling.

If you need to check e-mail on multiple devices, you can take advantage of how POP e-mail messages are delivered over the Internet. When someone sends you a message, it doesn't come directly to your computer. Instead, it goes to the server that your Internet service provider (or your company) has set up to handle incoming messages. When you ask Apple Mail to check for new messages, it communicates with the POP server to see if any messages are waiting in your account. If so, Mail downloads those messages to your computer and then instructs the server to delete the copies of the messages that are stored on the server.

The trick, then, is to configure Mail so that it leaves a copy of the messages on the POP server after you download them. That way, the messages are still available when you check messages using another device. Fortunately, the intuitive folks who designed the version of Mail on your iPhone must have understood this, because the program automatically sets up POP accounts to do just that. Specifically, after you download any messages from the POP server to your iPhone, Mail leaves the messages on the server.

Here's a good overall strategy that ensures you can download messages on all your devices, but prevents messages from piling up on the server:

- Let your main computer be the computer that controls deleting the messages from the server. In OS X, the default setting in Mail is to delete messages from the server after one week, and that's fine.

- Set up all your other devices — particularly your iPhone — to not delete messages from the server.

Note

To leave messages on the server in Outlook, choose Tools ➪ Account Settings, click the account, click Change, and then click More Settings. Click the Advanced tab and select the Leave a copy of messages on the server check box. In Outlook Express or Windows Live Mail, choose Tools ➪ Accounts, click your e-mail account, and click Properties. Click the Advanced tab and then select the Leave a copy of messages on server check box.

It's a good idea to check your iPhone POP accounts to ensure they're not deleting messages from the server. To do that, or to use a different setting — such as deleting messages after a week or when you delete them from your Inbox — follow these steps:

1. **On the Home screen, tap Settings.** The Settings app appears.

2. **Tap Mail, Contacts, Calendars.** Your iPhone opens the Mail, Contacts, Calendars settings screen.

3. **Tap the POP account you want to configure.** The account's settings screen appears.

4. **Near the bottom of the screen, tap Advanced.** Your iPhone displays the Advanced screen.

5. **Tap Delete from server.** The Delete from server screen appears, as shown in Figure 5.5.

6. **Tap Never.** If you prefer that your iPhone delete messages from the server automatically, tap either Seven days or When removed from Inbox.

Fixing outgoing e-mail problems by using a different server port

5.5 Use the Delete from server screen to ensure your iPhone is leaving messages on your POP server.

For security reasons, some Internet service providers (ISPs) insist that all their customers' outgoing mail must be routed through the ISP's Simple Mail Transport Protocol (SMTP) server. This usually isn't a big deal if you're using an e-mail account maintained by the ISP, but it can lead to the following problems if you are using an account provided by a third party (such as your website host):

- Your ISP might block messages sent using the third-party account because it thinks you're trying to relay the message through the ISP's server (a technique often used by spammers).

- You might incur extra charges if your ISP allows only a certain amount of SMTP bandwidth per month or a certain number of sent messages, whereas the third-party account offers higher limits or no restrictions at all.

- You might have performance problems, with the ISP taking much longer to route messages than the third-party host.

- You might think you can solve the problem by specifying that the third-party host's outgoing mail is sent by default through port 25. When you use this port, the outgoing mail goes through the ISP's SMTP server.

To work around the problem, many third-party hosts offer access to their SMTP server via a port other than the standard port 25. For example, the iCloud SMTP server (smtp.icloud.com) also accepts connections on ports 465 and 587. Here's how to configure an e-mail account to use a nonstandard SMTP port.

1. **On the Home screen, tap Settings.** You see the Settings app.

2. **Tap Mail, Contacts, Calendars.** The Mail, Contacts, Calendars settings screen appears.

3. **Tap the POP account you want to configure.** The account's settings screen appears.

4. **Near the bottom of the screen, tap SMTP.** Your iPhone displays the SMTP screen.

5. **In the Primary Server section, tap the server.** Your iPhone displays the server settings.

6. **In the Outgoing Mail Server section, tap Server Port.** Your iPhone displays a keypad so you can type the port number, as shown in Figure 5.6.

5.6 In the server settings screen's Outgoing Mail Server area, tap Server Port to type the new port number to use for outgoing messages.

Configuring authentication for outgoing mail

Because spam is such a big problem these days, many ISPs now require SMTP authentication for outgoing mail, which means that you must log on to the SMTP server to confirm that you're the person sending the mail (as opposed to some spammer spoofing your address). If your ISP requires authentication on outgoing messages, you need to configure your e-mail account to provide the proper credentials.

If you're not too sure about any of this, check with your ISP. If that doesn't work out, by far the most common type of authentication is to specify a username and password (this happens behind the scenes when you send messages). Follow these steps to configure your iPhone e-mail account with this kind of authentication:

1. **On the Home screen, tap Settings.** Your iPhone displays the Settings app.

2. **Tap Mail, Contacts, Calendars.** The Mail settings screen appears.

3. **Tap the POP account you want to configure.** The account's settings screen appears.

4. **Near the bottom of the screen, tap SMTP, and then tap Primary Server.** Your iPhone displays the server's settings screen.

5. **In the Outgoing Mail Server section, tap Authentication.** Your iPhone displays the Authentication screen.

6. **Tap Password.**

7. **Tap the server address to return to the server settings screen.**

8. **In the Outgoing Mail Server section, enter your account username in the User Name box and the account password in the Password box.**

Configuring E-mail Messages

The rest of this chapter takes you through a few useful and timesaving techniques for handling e-mail messages on your iPhone.

Setting the number of messages to display

By default, the Mail app displays the 50 most recent messages in an e-mail account Inbox. If you want to see more messages, you must scroll to the bottom of the message list and then tap Load More Messages. That's not a big deal if you just have a few more messages to display, but if you have hundreds of messages on the server and you need to see them, constantly loading a new batch of 50 can get old in a hurry.

The iOS 5 version of Mail solves that problem by letting you set a higher default number of messages to display. You can display 100, 200, 500, or even 1,000 recent messages. Here's what you do:

1. **On the Home screen, tap Settings.** You see the Settings app.

2. **Tap Mail, Contacts, Calendars.** The Mail, Contacts, Calendars settings screen appears.

3. **Tap Show.** The Show screen appears, as displayed in Figure 5.7.

4. **Tap the number of recent messages you want to display.** Your iPhone puts the new setting into effect.

Processing e-mail faster by identifying messages sent to you

In the Mail app on your iPhone, the Inbox folder tells you who sent you each message, but it doesn't tell you to whom the message was sent (that is, which addresses appeared on the To line or the Cc line). No big deal, right? Maybe, maybe not. You see, bulk mailers — I'm talking newsletters, mailing lists, and, notoriously, spammers — often don't send messages directly to each person on their subscriber lists. Instead, they use a generic bulk address, which means, significantly, that your e-mail address doesn't appear on the To or Cc lines. That's significant because most newsletters and mailing lists — and all spam — are low-priority messages that you can ignore when you're processing a stuffed Inbox.

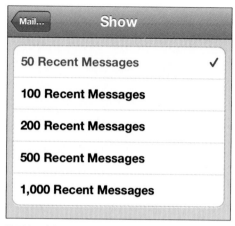

5.7 Use this screen to set the default number of recent messages that you see in your Inbox.

Okay, great, but what good does all this do you if Mail doesn't show the To and Cc lines? No, it doesn't show those lines, but you can configure Mail to show a little icon for messages that were sent directly to you.

- If the message includes your address in the To field, you see a To icon beside the message.

- If the message includes your address in the Cc field, you see a Cc icon beside the message.

Neat! Here's how to make this happen:

1. **On the Home screen, tap Settings.** The Settings app appears.

2. **Tap Mail, Contacts, Calendars.** The Mail, Contacts, Calendars screen appears.

3. **Tap the Show To/Cc Label switch to On.**

When you examine your Inbox, you see the To and Cc icons on messages addressed to you, and you don't see either icon on bulk messages, as shown in Figure 5.8.

Placing a phone call from an e-mail message

E-mail messages often include a signature — a line or three of text that appears at the bottom of the message. In business e-mail, a person's signature often includes contact information — what hipster business types like to refer to as their "coordinates" — such as their address (e-mail and postal) and their phone numbers (land and cell). (I show you how to create your own custom iPhone signature a bit later in this chapter.)

In a run-of-the-mill e-mail program, if you wanted to call one of your correspondents based on this signature information, you'd

▪▪▪▪ TELUS 📶	**11:49 AM** 🔋
◀ POP	**Inbox (6)**	Edit

Paul, However, I am going to need the
Quick Guide from you. You'll recall tha…

Wolfgang, Christina… Yesterday
🔲 Beginning 9781118186183 AR   **3** >
Hi, Paul, Just dropped off ch01 here:
\\in-docs\ftp Info\Editorial_Transfer\18…

Baldwin & Frankli… 📎 Yesterday
🔲 28 Galt   >
Vitas Welcome back. Could you please look
at the attached sketch? The owner wants…

Karen Hammond Yesterday
🔲 Update on Parents   >
Hi Paul, I talked to your mother today and
she had much news of happenings. Your…

LinkedIn Updates Yesterday
🔲 LinkedIn Network Updates, 8/30/…   >
Better. Faster. The New LinkedIn Mobile
App for iPhone and Android. LinkedIn Net…

Karen Hammond 📎 Yesterday

🔄   Updated 8/31/11 11:48 AM   📝

5.8 With the Show To/Cc Label switch turned on, Mail shows you which messages were addressed directly to you.

open the message, perhaps jot down the number if there was no phone nearby, and then make the call. As you know, your iPhone isn't run-of-the-mill *anything*, so you can just forget all that rigmarole. Why? Because when it sees a phone number in an e-mail message, your iPhone does something quite smart: It converts that number into a link. The number appears in blue, underlined text, much like a link on a web page. Figure 5.9 shows an example. Tap the number, tap Call in the dialog that appears, and your iPhone immediately dials the number for you. Thanks!

Genius

The Mail app converts phone numbers into fake links that you can tap, so it's not even remotely surprising that Mail also converts web addresses into actual links. That is, when you tap an address that appears in an e-mail message, your iPhone fires up Safari and takes you to that address. Even better, if the sender includes a link in the message, you can tap and hold the link to see a pop-up bubble that tells you the link address.

E-mailing a link to a web page

The web is all about finding content that's interesting, educational, and, of course, fun. And if you stumble across a page that meets one or more of these criteria, then the only sensible thing to do is share your good fortune with someone else, right? So, how do you do that? Some pages are kind enough to include an E-mail This Page link (or something similar), but you can't count on having one of those around. Instead, the usual method is to copy the page address, switch to your e-mail program, paste the address into the message, choose a recipient, and then send the message.

And, yes, with the copy-and-paste feature, you can do all that on your iPhone, but boy, that sure seems like a ton of work. So are you stuck using this unwieldy method? Not a chance (you probably knew that). Your iPhone includes a great little feature that enables you

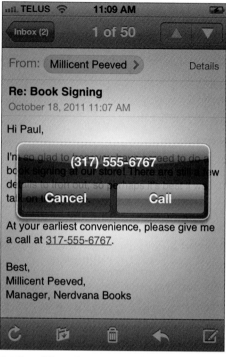

5.9 Your iPhone is savvy enough to convert a phone number in an e-mail message into a link that you can tap to call.

to plop the address of the current Safari page into an e-mail message with just a couple of taps. You then ship out the message and you've made the world a better place.

Here's how it works:

1. **Use Safari to navigate to the page you want to share.**

2. **Tap the Actions icon (the arrow) in the menu bar.** Safari displays a dialog with several options.

3. **Tap Mail Link to this Page.** This opens a new e-mail message. As you can see in Figure 5.10, the new message already includes the page title as the Subject and the page address in the message body.

5.10 When you tap the Mail Link to this Page option, your iPhone creates a new e-mail message with the page title and address already inserted.

4. **Choose a recipient for the message.**

5. **Edit the message text as you see fit.**

6. **Tap Send.** Your iPhone fires off the message and returns you to Safari.

Creating iCloud message folders

In your e-mail program on your computer, you've no doubt created lots of folders to hold different types of messages that you want or need to save: projects, people, mailing list gems, and so on. This is a great way to reduce Inbox clutter and organize the e-mail portion of your life.

Of course, these days the e-mail portion of your life extends beyond your computer and probably includes lots of time spent on your iPhone. Wouldn't it be great to have that same folder convenience and organization on your favorite phone? Happily, you can. If you have an iCloud account, any folders (technically, Apple calls them mailboxes) that you create on your iCloud account — either on your computer or on the iCloud site — are automatically mirrored on the iPhone Mail app.

Even better, you can create new iCloud message folders right from the comfort of your iPhone. Here's how:

1. **On the Home screen, tap Mail to open the Mail app.**

2. **Tap the Mailbox button in the top-left corner of the screen.** The Mail app displays the Mailboxes screen.

3. **In the Accounts section, tap your iCloud account.** Mail displays the iCloud folders list.

4. **Tap Edit.** Mail opens the iCloud folders list for editing.

5. **Tap New Mailbox.** The Edit Mailbox screen appears, as shown in Figure 5.11.

6. **Type a name for the new folder.**

7. **Tap the Mailbox Location and then tap the folder in which you want to store your new folder.**

8. **Tap Save.** Mail adds the folder, and iCloud propagates the change to the cloud.

9. **Tap Done.**

5.11 Use the Edit Mailbox screen to type a name and select a location for the message folder.

Note

To move a message to your new folder, display the iCloud Inbox folder, tap the message, tap the Move icon (the folder), and then tap the new folder.

Formatting e-mail text

We're all used to rich text e-mail messages by now, where formatting such as bold and italics is used to add pizzazz or emphasis to our e-musings. Until iOS 5 came along, the Mail app was having none of that. Oh, sure, it could *display* rich text formatting, but the missives you composed in the Mail app were as plain as plain text could get.

The iOS 5 version of Mail changes all that by giving you a limited set of formatting options for text: bold, italics, and underline. It's not much, but it's a start. Here are the steps to follow to format text in the Mail app:

1. **In your e-mail message, tap within the word or phrase you want to format.** The Mail app displays the cursor.

2. **Tap the cursor.** Mail displays a set of options.

3. **Tap Select.** Mail selects the word closest to the cursor.

4. **If needed, drag the selection handles to select the entire phrase you want to format.** Mail displays a set of options for the selected text.

5. **Tap the arrow on the right side of the options.** Mail displays more options.

6. **Tap the BIU button.** Mail displays the Bold, Italics, and Underline buttons, as shown in Figure 5.12.

7. **Tap the formatting you want to apply.** Mail leaves the formatting options on the screen, so feel free to apply multiple formats, if needed.

8. **Tap another part of the screen to hide the formatting options.**

5.12 You can now format e-mail text with bold, italics, or underline.

Genius

If you're composing a message on your computer and decide to work on it later, your mail program stores the message as a draft that you can reopen any time. The Mail app doesn't *appear* to have that option, but it does. In the message window, tap Cancel (unintuitive, I know!) and then tap Save Draft. When you're ready to resume editing, open the account in the Mailboxes screen, tap Drafts, and then tap your saved message.

Setting a minimum message font size

Some people who send e-mails must have terrific eyesight because the font they use for the message text is positively microscopic. Such text is tough to read even on a big screen, but when it's crammed into the iPhone touchscreen, you'll be reaching for the nearest magnifying glass. Of course, that same touchscreen can also solve this problem: a quick finger spread magnifies the text accordingly.

That's easy enough if you just get the occasional message with nanoscale text, but if a regular correspondent does this, or if your eyesight isn't quite what it used to be (so all your messages appear ridiculously teensy), then a more permanent solution might be in order. Your iPhone rides to the rescue once again by letting you configure a minimum font size for your messages. This means that if the message font size is larger than what you specify, your iPhone displays the message as is; however, if the font size is smaller than your specification, your iPhone scales up the text to your minimum size. Your tired eyes will be forever grateful.

Follow these steps to set your minimum font size:

1. **On the Home screen, tap Settings.** The Settings app appears.

2. **Tap Mail, Contacts, Calendars.** Your iPhone displays the Mail, Contacts, Calendars settings screen.

3. **Tap Minimum Font Size.** The Minimum Font Size screen appears.

4. **Tap the minimum font size you want to use: Small, Medium, Large, Extra Large, or Giant.** Mail uses the font size you select (or larger) when displaying your messages.

Creating a custom iPhone signature

E-mail signatures can range from the simple — a signoff such as "Cheers," or "All the best," followed by the sender's name — to baroque masterpieces filled with contact information, snappy quotations, even text-based artwork! On your iPhone, the Mail app takes the simple route by adding the following signature to all your outgoing messages (new messages, replies, and forwards):

Sent from my iPhone.

I really like this signature because it's short, simple, and kind of cool (I, of course, *want* my recipients to know that I'm using my iPhone). If that default signature doesn't rock your world, you can create a custom one that does. Follow these steps:

1. **On the Home screen, tap Settings.** Your iPhone opens the Settings app.

2. **Tap Mail, Contacts, Calendars.** You see the Mail, Contacts, Calendars settings screen.

3. **Tap Signature.** The Signature screen appears, as shown in Figure 5.13.

4. **Type the signature you want to use.**

5. **Tap Mail.** Mail saves your new signature and uses it on all outgoing messages.

5.13 Use the Signature screen to create your custom iPhone e-mail signature.

Caution

Mail doesn't give any way to cancel your edits and return to the original signature, so type your text carefully. If you make a real hash of things, tap Clear to get a fresh start.

Disabling remote images in messages

Lots of messages nowadays come not just as plain text, but also with fonts, colors, images, and other flourishes. This fancy formatting, called either rich text or HTML, makes for a more pleasant e-mail experience, particularly when using images in messages, because who doesn't like a bit of eye candy to brighten his day?

Unfortunately, getting images into your e-mail messages can sometimes be problematic:

● **A cellular connection might cause trouble.** For example, it might take a long time to load the images, or if your data plan has an upper limit, you might not want a bunch of e-mail images taking a big bite out of that limit.

● **Not all e-mail images are benign.** A *web bug* is an image that resides on a remote server and is added to an HTML-formatted e-mail message by referencing an address on the remote server. When you open the message, Mail uses the address to download the image for display within the message. That sounds harmless enough, but if the message is junk e-mail, it's likely that the address also contains either your e-mail address or a code that points to your e-mail address. So when the remote server gets a request to load the image, it knows not only that you've opened the message, but also that your e-mail address is legitimate. So, not surprisingly, spammers use web bugs all the time because, for them, valid e-mail addresses are a form of gold.

The iPhone Mail app displays remote images by default. To disable remote images, follow these steps:

1. **On the Home screen, tap Settings.** Your iPhone opens the Settings app.
2. **Tap Mail, Contacts, Calendars.** You see the Mail, Contacts, Calendars settings screen.
3. **Tap the Load Remote Images switch to Off.** Mail saves the setting and no longer displays remote images in your e-mail messages.

Preventing Mail from organizing messages by thread

In the Mail app, your messages get grouped by thread, which means the original message and all the replies you've received are grouped together in the account's Inbox folder. This is usually remarkably handy, because it means you don't have to scroll through a million messages to locate the reply you want to read.

Mail indicates a thread by displaying the number of messages in the thread on the right side of the latest thread message, as shown in Figure 5.14. Tap the message to see a list of the messages in the thread, and then tap the message you want to read.

Organizing messages by thread is usually convenient, but not always. For example, sometimes you view your messages and scroll through them by tapping the Next and Previous buttons. When you come to a thread, Mail jumps into the thread and you then scroll through each message in the thread, which can be a real hassle if the thread contains a large number of replies.

If you find that threads are more hassle than they're worth, you can follow these steps to configure Mail to no longer organize messages by thread:

1. **On the Home screen, tap Settings.** Your iPhone opens the Settings app.

2. **Tap Mail, Contacts, Calendars.** You see the Mail, Contacts, Calendars settings screen.

3. **Tap the Organize By Thread switch to Off.** Your iPhone saves the setting and no longer organizes your images by thread.

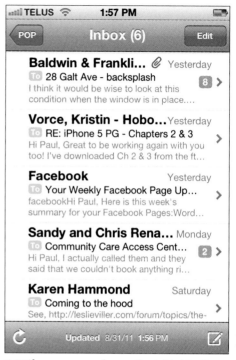

5.14 If you see a number on the right side of a message, that number tells you how many messages are in the thread.

Deleting Gmail messages instead of archiving them

With most e-mail accounts, you can tidy up the Inbox folder by tapping Edit, choosing one or more messages you no longer need, and then tapping Delete. Not so in your Gmail account. However, when you open your Gmail Inbox, tap Edit, and then select one or more messages, you see an Archive button instead of a Delete button, as shown in Figure 5.15. Tapping Archive moves the selected messages to the All Mail folder.

If you'd really prefer to delete your Gmail messages instead of archiving them, follow these steps to knock some sense into the Mail app:

1. **On the Home screen, tap Settings.**
   Your iPhone opens the Settings app.

2. **Tap Mail, Contacts, Calendars.** You
   see the Mail, Contacts, Calendars settings screen.

3. **Tap your Gmail account.** Your iPhone
   opens the Gmail settings.

4. **Tap the Archive Messages switch to
   Off.** Your iPhone saves the setting and
   no longer archives your Gmail messages.

Configuring your Exchange ActiveSync settings

If you have an account on a Microsoft Exchange
Server 2003 or 2007 network and that server
has deployed Exchange ActiveSync, then
you're all set to have your iPhone and Exchange
account synchronized automatically. That's
because ActiveSync supports wireless push
technology, which means that if anything changes on your Exchange server account, that change is
immediately synced with your iPhone:

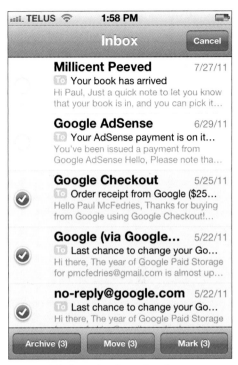

5.15 By default, Mail archives Gmail messages
instead of deleting them.

- **E-mail.** If you receive a new message on your Exchange account, ActiveSync immediately displays that message in the Mail app on your iPhone.

- **Contacts.** If someone at work adds or edits data in the server address book, those
  changes are immediately synced to your iPhone Contacts list.

- **Calendars.** If someone at work adds or edits an appointment in your calendar, or if
  someone requests a meeting with you, that data is immediately synced with the
  Calendar app on your iPhone.

- **Reminders.** If someone at work adds or edits a reminder, that data is immediately
  synced with the Reminders app on your iPhone.

ActiveSync works both ways, too, so if you send e-mail messages, add contacts or appointments, or accept meeting requests, your server account is immediately updated with the changes. And all this data whizzing back and forth is safe, because it's sent over a secure connection.

Your iPhone also gives you a few options for controlling ActiveSync, and the following steps show you how to set them:

1. **On the Home screen, tap Settings.** Your iPhone opens the Settings app.

2. **Tap Mail, Contacts, Calendars.** The Mail, Contacts, Calendars settings screen appears.

3. **Tap your Exchange account.** The Exchange account settings screen appears.

4. **To sync your Exchange e-mail account, tap the Mail switch to On.**

5. **To sync your Exchange address book, tap the Contacts switch to On.**

6. **To sync your Exchange calendar, tap the Calendars switch to On.**

7. **To sync your Exchange reminders, tap the Reminders switch to On.**

8. **To control the amount of time that gets synced on your e-mail account, tap Mail Days to Sync, and then tap the number of days, weeks, or months you want to sync.**

9. **If you want more folders pushed to you, tap Mail Folders to Push, and then tap each folder you want: Sent items, Deleted Items, or Junk E-Mail.**

Controlling e-mail with Siri voice commands

If you have an iPhone 4S, you can use the Siri voice recognition app to check, compose, send, and reply to messages, all with simple voice commands. Tap and hold the Home button (or press and hold the Mic button of the iPhone headphones, or the equivalent button on a Bluetooth headset) until Siri appears.

To check for new iCloud e-mail messages, you need only say "Check e-mail" (or just "Check mail"). You can also view a list of iCloud messages as follows:

- **Displaying unread messages.** Say "Show new e-mail."

- **Displaying messages where the subject line contains a specified topic.** Say "Show e-mail about *topic*," where *topic* is the topic you want to view.

- **Displaying messages from a particular person.** Say "Show e-mail from *name*," where *name* is the name of the sender.

If you want to start a new e-mail message, Siri gives you lots of options:

- **Creating a new message addressed to a particular person.** Say "E-mail *name,*" where *name* is the name of the recipient. This name can be a name from your Contacts list, or someone with a defined relationship, such as "Mom" or "my brother."
- **Creating a new message with a particular subject line.** Say "Email *name* about *subject,*" where *name* defines the recipient, and *subject* is the Subject line text.
- **Creating a new message with a particular body.** Say "Email *name* and say *text,*" where *name* is the recipient, and *text* is the message body text.

In each case, Siri creates the new message, displays it, and then asks if you want to send it. If you do, you can either say "Send" or tap the Send button.

If you have a message displayed, you can send back a response by saying "Reply." If you want to add some text to the response, say "Reply *text,*" where *text* is your response.

You can also use Siri within Mail to dictate a message. When you tap inside the body of a new message, the keyboard that appears shows a Mic icon beside the spacebar. Tap the Mic icon and then start dictating. Here are some notes:

- For punctuation, you can say the name of the mark you need, such as "comma" (,), "semicolon" (;), "colon" (:), "period" or "full stop" (.), "question mark" (?), "exclamation point" (!), "dash" (–), or "at sign" (@).
- You can enclose text in parentheses by saying "open parenthesis," then the text, and then "close parenthesis."
- To surround text with quotation marks, say "open quote," then the text, and then "close quote."
- To render a word in all uppercase letters, say "all caps" and then say the word.
- To start a new paragraph, say "new line."
- You can have some fun by saying "smiley face" for :-), "wink face" for ;-), and "frown face" for :-(.

To spell out a word (such as "period" or "colon"), say "No caps on, no space on," spell the word, and then say "No space off, no caps off." When you're finished, tap Done.

How Do I Synchronize My iPhone?

Your iPhone can function perfectly well on its own. After all, you can use it to create your own bookmarks, e-mail accounts, contacts, and appointments; you can download music and other media from the iTunes Store; and you can take your own photos using its built-in cameras. If you want to use your iPhone as a stand-alone device, no one can stop you, but I'm not sure why you'd want to. With all the great iPhone synchronization features, tons of the useful and fun content on your computer can also be shared with your iPhone. This chapter shows you how to master syncing your iPhone and your Mac or Windows computer.

Connecting Your iPhone to Your Computer

When the iPhone was first released, it looked as though we might have finally arrived at that glorious day when computers and devices could just sort of *sense* each other's presence, and begin a digital conversation without requiring something as inelegant as a *physical* connection. Ugh. However, even though the fancy-schmancy iPhone supported *three* wireless technologies — Wi-Fi, Bluetooth, and cellular — exchanging data between it and a Mac or PC required a wired connection.

Well, I'm happy to report that those days are behind us. Sort of. Yes, you can still use a cable to connect your iPhone and your computer, but iOS 5 now also supports *wireless* connections via Wi-Fi. The next couple of sections provide the details.

Connecting via USB

Although iOS 5 supports Wi-Fi syncing, USB connections are still important for those times when you want to use iTunes to change your sync settings. To make an old-fashioned USB-style connection, you can proceed in a couple of ways:

- **USB cable.** Use the cable that came with your iPhone to attach the USB connector to a free USB port on your Mac or Windows PC. Then, attach the dock connector to the 30-pin connector port on the bottom of the iPhone.

- **Dock.** If you shelled out the bucks for an optional Apple Universal Dock, plug it into a power outlet. Using the iPhone cable, attach the USB connector to a free USB port on your Mac or Windows PC and then attach the dock connector to the 30-pin connector port on the back of the dock. Now insert your iPhone into the dock cradle.

Connecting via Wi-Fi

As long as your iPhone and your computer are connected to the same Wi-Fi network, the Wi-Fi connection happens automatically, but only if you prepare your iPhone. Specifically, you need to follow these steps:

1. **Connect your iPhone to your computer.**

2. **When your iPhone appears in the iTunes Devices list, click it.**

3. **In the Summary tab, select the Sync with this iPhone over Wi-Fi check box.**

4. **Click Apply.** iTunes configures your iPhone to sync over Wi-Fi.

5. **Eject and then disconnect your iPhone.**

6. **Shut down and restart iTunes.**

7. **Turn off your iPhone and then turn it back on.** Your iPhone appears in the iTunes Devices list without being physically connected to your computer.

After you do all that, you're ready to sync over Wi-Fi, as I describe a bit later in this chapter.

Synchronizing Your iPhone Automatically

Start with the look-ma-no-hands syncing scenario, where you don't have to pay the slightest attention: automatic syncing. If the amount of iPhone-friendly digital content you have on your Mac or Windows PC is less than the capacity of your iPhone, then you have no worries because you know it's all going to fit. All you have to do is turn on your iPhone and connect it to your computer.

That's it! iTunes opens automatically and begins syncing your iPhone (and, as an added bonus, it also begins charging the iPhone battery). Your iPhone displays the Sync icon in the menu bar (see Figure 6.1) while the sync runs, and, unlike in previous versions of iOS, you can use your iPhone while the sync is running.

6.1 While your iPhone is in midsync, you see the Sync icon in the menu bar.

Bypassing the automatic sync

What do you do if you want to connect your iPhone to your computer, but you don't want it to sync? I'm not talking about switching to manual syncing full time (I get to that in a second). Instead, I'm talking about bypassing the sync one time only. For example, you might want to connect your iPhone to your computer just to charge it (assuming you either don't have the optional dock or don't have it with you). Or perhaps you just want to use iTunes to eyeball how much free space is left on your iPhone or check for software updates.

Genius You don't need to use iTunes to see how much free space is left on your iPhone. On the Home screen, tap Settings, tap General, and then tap About. In the About screen that slides in, the Available value tells you how many gigabytes (or megabytes) of free space you have to play with.

Whatever the reason, you can tell iTunes to hold off the syncing this time by using one of the following techniques:

- **Mac.** Connect the iPhone to the Mac and then quickly press and hold the Option and ⌘ keys.

- **Windows.** Connect the iPhone to the Windows PC and then quickly press and hold the Ctrl and Shift keys.

When you see that iTunes has added your iPhone to the Devices list, you can release the keys.

Troubleshooting automatic syncing

Okay, so you connect your iPhone to your computer and then nothing happens. iTunes doesn't wake from its digital slumber or, if iTunes is already running, it sees the iPhone but refuses to start syncing. What's up with that?

It could be a couple of things. First, connect your iPhone, switch to iTunes on your computer, and then click your iPhone in the Devices list. On the Summary tab (see Figure 6.2), make sure the Open iTunes when this iPhone is connected check box is selected.

If that check box was already selected, then you need to delve a bit deeper to solve the mystery. Follow these steps:

1. **Open the iTunes preferences:**
   - **Mac.** Choose iTunes ➪ Preferences, or press ⌘+. (period).
   - **Windows.** Choose Edit ➪ Preferences, or press Ctrl+. (period).
2. **Click the Devices tab.**
3. **Deselect the Prevent iPods, iPhones and iPads from syncing automatically check box.**
4. **Click OK to put the new setting into effect and enable automatic syncing once again.**

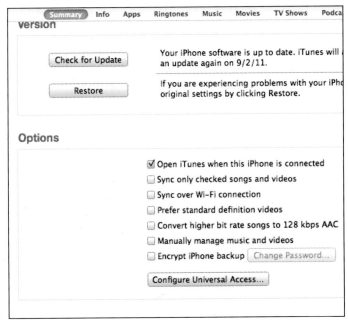

6.2 Select the Open iTunes when this iPhone is connected check box.

Synchronizing Your iPhone Manually

One fine day, you'll be minding your own business and performing what you believe to be a routine sync operation when a dialog like the one shown in Figure 6.3 will rear its nasty head.

Groan! This most unwelcome dialog means just what it says: there's not enough free space on your iPhone to sync all the content from your computer. You've got a couple of ways you can handle this:

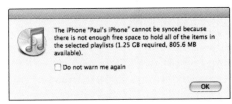

6.3 You see this dialog if iTunes can't fit all of your stuff on your iPhone.

● **Remove some of the content from your computer.** This is a good way to go if your iPhone is really close to having enough space. For example, the dialog may say that your computer wants to send 100MB of data but your iPhone has only 98MB of free space. In this case, you can get rid of a few megabytes of stuff on your computer, and you're back in the sync business.

- **Synchronize your iPhone manually.** This means that you no longer sync everything on your computer. Instead, you handpick which playlists, podcasts, audiobooks, and so on are sent to your iPhone. It's a bit more work, but it's the way to go if there's a big difference between the amount of content on your computer and the amount of space left on your iPhone.

The rest of this chapter shows you how to manually sync the various content types: contacts, calendars, e-mail, bookmarks, documents, music, podcasts, audiobooks, movies, TV shows, eBooks, photos, and videos.

Syncing Your iPhone Via Wi-Fi

The capability to sync your iPhone with your computer without a wire in sight is one of the nicest new iOS 5 features. If you're sitting in your easy chair or relaxing on the front porch, who wants to get up, go to the computer, connect your iPhone, and then run a sync just to get, say, the latest podcasts? With iOS 5, as long as your iPhone is on AC and is connected to the same Wi-Fi network as your computer, you can run the sync by barely moving a muscle.

Follow these steps to sync with iTunes right where you are by using Wi-Fi:

1. **Make sure your computer is running and connected to the same Wi-Fi network as your iPhone.**

2. **On the iPhone Home screen, tap Settings.** The Settings app appears.

3. **Tap General.**

4. **Tap iTunes Wi-Fi Sync.**

5. **Tap Sync.** Your iPhone syncs with iTunes on your computer.

Synchronizing Information with Your iPhone

If you step back a pace or two to take in the big picture, you see that your iPhone deals with two broad types of data: media — all that audio and video stuff — and information such as contacts, appointments, e-mail, websites, and notes. You need both types of data to get the most out of your iPhone investment and, happily, both types of data are eminently syncable. I get to the media syncing portion of the show a bit later. For now, the next few sections show you how to take control of syncing your information between your iPhone and your computer.

Syncing your contacts

Although you can certainly add contacts directly on your iPhone — and I show you how to do just that in Chapter 9 — adding, editing, grouping, and deleting contacts is a lot easier on a computer. So, a good way to approach contacts is to manage them on your Mac or Windows PC, and then sync them with your iPhone.

However, do you really need to sync all your contacts? For example, if you only use your iPhone to contact friends and family, then why clog your phone's Contacts list with work contacts? I don't know!

You can control which contacts are sent to your iPhone by creating groups of contacts and then syncing only those that you want. Here are some quickie instructions for creating groups:

- **Address Book (Mac).** Choose File ➪ New Group, type the group name, and then press Return. Now populate the new group by dragging and dropping contacts on it.

- **Contacts (Windows 7 and Windows Vista).** Click New Contact Group, type the group name, and then click Add to Contact Group. Choose all the contacts you want in the group and then click Add. Click OK.

Note   If you're an Outlook user, note that iTunes doesn't support Outlook-based contact groups, so you're stuck with syncing everyone in your Outlook Contacts folder. Also note that iTunes doesn't support Windows Live Mail at all, so you can't use that application to sync your contacts.

With your group (or groups) all figured out, follow these steps to sync your contacts with your iPhone:

1. **Connect your iPhone to your computer.**

2. **In iTunes, click your iPhone in the Devices list.**

3. **Click the Info tab.**

4. **Turn on contacts syncing by using one of the following techniques:**

    - **Mac.** Select the Sync Address Book Contacts check box.

    - **Windows.** Select the Sync Contacts with check box, and then use the list to choose the program you want to use (such as Outlook). For Yahoo! contacts, see Step 7; for Google contacts, see Step 8.

5. **Select an option:**

   - **All contacts.** Select this option to sync all your Address Book contacts.

   - **Selected groups.** Select this option to sync only the groups you pick. In the group list, select the check box beside each group that you want to sync, as shown in Figure 6.4.

6. **If you want to make the sync a two-way street, select the Add contacts created outside of groups on this iPhone to option, and then choose a group from the menu.**

7. **In Mac OS X, if you have a Yahoo! account and you also want your Yahoo! Address Book contacts synced, select the Sync Yahoo! Address Book contacts check box.** In Windows, use the Sync Contacts with list to select Yahoo! Address Book. In either case, you then type your Yahoo! ID and password and click OK.

8. **In Mac OS X, if you have a Google account and you also want your Google Contacts synced, select the Sync Google Contacts check box.** In Windows, use the Sync Contacts with list to select Google Contacts. In either case, you then type your Google username and password, and click OK.

9. **Click Apply.** iTunes syncs the iPhone using your new contacts settings.

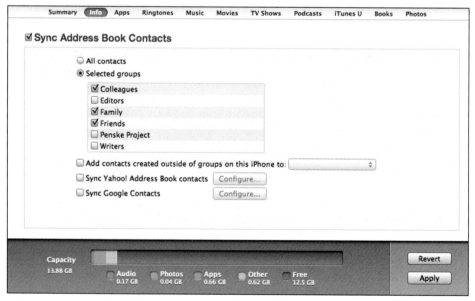

6.4 You can sync selected Address Book groups with your iPhone.

Syncing your calendar

When you're tripping around town with your trusty iPhone at your side, you certainly don't want to be late if you've got a date. The best way to ensure that you don't miss an appointment, meeting, or rendezvous is to always have the event details at hand, which means adding those details to your iPhone Calendar. You can add the appointment to Calendar right on the iPhone (a technique I take you through in Chapter 9), but it's easier to create it on your computer and then sync it to your iPhone. This gives you the added advantage of having the appointment listed in two places, so you're sure to arrive on time.

Most people sync all appointments, but it's not unusual to keep track of separate schedules — for example, business and personal. You can control which schedule is synced to your iPhone by creating separate calendars and then syncing only those that you want. In the iCal application on your Mac, choose File ⇨ New Calendar, type the calendar name, and then press Return.

Note   Although you can create extra calendars in Outlook, iTunes doesn't recognize them, so you have to sync everything in your Outlook Calendar folder. Also, iTunes doesn't support Windows Calendar (available with Windows Vista), so you're out of luck if you use that to manage your schedule.

Now follow these steps to sync your calendar with your iPhone:

1. **Connect your iPhone to your computer.**

2. **In iTunes, click your iPhone in the Devices list.**

3. **Click the Info tab.**

4. **Turn on calendar syncing by using one of the following techniques:**

    - **Mac.** Select the Sync iCal Calendars check box.

    - **Windows.** Select the Sync Calendars with check box, and then use the list to choose the program you want to use (such as Outlook).

5. **Select an option:**

    - **All calendars.** Select this option to sync all your calendars.

    - **Selected calendars.** Select this option to sync only the calendars you pick. In the calendar list, select the check box beside each calendar that you want to sync, as shown in Figure 6.5.

6. **To control how far back the calendar sync goes, select the Do not sync events older than *X* days check box.** Next, type the number of days of calendar history you want to see on your iPhone.

7. **Click Apply.** iTunes syncs the iPhone using your new calendar settings.

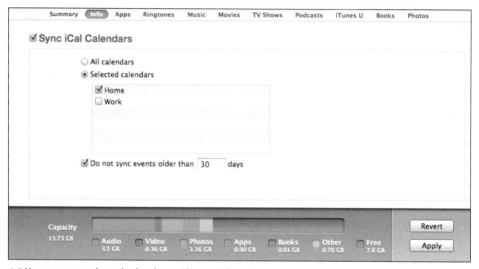

6.5 You can sync selected calendars with your iPhone.

Syncing your e-mail account

By far the easiest way to configure your iPhone with an e-mail account is to let iTunes do all the heavy lifting. If you have an existing account — whether it's a Mail account on your Mac or an Outlook or Windows Mail account on your PC — you can convince iTunes to gather all the account details and pass them along to your iPhone. Here's how it works:

1. **Connect your iPhone to your computer.**

2. **In the iTunes sources list, click the iPhone.**

3. **Click the Info tab.**

4. **In the Mail Accounts section, use one of the following techniques:**

   ● **Mac.** Select the Sync Mail Accounts check box, and then select the check box beside each account you want to add to your iPhone, as shown in Figure 6.6.

   ● **Windows.** Select the Sync Mail Accounts from check box, select your e-mail program from the drop-down list, and then select the check box beside each account you want to add to your iPhone.

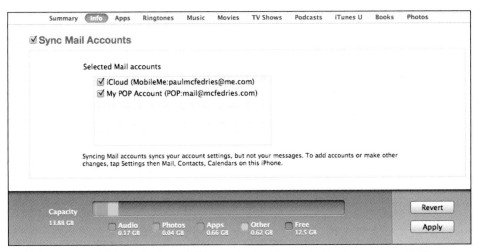

6.6 Make sure you click both the Sync Mail Accounts check box and at least one account in the Selected Mail accounts list.

5. **Click Apply.** You may see a message asking if AppleMobileSync can be allowed access to your keychain (your Mac's master password list).

6. **If you see that message, click Allow.** iTunes begins syncing the selected e-mail account settings from your computer to your iPhone.

Syncing your bookmarks

The easiest way to get bookmarks for your favorite sites into your iPhone is to take advantage of your best bookmark resource: the Safari browser on your Mac (or PC) or the Internet Explorer browser on your Windows PC (which calls them Favorites). Whichever browser you prefer, you've probably used it for a while and have all kinds of useful and fun bookmarked sites at your meta-phorical fingertips. To get these at your literal fingertips — that is, on your iPhone — you need to include bookmarks as part of the synchronization process between the iPhone and iTunes.

Note

Having used Safari or Internet Explorer for a while means having lots of great sites bookmarked, but it also likely means that you've got lots of digital dreck — that is, sites you no longer visit or that have gone belly-up. Before synchronizing your bookmarks with the iPhone, consider taking some time to clean up your existing bookmarks. You'll thank yourself in the end.

Follow these steps to activate bookmark syncing:

1. **Connect your iPhone to your computer.**

2. **In the iTunes sources list, click the iPhone.**

3. **Click the Info tab.**

4. **Scroll down to the Other section, and then use one of the following techniques:**

   ● **Mac.** Select the Sync Safari bookmarks check box, as shown in Figure 6.7.

   ● **Windows.** Select the Sync bookmarks with check box, and then select your web browser from the drop-down list.

5. **Click Apply.** iTunes begins syncing the bookmarks from your computer to your iPhone.

Genius

What's that? You've already synced your bookmarks to your iPhone and you now have a bunch of useless sites clogging up the Safari app's bookmark arteries? Not a problem! Return to your desktop Safari (or Internet Explorer), purge the bogus bookmarks, and then resync your iPhone by following the bookmark syncing steps. Any bookmarks you blew away will also be trashed from iPhone.

6.7 Make sure the Sync Safari bookmarks check box is selected.

Syncing your notes

If you use the Notes app on your iPhone to jot down quick thoughts, ideas, and other mental tidbits, you might want to transfer them to your computer so you can incorporate them into another document, add them to a to-do list, or whatever. To do this in early versions of the iPhone OS, you had to e-mail the notes to yourself, which wasn't exactly convenient. Now, however, notes are full-fledged members of the iPhone information pantheon, which means you can sync your notes to your computer.

Note

To sync notes on your Mac, you must be running Mac OS X 10.5.7 or later.

Follow these steps to activate notes syncing:

1. **Connect your iPhone to your computer.**

2. **In the iTunes sources list, click the iPhone.**

3. **Click the Info tab.**

4. **Scroll down to the Other section (as shown previously in Figure 6.7), and then use one of the following techniques:**

   - **Mac.** Select the Sync notes check box.

   - **Windows.** Select the Sync notes with check box, and then select an application from the drop-down list (such as Outlook).

5. **Click Apply.** iTunes begins syncing the notes between your computer and your iPhone.

Merging data from two or more computers

Long gone are the days when your information resided on a single computer. Now it's common to have a desktop computer (or two) at home, a work computer, and perhaps a notebook computer to take on the road. It's nice to have all that digital firepower, but it creates a big problem: You end up with contacts, calendars, and other information scattered over several machines. How are you supposed to keep track of it all?

The latest solution from Apple is iCloud, which provides seamless information integration across multiple computers (Mac and Windows) and, of course, the iPhone. This is the topic I cover in Chapter 12.

However, if you don't have an iCloud account, you can still achieve a bit of data harmony. That's because iTunes offers the welcome capability of merging information from two or more computers on the iPhone. For example, if you have contacts on your home computer, you can sync them with your iPhone. If you have a separate collection of contacts on your notebook, you can also sync them with your iPhone, but iTunes gives you two choices:

- **Merge Info.** With this option, your iPhone keeps the information synced from the first computer and merges it with the information synced from the second.

- **Replace Info.** With this option, your iPhone deletes the information synced from the first computer and replaces it with the information synced from the second.

Here are the general steps to follow to set up your merged information:

1. **Sync your iPhone with information from one computer.** This technique works with contacts, calendars, e-mail accounts, and bookmarks.

2. **Connect your iPhone to the second computer.**

3. **In iTunes, click your iPhone in the Devices list.**

4. **Click the Info tab.**

5. **Select the Sync check boxes that correspond with information already synced on the first computer.** For example, if you synced contacts on the first computer, select the Sync Address Book contacts check box.

6. **Click Apply.** iTunes displays a dialog like the one shown in Figure 6.8.

7. **Click Merge Info.** iTunes syncs your iPhone and merges the second computer's information with the existing information from the first computer.

6.8 You can merge contacts, calendars, e-mail accounts, bookmarks, and notes from two or more computers.

Handling sync conflicts

When you sync information between your iPhone and a computer, any edits you make to that information are included in the sync. For example, if you change someone's e-mail address on your iPhone, the next time you sync, iTunes updates the e-mail address on the computer, which is exactly what you want.

However, what if you already changed that person's address on the computer? If you made the same edit, then it's no biggie because there's nothing to sync. But what if you made a different edit? Ah, that's a problem, because now iTunes doesn't know which version has the correct information. In that case, it shrugs its digital shoulders and passes off the problem to a program called Conflict Resolver, which displays the dialog shown in Figure 6.9.

6.9 If you make different edits to the same bit of information on your iPhone and your computer, the Conflict Resolver springs into action.

If you want to deal with the problem now, click Review Now. Conflict Resolver then offers you the details of the conflict. For example, in Figure 6.10 you can see that a contact's company name and picture are different in Address Book and on the iPhone. To settle the issue once and for all (you hope), click the correct version of the information and then click Continue to move on to the next conflict. When you've gone through all the conflicts, click Done. When Conflict Resolver tells you it will fix the problem during the next sync, click Sync Now to make it happen right away.

6.10 Clicking Review Now shows you the details of any sync conflicts.

Handling large iPhone-to-computer sync changes

Syncing works both ways, meaning that not only does your iPhone receive content from your computer, but your computer also receives content from your iPhone. For example, if you create any bookmarks, contacts, or appointments on your iPhone, those items are sent to your computer during the sync.

However, it's implied that the bulk of the content flows from your computer to your iPhone, which makes sense because, in most cases, it's easier to add, edit, and delete stuff on the computer. So that's why, if you make lots of changes to your iPhone content, iTunes displays a warning that the sync is going to, likewise, change a lot of the content on your computer. The threshold is five percent, which means that if the sync changes more than five percent of a particular type of content on your computer — such as bookmarks or calendars — the warning appears, as shown in Figure 6.11.

If you're expecting this (because you did change lots of stuff on your iPhone), click the Sync *Whatever* button (where *Whatever* is the type of data you want to sync: Bookmarks,

6.11 iTunes warns you if the sync will mess with more than five percent of your computer's content.

Calendars, and so on). If you're not sure, click Show Details to see what the changes are. If you're still scratching your head, click Cancel to skip that part of the sync.

If you're running iTunes for Windows, you can either turn off this warning or adjust the threshold. (For some unfathomable reason, iTunes for Mac doesn't offer this handy option.) Follow these steps:

1. **Choose Edit ⇨ Preferences, or press Ctrl+, (comma).** The iTunes dialog box comes aboard.

2. **Click the Devices tab.**

3. **If you want to disable the sync alerts altogether, deselect the Warn when check box.** Otherwise, leave that check box selected and move on to Step 4.

4. **Use the Warn when *percent* of the data on the computer will be changed list to set the alert threshold, where *percent* is one of the following:**

   - **any.** Select this option to see the sync alert whenever syncing with the iPhone will change data on your computer. iPhone syncs routinely modify data on the computer, so be prepared to see the alerts every time you sync. (Of course, that may be exactly what you want.)

   - **more than *X*.** Where *X* is 5% (the default), 25%, or 50%. You'll see the alert only when the sync will change more than the chosen percentage of data on the computer.

5. **Click OK to put the new settings into effect.**

Replacing your iPhone data with fresh info

Once you know what you're doing, syncing contacts, calendars, e-mail accounts, and bookmarks to your iPhone is a relatively bulletproof procedure that should happen without a hitch each time. Of course, this is technology we're dealing with here, so hitches do happen every now and then. As a result, you might end up with corrupt or repeated information on your iPhone.

Or perhaps you've been syncing your iPhone with a couple of different computers, and you decide to cut one of the computers out of the loop and revert to a single machine for all of your syncs.

In both of these scenarios, you need to replace the existing information on your iPhone with a freshly baked batch of data. Fortunately, iTunes has a feature that lets you do exactly that. Here's how it works:

1. **Connect your iPhone to your computer.**

2. **In the iTunes sources list, click the iPhone.**

3. **Click the Info tab.**

4. **Select the Sync check boxes for each type of information you want to work with (contacts, calendars, e-mail accounts, bookmarks, or notes).** If you don't select a check box, iTunes won't replace that information on your iPhone. For example, if you like your iPhone bookmarks just the way they are, don't select the Sync bookmarks check box.

5. **In the Advanced section, select the check box beside each type of information you want to replace.** As shown in Figure 6.12, there are five check boxes: Contacts, Calendars, Mail Accounts, Bookmarks, and Notes.

6. **Click Apply.** iTunes replaces the selected information on your iPhone.

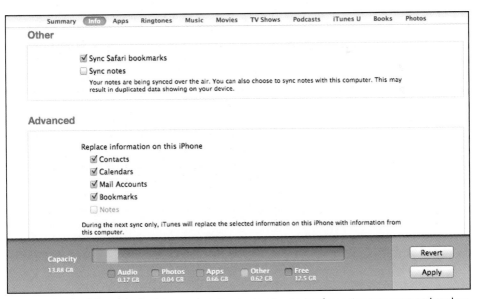

6.12 Use the check boxes in the Advanced section to decide which information you want replaced on your iPhone.

Note

If a check box in the Advanced section is disabled, it's because you didn't select the corresponding Sync check box. For example, in Figure 6.12 you see that the Sync Notes check box in the Other section is deselected, so in the Advanced section, the Notes check box is disabled.

Synchronizing Media with Your iPhone

The brainy Phone app and the sleek Safari browser may earn the lion's share of kudos for the iPhone, but many people reserve their rave reviews for its Music app. The darn thing is just so versatile! It can play music, of course, but it also happily cranks out audiobooks and podcasts, as well as music videos, movies, and TV shows. Ear and eye candy all in one package!

If there's a problem with this digital largesse, it's that the Music app might be too versatile. Even if you have a big 64GB iPhone, you may still find its confines a bit cramped, particularly if you're also loading up your iPhone with photos, contacts, and calendars, and you just can't seem to keep your hands out of the App Store cookie jar.

All this means is that you probably have to pay a bit more attention when it comes to syncing your iPhone, and the following sections show you how to do just that.

Syncing music and music videos

The Music app is a digital music player at heart, so you've probably already loaded up your iPhone with lots of audio content and music videos. To get the most out of the Music app's music and video capabilities, you need to know all the ways you can synchronize these items. For example, if you use the Music app primarily as a music player and your iPhone has more disk capacity than you need for all of your digital audio, feel free to throw all your music onto the player. On the other hand, your iPhone might not have much free space, or you might only want certain songs and videos on the player to make it easier to navigate. Not a problem! You can configure iTunes to sync only the songs that you select.

Genius

Something I like about syncing playlists is that you can estimate in advance how much space your selected playlists will usurp on the iPhone. In iTunes, click the playlist and then examine the status bar, which tells you the number of songs in the playlist, its total duration, and — most significantly — its total size.

Before getting to the specific sync steps, you need to know that there are three ways to manually sync music and music videos:

- **Playlists.** With this method, you specify the playlists that you want iTunes to sync. Those playlists also appear on your iPhone's Music app. This is by far the easiest way to manually sync music and music videos because you usually just have a few playlists to select. The downside is if you have large playlists and run out of space on your iPhone, the only way to fix the problem is to remove an entire playlist. Another bummer with this method is that you can only sync all or none of your music videos.

- **Check boxes.** With this method, you specify which songs and music videos are synced by selecting the little check boxes that appear beside every song and video in iTunes. This is precise syncing for sure, but because your iPhone can hold thousands of songs, it's also a lot of work.

- **Drag and drop.** With this method, you click and drag individual songs and music videos, and drop them on the iPhone icon in the iTunes Devices list. This is an easy way to get a bunch of tracks on your iPhone quickly. However, iTunes doesn't give you any way of tracking which files you've dragged and dropped.

Genius

What do you do if you only want to select a few tracks from a large playlist? Waste a big chunk of your life deselecting a few hundred check boxes? Pass. Here's a better way: Press ⌘+A (Mac) or Ctrl+A (Windows) to select every track, right-click any track, and then click Uncheck Selection. Voila! iTunes deselects every track in seconds flat. Now you can select only the tracks you want. You're welcome.

Here are the steps to follow to sync music and music videos using playlists:

1. **In iTunes, click your iPhone in the Devices list.**

2. **Click the Music tab.**

3. **Select the Sync Music check box.** iTunes asks you to confirm that you want to sync music.

4. **Click Sync Music.**

5. **Select the Selected playlists, artists, albums, and genres option.**

6. **Select the check box beside each playlist, artist, album, and genre you want to sync, as shown in Figure 6.13.**

147

7. **Select the Include music videos check box if you also want to add your music videos into the sync mix.**

8. **Select the Include voice memos check box if you also want to sync voice memos recorded on your iPhone.**

Genius If you have lots of music that has been ripped at a high bit rate (say, 256 Kbps or higher), those songs will take up a lot of disk space on your iPhone. To fix this, click the Summary tab and then select the Convert higher bit rate songs to 128 Kbps AAC check box.

9. **If you want iTunes to fill up any remaining free space on your iPhone with a selection of related music from your Library, select the Automatically fill free space with songs check box.**

10. **Click Apply.** iTunes syncs your iPhone using the new settings.

6.13 Choose the Selected playlists, artists, albums, and genres option and then select the playlists you want to sync.

Here are the steps to follow to sync using the check boxes that appear beside each track in your iTunes Music Library:

1. **In iTunes, click your iPhone in the Devices list.**

2. **Click the Summary tab.**

3. **Select the Sync only checked songs and videos check box.**

4. **Click Apply.** If iTunes starts syncing your iPhone, click the Cancel button (X) in the iTunes status window to stop it.

5. **Either click Music in the Library list or click a playlist that contains the tracks you want to sync.** If a track's check box is selected, iTunes syncs it with your iPhone. If a track's check box is deselected, iTunes doesn't sync it with your iPhone. If the track is already on your iPhone, iTunes removes it.

6. **In the Devices list, click your iPhone.**

7. **Click the Summary tab.**

8. **Click Sync.** iTunes syncs just the selected tracks.

Genius

If you download a music video from the web and then import it into iTunes (by choosing File ➪ Import), iTunes adds the video to its Movies Library. To display it in the Music Library instead, open the Movies Library, right-click the music video, and then click Get Info. Click the Video tab and use the Kind list to choose Music Video. Click OK. iTunes moves the music video to the Music folder.

You can also configure iTunes to let you drag tracks from the Music Library (or any playlist) and drop them on your iPhone. Here's how this works:

1. **In iTunes, click your iPhone in the Devices list.**

2. **Click the Summary tab.**

3. **Select the Manually manage music and videos check box.**

Note

When you select the Manually manage music and videos check box, iTunes automatically deselects the Sync music check box in the Music tab. However, iTunes doesn't mess with the music on your iPhone. Even when it syncs after a drag and drop, it only adds the new tracks — it doesn't delete any of your phone's existing music.

4. **Click Apply.** If iTunes starts syncing your iPhone, click the Cancel button (X) in the iTunes status window to stop it.

5. **Either click Music in the Library list or click a playlist that contains the tracks you want to sync.**

6. **Choose the tracks you want to sync:**

   - If all the tracks are together, Shift+click the first track, hold down Shift, and then click the last track.

   - If the tracks are scattered all over the place, hold down ⌘ (or Ctrl in Windows) and click each track.

7. **Click and drag the selected tracks to the Devices list and drop them on the iPhone icon.** iTunes syncs the selected tracks.

Caution If you decide to return to playlist syncing by selecting the Sync music check box in the Music tab, iTunes removes all tracks that you added to your iPhone via the drag-and-drop method.

Syncing podcasts

In many ways, podcasts are the most problematic of the various media you can sync with your iPhone. Not that the podcasts themselves pose any concern. Quite the contrary: they're so addictive that it's not unusual to collect them by the dozens. Why is that a problem? Because most professional podcasts are at least a few megabytes in size and many are tens of megabytes. A large-enough collection can put a serious dent in your iPhone's remaining storage space.

All the more reason to take control of the podcast-syncing process. Here's how you do it:

1. **In iTunes, click your iPhone in the Devices list.**

2. **Click the Podcasts tab.**

3. **Select the Sync Podcasts check box.**

4. **If you want iTunes to choose some of the podcasts automatically, select the Automatically include check box and proceed to Steps 5 and 6.** If you prefer to choose all the podcasts manually, deselect the Automatically include check box and skip to Step 7.

5. **Choose an option from the first pop-up menu, shown in Figure 6.14:**

    - **All.** Choose this item to sync every podcast.

    - **X Most Recent.** Choose this item to sync the X most recent podcasts (where X is a number you choose).

    - **All Unplayed.** Choose this item to sync all the podcasts you haven't yet played.

    - **X Most Recent Unplayed.** Choose this item to sync the X most recent podcasts that you haven't yet played.

    - **X Least Recent Unplayed.** Choose this item to sync the X oldest podcasts that you haven't yet played.

    - **All New.** Choose this item to sync all the podcasts published since the last sync.

    - **X Most Recent New.** Choose this item to sync the X most recent podcasts published since the last sync.

    - **X Least Recent New.** Choose this item to sync the X oldest podcasts published since the last sync.

6.14 To sync specific podcasts, choose the selected podcasts option and then select the check boxes for each podcast you want synced.

151

Note A podcast episode is unplayed if you haven't yet played at least part of it, either in iTunes or on your iPhone. If you play an episode on your iPhone, the player sends this information to iTunes when you next sync. Even better, your iPhone also lets iTunes know if you paused in the middle of an episode, so when you play that episode in iTunes, it starts at the point where you left off.

6. **Choose an option from the second pop-up menu:**

   - **All podcasts.** Select this to apply the option from Step 4 to all your podcasts.

   - **Selected podcasts.** Select this to apply the option from Step 4 only to the podcasts you select.

7. **Select the check box beside any podcast or podcast episode you want to sync.**

8. **Click Apply.** iTunes syncs the iPhone using your new podcast settings.

Genius To mark a podcast episode as unplayed, in iTunes choose the Podcasts Library, right-click the episode, and then choose Mark as New.

Syncing audiobooks

The iTunes sync settings for your iPhone have tabs for Music, Photos, Podcasts, and Video, but not one for Audiobooks. What's up with that? It's not, as you might think, some sort of antibook conspiracy, or even forgetfulness on the part of Apple. Instead, iTunes treats audiobook content as a special type of book (not surprisingly). To get audiobooks on your iPhone, follow these steps:

1. **In iTunes, click your iPhone in the Devices list.**

2. **Click the Books tab.**

3. **Select the Sync Audiobooks check box.**

4. **Select the Selected audiobooks option.**

5. **Select the check box beside each audiobook you want to sync.**

6. **Click Apply.** iTunes syncs your audiobooks to your iPhone.

Syncing movies

It wasn't all that long ago when technology prognosticators and pundits laughed at the idea of people watching movies on a 2-inch by 3-inch screen. Who could stand to watch even a music video on such a tiny screen? The pundits were wrong, of course, because now it's not at all unusual for people to use their iPhones to watch not only music videos, but also short films, animated shorts, and even full-length movies.

The major problem with movies is that their file size tends to be quite large — even short films lasting just a few minutes weigh in at dozens of megabytes, and full-length movies are several gigabytes. Clearly there's a compelling need to manage your movies to avoid filling up your iPhone and leaving no room for the latest album from your favorite band.

Follow these steps to configure and run the movie synchronization:

1. **In iTunes, click your iPhone in the Devices list.**

2. **Click the Movies tab.**

3. **Select the Sync Movies check box.** iTunes asks you to confirm that you want to sync movies.

4. **Click Sync Movies.**

5. **If you want iTunes to choose some of the movies automatically, select the Automatically include check box and proceed to Step 6.** If you prefer to choose all the movies manually, deselect the Automatically include check box and skip to Step 7.

6. **Choose an option from the pop-up menu:**

   - **All.** Choose this item to sync every movie.

   - *X* **Most Recent.** Choose this item to sync the *X* most recent movies you've added to iTunes (where *X* is a number you choose).

   - **All Unwatched.** Choose this item to sync all the movies you haven't yet played.

   - *X* **Most Recent Unwatched.** Choose this item to sync the *X* most recent movies you haven't yet played.

   - *X* **Least Recent Unwatched.** Choose this item to sync the *X* oldest movies you haven't yet played.

7. **Select the check box beside any other movie you want to sync.**

Note A movie is unwatched if you haven't yet viewed it either in iTunes or on your iPhone. If you watch a movie on your iPhone, the player sends this information to iTunes when you next sync.

8. **If you want to watch rented movies on your iPhone, in the Rented Movies section, click the Move button beside the rented movie you want to shift to your iPhone.** iTunes adds it to the On *iPhone* list (where *iPhone* is the name of your iPhone).

9. **Click Apply.** iTunes syncs the iPhone using your new movie settings.

Syncing TV show episodes

If the average iPhone is at risk of being filled by a few large movie files, it's probably also at grave risk of being overwhelmed by a large number of TV show episodes. A single half-hour episode can eat up approximately 250MB, so even a modest collection of shows will consume multiple gigabytes of precious iPhone disk space.

This means it's crucial to monitor your TV episode collection and keep your iPhone synced with only the episodes you need. Fortunately, iTunes gives you a decent set of tools to handle this:

1. **In iTunes, click your iPhone in the Devices list.**

2. **Click the TV Shows tab.**

3. **Select the Sync TV Shows check box.** iTunes asks you to confirm that you want to sync TV shows.

4. **Click Sync TV Shows.**

5. **If you want iTunes to choose some of the episodes automatically, select the Automatically include check box and proceed to Steps 6 and 7.** If you prefer to choose all the episodes manually, deselect the Automatically include check box and skip to Step 8.

6. **Choose an option from the drop-down menu:**
   - **All.** Choose this item to sync every TV show episode.
   - **X Most Recent.** Choose this item to sync the X most recent episodes (where X is a number you choose).
   - **All Unwatched.** Choose this item to sync all the episodes you haven't yet viewed.
   - **X Most Recent Unwatched.** Choose this item to sync the X most recent episodes that you haven't yet viewed.
   - **X Least Recent Unwatched.** Choose this item to sync the X oldest episodes that you haven't yet viewed.

Note

A TV episode is unwatched if you haven't yet viewed it either in iTunes or on your iPhone. If you watch an episode on your iPhone, the player sends this information to iTunes when you next sync.

7. **Choose an option from the second pop-up menu:**

   - **All shows.** Select this option to apply the choice from Step 6 to all of your TV shows.

   - **Selected Shows.** Select this option to apply the choice from Step 6 to only the TV shows you select, as shown in Figure 6.15.

8. **Select the check box beside any TV show or episode you want to sync.**

9. **Click Apply.** iTunes syncs the iPhone using your new TV show settings.

6.15 To sync specific TV shows, select the Sync TV shows check box, and then select the check boxes for each show you want synced.

Note

To mark a TV episode as unwatched, in iTunes choose the TV Shows Library, right-click the episode, and then choose Mark as New.

Syncing eBooks

If you've used your computer to purchase eBooks from the iTunes Store or to add some down-loaded eBooks to the iTunes Library, you'll want to get those onto your iPhone as soon as possible. Similarly, if you've grabbed some eBooks from the iBookstore on your iPhone, it's a good idea to back them up to your computer.

You can do both by syncing eBooks between your computer and your iPhone:

1. **In iTunes, click your iPhone in the Devices list.**

2. **Click the Books tab.**

3. **Select the Sync Books check box.**

4. **In the book list, select the check box beside each book that you want to sync, as shown in Figure 6.16.**

5. **Click Apply.** iTunes syncs the iPhone using your new book settings.

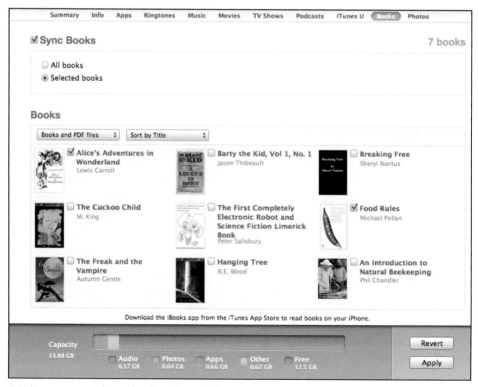

6.16 You can sync selected books with your iPhone.

Syncing computer photos to your iPhone

No media collection on an iPhone is complete without a few choice photos to show off around the water cooler. One way to get those photos is to take them with the built-in digital cameras on your iPhone. However, if you have some good pics on your computer, you can use iTunes to send them to the iPhone. Note that Apple supports a number of image file types in addition to the most common TIFF and JPEG formats, including BMP, GIF, JPG2000 or JP2, PICT, PNG, PSD, and SGI.

Note If you have another photo-editing application installed on your computer, chances are it will also appear in the Sync photos from list.

If you use your computer to process lots of photos and you want to take copies of some (or all) of them with you on your iPhone, then follow these steps to sync them:

1. **In iTunes, click your iPhone in the Devices list.**

2. **Click the Photos tab.**

3. **Select the Sync Photos from check box.**

4. **Choose an option from the drop-down menu:**

    - **iPhoto (Mac only).** Choose this item to sync the photos, albums, and events you've set up in iPhoto.

    - **Choose folder.** Choose this command to sync the images contained in a folder you specify.

    - **My Pictures (or Pictures on Windows Vista).** Choose this item to sync the images in the My Pictures (or Pictures) folder.

5. **Select the photos you want to sync.** The controls you see depend on what you chose in Step 4:

    - **If you chose iPhoto.** In this case, you get two further options: Select the All photos, albums, Events, and Faces option to sync your entire iPhoto library. Select the Selected albums, Events, and Faces option, and then select the check box beside each item you want to sync, as shown in Figure 6.17.

    - **If you chose either My Pictures or Choose folder.** In this case, select either the All photos option or the Selected folders option. If you select the latter, select the check box beside each subfolder you want to sync.

6. **Click Apply.** iTunes syncs the iPhone using your new photo settings.

Note iTunes doesn't sync exact copies of your photos to the iPhone. Instead, it creates what Apple calls TV-quality versions of each image. These are copies of the images that have been reduced in size to match the iPhone screen size. This not only makes the sync go faster, but it also means the photos take up much less room on your iPhone.

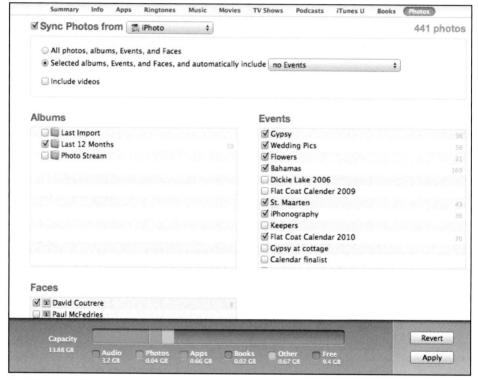

6.17 If you have iPhoto on your Mac, you can sync specified albums, Events, and Faces to your iPhone.

Syncing iPhone photos to your computer

If you create a Safari bookmark on your iPhone and then sync with your computer, that bookmark is transferred from the iPhone to the default web browser on your computer. That's a sweet deal and it also applies to contacts and appointments. Unfortunately, it doesn't apply to media files that, with one exception, travel along a one-way street from your computer to your iPhone.

Ah, but then there's that one exception, and it's a good one. If you take any photos using your iPhone's built-in (and pretty good) cameras, the sync process reverses itself and enables you to send some (or all) of those images to your computer. Sign me up!

Note

Actually, there's a second exception to the one-way media syncing rule. If you use the iTunes app on your iPhone to purchase or download music, those files are transferred to your computer during the next sync. iTunes creates a Store category called Purchased on *iPhone* (where *iPhone* is the name of your iPhone). When the sync is complete, you can find your music there, as well as in the Music Library.

The iPhone-to-computer sync process bypasses iTunes entirely. Instead, your computer deals directly with your iPhone and treats it just as though it was some garden-variety digital camera. How this works depends on whether your computer is a Mac or a Windows PC, so I use separate sets of steps.

To sync your iPhone camera photos to your Mac, follow these steps:

1. **Connect your iPhone to your Mac.** iPhoto opens, adds your iPhone to the Devices list, and displays the photos from your iPhone's Camera Roll album, as shown in Figure 6.18.

6.18 When you connect your iPhone to your Mac, iPhoto shows up to handle the import of the photos.

159

2. **Use the Event Name text box to name the event that these photos represent.**

3. **Choose how you want to import the photos:**

    ● **If you want to import every photo, click Import *X* Photos, where *X* is the number of photos in your iPhone's Camera Roll.** Technically, it's the number of photos in your iPhone's Camera Roll that you haven't previously imported. Any photos that you've already imported appear separately in the Already Imported section.

    ● **If you want to import only some of the photos, select those you want and then click Import Selected.**

4. **Using the dialog that appears after the import is complete, choose what you want iPhoto to do with the photos on your iPhone:**

    ● **If you want to leave the photos on your iPhone, click Keep Photos.**

    ● **If you prefer to clear the photos from your iPhone, click Delete Photos.**

Here's how things work if you're syncing with a Windows 7 PC (these steps assume you've installed Windows Live Photo Gallery from the Windows Live Essentials site):

Genius If you don't have Windows Live Photo Gallery installed, you can still access your iPhone photos in Windows 7. Choose Start ⇨ Computer, and then double-click your iPhone in the Portable Devices group. Open the Internal Storage folder, then the DCIM folder, and then the folder that appears (which will have a name such as 800AAAAA). Your iPhone photos appear and you can then copy them to your computer.

1. **Connect your iPhone to your Windows PC.**

2. **Open Windows Live Photo Gallery.**

3. **Choose Home ⇨ Import.** The Import Photos and Videos dialog box appears.

4. **Click the icon for your iPhone, and then click Import.** Windows Live Photo Gallery connects to your iPhone to gather the photo information.

5. **Select the Import all new Items now option.** If you'd prefer to select the photos you want to import, select the Review, organize and group Items to import option. Then, click Next, use the dialog box to choose the photos you want, and skip to Step 7.

6. **Type a tag for the photos.** A tag is a word or short phrase that identifies the photos.

7. **Click Import.** Windows Live Photo Gallery imports the photos.

Here's how things work if you're syncing with a Windows Vista PC:

1. **Connect your iPhone to your Windows Vista PC.** The AutoPlay dialog box appears.

2. **Click Import pictures using Windows.** The rest of these steps assume you selected this option. However, if you have another photo-management application installed, it should appear in the AutoPlay list. Click it to import photos via that program.

3. **Type a tag for the photos.** A tag is a word or short phrase that identifies the photos.

4. **Click Import.** Vista imports the photos and then opens Windows Photo Gallery to display them.

Note Configuring your computer not to download photos from your iPhone means that in the future, you'll either need to reverse the setting to get photos or manually import them.

Syncing photos via iCloud

Syncing photos from your computer isn't difficult, but it seems more than a little old-fashioned in this increasingly wireless age. Fortunately, if you have an iCloud account, you can place your feet firmly in the modern era by using the Photo Stream feature to sync photos without even looking at a USB cable. Photo Stream automatically syncs photos you take using your iPhone cameras to your iCloud account, which then downloads them to your computer, your iPad, or any other device associated with your account. Similarly, if you upload photos to iCloud using another device, those photos are synced automatically to your iPhone.

Follow these steps to activate Photo Stream on your iPhone:

1. **In the iPhone Home screen, tap Settings.** The Settings app appears.

2. **Tap Photos.**

3. **Tap the Photo Stream switch to On.**

Preventing your iPhone from sending photos to your computer

Each time you connect your iPhone to your computer, you see iPhoto (on your Mac), the AutoPlay dialog box (in Windows Vista), or the Scanner and Camera Wizard (in Windows XP). (Windows 7 doesn't display the AutoPlay dialog box when you connect your iPhone.) This is certainly convenient if you actually want to send photos to your computer, but you might find that you only do that once in a blue moon. In that case, having to deal with iPhoto or a dialog box every time could cause even the most mild-mannered among us to start pulling his hair out.

If you prefer to keep your hair, you can configure your computer not to pester you about getting photos from your iPhone.

Here's how you set this up on your Mac:

1. **Choose Finder ⇨ Applications to open the Applications folder.**

2. **Double-click Image Capture.** The Image Capture application opens.

3. **In the Devices list, click your iPhone.**

4. **Click the Connecting this iPhone opens menu, and then choose No application, as shown in Figure 6.19.**

5. **Choose Image Capture ⇨ Quit Image Capture.** Image Capture saves the new setting and then shuts down. The next time you connect your iPhone, iPhoto ignores it.

Follow these steps to convince Windows 7 and Windows Vista not to open the AutoPlay dialog box each time you connect your iPhone:

1. **Choose Start ⇨ Default Programs to open the Default Programs window.**

2. **Click Change AutoPlay settings.** The AutoPlay dialog box appears.

6.19 In the Image Capture Preferences window, choose No application to prevent iPhoto from starting when you connect your iPhone.

3. **In the Devices section, open the Apple iPhone list and choose Take no action, as shown in Figure 6.20.**

4. **Click Save.** Windows saves the new setting. The next time you connect your iPhone, you won't be bothered by the AutoPlay dialog box.

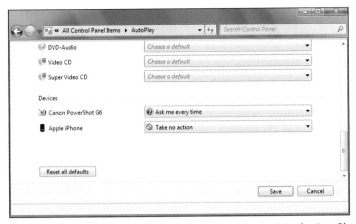

6.20 In the Apple iPhone list, choose Take no action to prevent the AutoPlay dialog box from appearing when you connect your iPhone.

Syncing media with two or more computers

It's a major drag, but you can't sync the same type of content to your iPhone from more than one computer. For example, suppose you're syncing photos from your desktop computer. If you then connect your iPhone to another computer (your notebook, for example), crank up iTunes, and then select the Sync photos from check box, iTunes coughs up the dialog in Figure 6.21. As you can see, iTunes is telling you that if you go ahead with the photo sync on this computer, it will blow away all your existing iPhone photos and albums!

6.21 Syncing the same type of content from two computers is a no-no in the iTunes world.

So there's no chance of syncing the same iPhone with two different computers, right? Not so fast, my friend! Let's try another thought experiment. Suppose you're syncing your iPhone with your desktop computer, but you're not syncing movies. Once again, you connect your iPhone to your notebook computer (or whatever), crank up iTunes, and then select the Sync movies check box. Hey, no ominous warning dialog! What gives?

The deal here is that if iTunes sees that you don't have any examples of a particular type of content (such as movies) on your iPhone, it lets you sync that type of content, no questions asked.

In other words, you can sync your iPhone with multiple computers, although in a roundabout kind of way. The secret is to have no overlapping content types on the various computers you use for the syncing. For example, let's say you have a home desktop computer, a notebook computer, and a work desktop computer. Here's a sample scenario for syncing your iPhone with all three machines:

- **Home desktop (music and video only).** Select the Sync Music check box in the Music tab, and select the Sync Movies check box in the Movies tab. Deselect the Sync Photos and Sync Podcasts check boxes on the Photos and Podcasts tabs, respectively.

- **Notebook (photos only).** Select the Sync Photos check box on the Photos tab. Deselect all the Sync check boxes in the Music, Podcasts, and Movies tabs.

- **Work desktop (podcasts only).** Select the Sync Podcasts check box in the Podcasts tab. Deselect the Sync check boxes in the Music, Photos, and Movies tabs.

How Can I Get More Out of My iPhone's Audio Features?

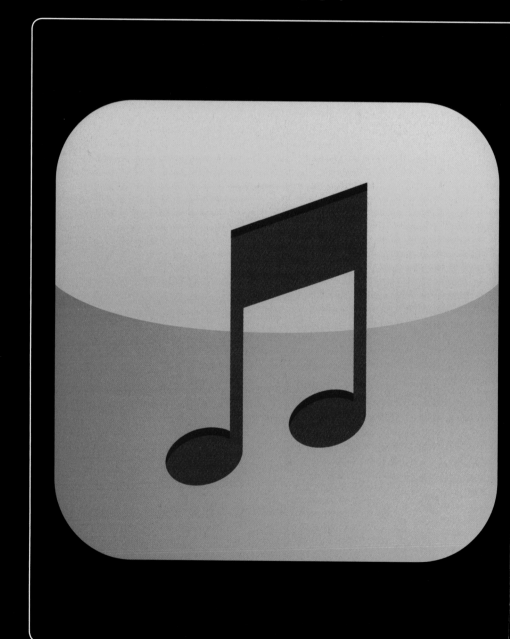

The eye candy of the iPhone's gorgeous screen garners the lion's share of kudos and huzzahs, but your iPhone offers quite a bit of ear candy as well. With numerous audio accessories available, and with the built-in Music and iTunes apps, your iPhone packs a real audio punch. This chapter takes you on a tour of these audio features and shows you how to get the most out of them to maximize your listening pleasure.

Using Audio Accessories with Your iPhone

As soon as the original iPhone was announced, a rather large cottage industry of iPhone accessories formed seemingly overnight. Suddenly, the world was awash in headsets (wired and Bluetooth), external speakers, FM transmitters, and all manner of cases, car kits, cables, and cradles. There are places that sell iPhone accessories scattered all over the web, but the following sites are faves with me:

- **Apple.** http://store.apple.com/us/browse/home/shop_iphone
- **Belkin.** www.belkin.com/iphone
- **Griffin.** www.griffintechnology.com/iphone
- **NewEgg.** www.newegg.com
- **EverythingiCafe.** http://store.everythingicafe.com

Here are a few notes to remember when shopping for and using audio-related accessories for your iPhone:

- **Look for the logo.** Your iPhone may appear to be an iPod in fancy phone clothes, but it's a completely different device that doesn't fit or work with many iPod accessories. To be sure what you're buying is iPhone friendly, look for the "Works with iPhone" logo.

- **Headsets, headphones, and earpieces.** All iPhones since the iPhone 3G use a standard headset jack, which means that just about any headset that uses a garden-variety stereo miniplug will fit your iPhone without a hitch and without requiring the purchase of an adapter (as was required for the original iPhone, which had a recessed audio jack).

- **External speakers.** There are legions of external speakers made for the iPod where you simply dock the iPod in the device and wail away. Unfortunately, the dimensions of the bottom panel of the iPhone are different than any of the iPod models, so you won't be able to just plug-and-play your iPhone. Instead, you need an adapter — such as the Apple Universal Dock Adapter — to ensure a proper fit.

- **FM transmitters.** These are must-have accessories for car trips because they send the output from your iPhone to an FM station, which you then play through your car stereo. The FM transmitters that work with the iPod don't generally work with iPhones, so look for one that's designed for the iPhone.

● **Electronic interference.** Because your iPhone is, after all, a phone, it generates a nice little field of electronic interference, which is why you need to switch it to Airplane mode
  when you're flying (see Chapter 2). That same interference can also wreak havoc on
  nearby external speakers and FM transmitters, so if you hear static when playing audio,
  switch to Airplane mode to get rid of it.

Getting More Out of the Music App

Your iPhone is a full-fledged digital music player thanks to its built-in Music app, which you can fire
up any time you want by tapping the Music icon in the Home screen's Dock. In the next few sections, you learn a few useful techniques that help you get more out of the Music app.

Rating a song

If you use song ratings to organize your tunes (as I describe later in this chapter), you might come
across some situations where you want to rate a song that's playing on your iPhone:

● You used your iPhone to download some music from the iTunes Store, and you want to
  rate that music.

● You're listening to a song on your iPhone and decide that you've given a rating that's
  either too high or too low and you want to change it.

In the first case, you could sync the music to your computer and rate it there; in the second case,
you could modify the rating on your computer and then sync with your iPhone. However, these
solutions are lame because you have to wait until you connect your iPhone to your computer. If
you're out and about, you want to rate the song now while it's fresh in your mind.

Yes, you can do that with your iPhone:

1. **Locate the song you want to rate and tap it to start the playback.** Your iPhone displays the album art and the name of the artist, song, and album at the top of the screen.

2. **Tap the Details icon in the upper-right corner of the screen (just below the battery
   status).** Your iPhone "turns" the album art and displays a list of the songs on the album.
   Above that list are the five rating dots.

3. **Tap the dot that corresponds to the rating you want to give the song.** For example, to
   give the song a four-star rating, tap the fourth dot from the left, as shown in Figure 7.1.

4. **Tap the Album Art icon in the upper-right corner.** Your iPhone saves the rating and returns you to the album art view.

The next time you sync your iPhone with your computer, iTunes notes your new ratings and applies them to the same tracks in the iTunes library.

Browsing music with Cover Flow

Here in the second decade of the twenty-first century, physical CD collections are suffering the same fate that vinyl LP collections went through in the 1980s — they're disappearing. I'm not crying in my beer over this trend because a large anthology of CDs is an eyesore. However, one thing I do miss is flipping through CD covers looking for something that catches my eye. You may not be able to do

7.1 Tap the dot that corresponds to the rating you want to give a playing track.

this anymore, but your iPhone gives you the next best thing with Cover Flow. This feature displays all of your album art as a kind of flip book. Only in this case, I should call it a "flick" book because you can use your finger to flick back and forth through the album art, just like flipping through a CD collection.

To give this a whirl, open the Music app and then rotate your iPhone into the landscape position. Your iPhone switches to the Cover Flow view and displays either the first album in your collection or the album associated with whatever's currently playing (or most recently played), as shown in Figure 7.2.

You can flick to the right and left to navigate the albums. To see the tracks on an album, tap the album art (or the *i* icon in the bottom-right corner). To return to the regular view, rotate your iPhone into the portrait position.

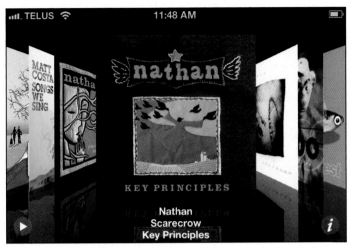

7.2 Open the Music app and rotate your iPhone into landscape mode to see the Cover Flow view.

Controlling music with Siri voice commands

If you're using your iPhone 4S in a hands-free environment, you can still control your music by using the convenient Siri app, which recognizes a number of music-related voice commands. To get started, tap and hold the Home button (or press and hold the Mic button of the iPhone headphones, or the equivalent button on a Bluetooth headset) until the Siri screen appears.

The most basic music voice commands mimic the on-screen controls you see when you play a song. That is, while a song is playing, you can speak any of the following commands to control the playback:

- "Pause."
- "Play."
- "Next track (or next song)."
- "Previous track (or previous song)."

In each case, your iPhone repeats the command back to you so you know whether it heard you correctly. You can also get more sophisticated by speaking commands that use roughly the following format:

Verb object subject.

171

Here, *verb* is the action you want the Music app to take, which will most often be play; *object* is the type of item you want to work with, such as a song, album, or playlist; and *subject* is the particular item you want included in the action, such as the name of a song, album, playlist, or artist. Here are a few examples:

- "Play songs by the Submarines."
- "Play album *Blue Horse.*"
- "Play some blues."
- "Play playlist My Top Rated."

Again, Siri confirms the command by saying it back to you (for example, "Playing songs by the Submarines").

Here are a few more voice commands to play with:

- **"Shuffle."** Activates the Music app's Shuffle mode.
- **"Shuffle *playlist.*"** Plays the specified playlist in Shuffle mode.
- **"Skip."** Skips to the next track.
- **"What song is this?"** Tells you the name of the current song and artist. Siri responds, "Now playing *name of song* by *name of artist.*"
- **"Play more songs like this."** Creates a playlist of songs that are similar to the current song. Siri responds, "Playing similar songs." This is called a Genius playlist, which is explained in more detail later in this chapter.

Turning off the Shake to Shuffle feature

One of the nice little audio bonuses you get with your iPhone is the Shake to Shuffle feature that lets you shuffle to a random song just by shaking your iPhone from side to side. If you're playing songs by a particular artist, you get a random song from the same artist. If you're playing an album, you get a random song from that album.

If you're not a fan of Shake to Shuffle (for example, you might find it shuffles when you don't want it to) or if you want to turn it off temporarily (for example, if you're taking the iPhone with you for a run or bull-riding session), here's how to disable it:

1. **On the Home screen, tap Settings.** The Settings app appears.
2. **Tap Music.** The Music screen appears.
3. **Tap the Shake to Shuffle switch to Off.**

Answering an incoming call while listening to music on the headset

If you're listening to music on your iPhone and a call comes in, you obviously don't want the caller to be subjected to Blitzen Trapper at top volume. Fortunately, your iPhone smartphone is smart enough to know this, and it automatically pauses the music. If you have your iPhone headset on when the call arrives, use the following techniques to deal with it:

- **Answer the call.** Press and release the headset mic button (it's the plastic button on one of the headset cords).

- **Decline the call (send it directly to voicemail).** Press and hold the mic button for about two seconds, and then release. If you hear a couple of beeps, you successfully declined the call.

- **End the call.** Press and release the mic button.

Listening to a Shared iTunes Library

You may be familiar with an iTunes feature called Home Sharing. It enables you to share your iTunes library with other people on your network as long as you're all logged in with the same Apple ID. Home Sharing is also available on the iPhone, which means you can use your iPhone to get wireless access to an iTunes library that's stored on a Mac or PC.

To set this up, you must first activate Home Sharing in iTunes. Here's how it's done:

1. **In iTunes on your Mac or PC, choose Advanced ⇨ Turn On Home Sharing.** iTunes prompts you for an Apple ID.

2. **Type your Apple ID and password.**

3. **Click Create Home Share.** iTunes configures your library for sharing on the network.

4. **Click Done.**

Genius

By default, iTunes shares the library with the name *User*'s Library, where *User* is the first name of the current user account. To change that, choose iTunes ⇨ Preferences, click the General tab, and then use the Library Name text box to type the new name.

With your iTunes library set up for sharing, your next task is to configure your iPhone with the same Home Sharing Apple ID and password. Here's what you do:

1. **On the iPhone Home screen, tap Settings.** The Settings app appears.

2. **Tap Music.** The Music screen appears.

3. **In the Home Sharing section, use the Apple ID and Password boxes to type the same account information that you used to set up Home Sharing in iTunes.**

Now open the Music app on your iPhone. If a tune is currently playing, tap the Back button (the left-pointing arrow) to return to the main Music screen. Tap More, and then tap Shared. As you can see in Figure 7.3, the Music app displays the Shared screen, which lists the available shared libraries. Tap the library you want to access, and the Music app displays the media in that library instead of the iPhone media.

7.3 Tap More and then Shared to see a list of the available shared libraries.

Using AirPlay to stream iPhone audio

If you have an Apple TV that supports AirPlay, you can use AirPlay to stream audio from your iPhone to your TV or other audio device. Here's how it works:

1. **Make sure your Apple TV is turned on.**

2. **On your iPhone, start the audio you want to stream.**

3. **Tap the AirPlay button, which appears to the right of the Next/Fast Forward button.** The Music app displays a menu of output choices, as shown in Figure 7.4.

4. **Tap the name of your Apple TV device.** Your iPhone streams the video to that device and, hence, to your TV or receiver.

7.4 Tap the AirPlay button on the multitasking bar to stream the audio to your Apple TV.

Getting More Out of the iTunes App

If you have a fast Wi-Fi connection going (a 3G cellular connection will do in a pinch), you can use your iPhone to purchase music directly from the iTunes Store. To get there, tap the iTunes icon in the Home screen.

Creating a custom iTunes menu bar

Just like the Music app, the iTunes app also presents you with a series of browse buttons, each one of which represents a section or feature of the mobile version of the iTunes Store (see Figure 7.5). For example, tapping the Search browse button enables you to search for artists, albums, songs, and more.

You see four browse buttons in the default menu bar: Music, Videos, Search, and Purchased. A fifth button called More displays a list of seven more browse buttons. Here's a summary of all eleven:

7.5 The iTunes app uses browse buttons to navigate the mobile iTunes Store.

- ⚬ **Music.** Enables you to browse and purchase music on the iTunes Store using the Featured, Top Tens, and Genres tabs.

- ⚬ **Videos.** Enables you to browse video content on the iTunes Store using the Movies, TV Shows, and Music Videos tabs.

- ⚬ **Search.** Enables you to search the iTunes Store.

- ⚬ **Purchased.** Displays a list of songs that you have purchased from the iTunes Store.

- ⚬ **Genius.** Creates a Genius playlist, as described later in this chapter.

- ⚬ **Ping.** Enables you to share music with friends on the Ping social network using the Activity, People, and My Profile tabs.

- ⚬ **Tones.** Enables you to browse ringtones on the iTunes Store using the Featured, Top Tens, and Genres tabs.

- **Podcasts.** Enables you to browse podcasts on the iTunes Store using the What's Hot, Top Tens, and Categories tabs.

- **Audiobooks.** Enables you to browse audiobooks on the iTunes Store using the Featured, Top Tens, and Categories tabs.

- **iTunes U.** Enables you to browse lessons on the iTunes Store using the What's Hot, Top Tens, and Categories tabs.

- **Downloads.** Lists the current downloads in progress.

If there's a browse button on the More list that you use all the time, you can move it to the menu bar for easier access. Here's how:

1. **On the Home screen, tap iTunes to open the iTunes app.**

2. **Tap More in the menu bar.**

3. **Tap Edit.** Your iPhone displays the Configure screen, which lists all ten browse buttons, as shown in Figure 7.6.

4. **Drag a browse button that you want to add to the menu bar and drop it on whatever existing menu bar browse button you want it to replace.** For example, if you want to replace the Purchased browse button with Audiobooks, drag the Audiobooks button and drop it on Purchased. Your iPhone replaces the old browse button with the new one.

5. **Repeat Step 4 to add any of your other preferred browse buttons to the menu bar.**

6. **Tap Done to save the new menu bar configuration.**

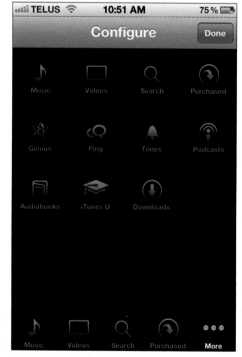

7.6 Use the Configure screen to create a custom iTunes menu bar.

Redeeming an iTunes gift card

If you've been lucky enough to receive an iTunes gift card or gift certificate for your birthday or some other special occasion (or just for the heck of it), you'd normally use the iTunes Store on your computer to redeem it. However, if you're not at your computer and the gift card is burning a hole in your pocket, don't fret: you can redeem the gift card right on your iPhone. Here's how:

1. **Sign in to the iTunes Store on your iPhone.** You do this by tapping Settings, tapping Store, tapping Sign In, tapping Use Existing Apple ID, and then typing your iTunes Store username and password.

2. **On the Home screen, tap iTunes.** The iTunes screen appears.

3. **Tap Music in the menu bar and then tap New Releases.**

4. **Scroll to the bottom of the New Releases screen and then tap Redeem.** iTunes displays the Redeem screen shown in Figure 7.7.

5. **Use the Code box to type the code from the gift card or gift certificate.**

6. **Tap Redeem.** iTunes asks you to sign in to your account.

7. **Tap Continue.** iTunes prompts you for your account password.

7.7 Use the Redeem screen to redeem an iTunes gift card or gift certificate.

8. **Type your iTunes password and then tap OK.** iTunes redeems the gift code and then displays your current account balance.

Creating a Custom Ringtone

Your iPhone comes stocked with 25 predefined ringtones. Although some of them are amazingly annoying, you ought to be able to find one you can live with. If you can't, or if you crave something unique, you can create a custom ringtone and use that.

In previous versions of iTunes, the easiest way to cobble together a custom ringtone was to convert a song you purchased through the iTunes Store. Unfortunately, that feature was removed in iTunes 10. You can always purchase ringtones in the iTunes Store, but there are still a couple of techniques you can use to create a custom (and free!) ringtone, as the next couple of sections show.

Using iTunes to create a custom ringtone

The old Create Ringtone command may be gone from iTunes 10, but that application still comes with features that enable you to create a custom ringtone. Here's how it works:

1. **In iTunes, play the track you want to use.** While the track is playing, watch the playback time and note the start time and end time of the portion of the track you want to use as your ringtone.

Note

Ringtones can be a maximum of 30 seconds long, so select a portion of the track that is no longer than 30 seconds.

2. **Choose File ⇨ Get Info, or press ⌘+I.** The track's Info dialog appears.

3. **Click the Options tab.**

4. **Use the Start Time and Stop Time text boxes to type the starting and ending points for your ringtone snippet (see Figure 7.8), and then click OK.**

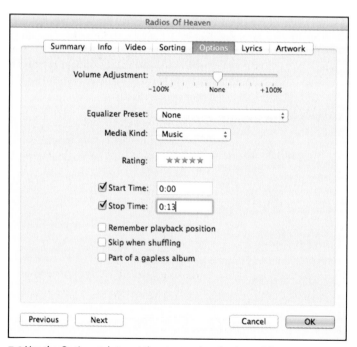

7.8 Use the Options tab to set the start and end points of the ringtone snippet.

5. **With the track still selected, choose Advanced ⇨ Create AAC Version.** iTunes creates a version of the track that includes only the snippet you specified in Step 4.

6. **Click the new version of the track, then choose File ⇨ Show in Finder, or press Shift+⌘+R.** A new Finder window appears with the short version of the track selected.

7. **Press Return to open the file name for editing, change the extension from m4a to m4r, and then press Return.** The m4r extension designates the file as a ringtone. Mac OS X asks you to confirm the extension change.

8. **Click Use .m4r.** Mac OS X converts the file to a ringtone.

9. **In iTunes, make sure the short version of the track is selected, and then choose Edit ⇨ Delete.** iTunes asks you to confirm.

10. **Click Remove.** iTunes asks if you want to move the file to the Trash.

11. **Click Keep File.**

12. **Return to the Finder window that contains the ringtone, and then double-click the file.** iTunes plays the ringtone, but more importantly, it adds the file to the Ringtone section of the library.

Using GarageBand to create a custom ringtone

The technique I showed you in the previous section is easy, for sure, but it's a bit convoluted. So let's look at a second, more straightforward, method that uses GarageBand, the Apple application for making homebrew music.

Genius There's no reason you have to use commercial music for your ringtone. GarageBand makes it easy to create your own music from scratch. For example, choose File ⇨ New, click Magic GarageBand, click a music genre, and then click Choose. GarageBand creates a whole song for you, and you can even add your own instruments! (Click Audition, and then click Create Project when you're done.)

First, here are the steps to follow to create a ringtone out of any song in your iTunes library:

1. **Click the GarageBand icon in the Dock, click iPhone Ringtone, click Choose, type a name for the project, and then click Create.** GarageBand starts a new project for you.

2. **Choose Track ⇨ Delete Track to get rid of the default track.**

3. **Switch to iTunes, click the song you want to use for your ringtone, and then choose File ⇨ Show in Finder, or press Shift+⌘+R.** Mac OS X displays the song's file in a Finder window.

4. **Click and drag the file and drop it inside GarageBand.** The program creates a new track for the song.

Note

If the song is protected by digital rights management (DRM), you won't be able to import it into GarageBand.

5. **Click and drag the Cycle Region to the approximate area of the song you want to use for the ringtone.** The Cycle Region, pointed out in Figure 7.9, defines the portion of the song that you would use for a ringtone. If you don't see the Cycle Region tool, click the Cycle Region button pointed out in Figure 7.9.

Cycle Region tool

Cycle Region button

7.9 Use the Cycle Region to define what part of the song you want to use for the ringtone.

6. **Click and drag the left edge of the Cycle Region to define the starting point of the ringtone.**

7. **Click and drag the right edge of the Cycle Region to define the ending point of the ringtone.**

8. **Choose Share ⇨ Send Ringtone to iTunes.** GarageBand converts the track to a ringtone, and then adds it to the Ringtones category in iTunes.

Note The maximum length for a GarageBand ringtone is 40 seconds. To see how long the Cycle Region is, choose Control ⇨ Show Time in LCD.

Syncing ringtones

The next time you sync your iPhone through iTunes, follow these steps to include one or more custom ringtones in the sync:

1. **Click your iPhone in the Devices list.**

2. **Click the Ringtones tab.**

3. **Select the Sync Ringtones check box.**

4. **Select the Selected ringtones option.**

5. **Select the check box beside each custom ringtone you want to use on your iPhone.**

6. **Click Apply.**

To apply the custom ringtone on your iPhone, tap Settings in the Home screen, tap Sounds, and tap Ringtone. Your ringtones appear at the top of the Ringtones list. Tap a custom ringtone to use the snippet as your ringtone.

Note You can also use the Sounds screen to apply a custom ringtone to other sound events, such as incoming text messages, voicemails, and e-mail messages.

Working with Playlists

Although you can purchase and download songs directly from the iTunes Store on your iPhone, I'm going to assume that the vast majority of your music library is cooped up on your Mac or PC, and that you're going to want to transfer that music to your iPhone. Or perhaps I should say that you're going to want to transfer *some* of that music to the iPhone. Most of us now have multigiga-byte music collections and, depending on the storage capacity of your iPhone and the amount of other content you've stuffed into it (particularly videos and movies), it's likely that you only want to copy a subset of your music library.

If that's the case, then iTunes gives you three choices when it comes to selecting which tunes to transfer: artist, genre, and playlists. The first two are self-explanatory (and, in any case, I gave you the audio syncing details in Chapter 6), but it's the last of these three where you can take control of syncing music to your iPhone.

A *playlist* is a collection of songs that are related in some way, and using your iTunes library, you can create customized playlists that include only the songs that you want to hear. For example, you might want to create a playlist of upbeat or festive songs to play during a party or celebration. Similarly, you might want to create a playlist of your current favorite songs.

Playlists are the perfect way to control music syncing for the iPhone, so before you start transferring tunes, consider creating a playlist or three in iTunes.

Creating a favorite tunes playlist for your iPhone

Your iTunes library includes a Rating field that enables you to supply a rating for your tracks: one star for songs you don't like so much, up to five stars for your favorite tunes. You click the song you want to rate, and then click a dot in the Rating column (click the first dot for a one-star rating, the second dot for a two-star rating, and so on). Rating songs is useful because it enables you to organize your music. For example, the Playlists section includes a My Top Rated playlist that includes all your four- and five-star-rated tunes, ordered by the Rating value.

Rating tracks comes in particularly handy when deciding which music to use to populate your iPhone. If you have tens of gigabytes of tunes, only some of them will fit on your iPhone. How do you choose? One possibility would be to rate your songs, and then just sync the My Top Rated playlist to your iPhone.

The problem with the My Top Rated playlist is that it includes only your four- and five-star-rated tunes. You can fit thousands of tracks on your iPhone, but it's unlikely that you've got thousands of songs rated at four stars or better. To fill out your playlist, you should also include songs rated at three stars, a rating that should include lots of good, solid tunes.

To set this up, you have two choices:

● **Modify the My Top Rated playlist.** Right-click the My Top Rated playlist, and then click Edit Playlist. In the Smart Playlist dialog, click the second star, and then click OK.

● **Create a new playlist.** This is the way to go if you want to leave My Top Rated as your best music. Choose File ⇨ New Smart Playlist to open the Smart Playlist dialog. Choose Rating in the Field list, choose Is Greater Than in the Operator list, and then click the second star. Figure 7.10 shows the configured dialog. Click OK, type a title for the playlist (such as Favorite Tunes), and then press Return (or Enter).

7.10 Use the Smart Playlist dialog to create a playlist that contains your tracks rated at three stars or more.

The next time you sync your iPhone, be sure to include either the My Top Rated playlist or the Smart Playlist you created.

Creating a playlist on your iPhone

The playlists on your iPhone are those you've synced via iTunes, and those playlists are either generated automatically by iTunes or they're ones you've cobbled together yourself. However, when you're out in the world and listening to music, you might come up with an idea for a different collection of songs. It might be girl groups, boy bands, or songs with animals in the title.

Whatever your inspiration, don't do it the hard way by picking out and listening to each song one at a time. Instead, you can use your iPhone to create a playlist on the fly.

To create a playlist using the Music app, follow these steps:

1. **Open the Music app.**

2. **Tap the Playlists browse button.** This displays your playlists.

3. **Tap Add Playlist.** The Music app displays the New Playlist dialog.

4. **Type the name of your playlist, and then tap Save.** The Music app displays the Songs screen, which contains a list of all of your songs.

5. **Scroll through the list and tap each song you want to add to your list.**

6. **When you've added all the songs you want, tap Done.** The Music app displays the playlist.

Your playlist isn't set in stone by any means. You can get rid of songs, change the song order, and add more songs. Follow these steps:

1. **In the Music app, tap the Playlists icon to see your playlists.**

2. **Tap your playlist.** The Music app displays the playlist settings and music.

3. **Tap Edit.** This changes the list to the editable version, as shown in Figure 7.11.

4. **To remove a song, tap the red Minus (–) icon to the left of the song.** Then, tap the Delete button that appears. If you change your mind, tap the red Minus icon again to cancel the deletion.

5. **To move a song within the playlist, slide the song's Drag icon (it's on the right) up or down to the position you prefer.**

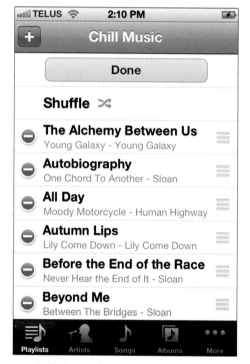

7.11 A playlist in Edit mode.

6. **To add more tracks, tap the + button in the upper-left corner, select another playlist, and then tap the blue + key next to each song you want to add.**

7. **When you finish editing, tap Done.** This sets the playlist.

Note If your playlist is a bit of a mess, or if your mood suddenly changes, don't delete all the tracks one by one. Instead, open the playlist, tap Edit, and then tap Clear. When your iPhone asks you to confirm, tap Clear Playlist.

Creating a Genius playlist on your iPhone

You may be familiar with the iTunes Genius sidebar, which shows you songs from the iTunes Store that are similar to a particular song in your library. It's a great way to find new music. The Music app on your iPhone doesn't have a Genius sidebar, but it has something sort of similar: a Genius playlist. The idea here is that you pick a song on your iPhone, and the Music app creates a playlist of other songs on your iPhone that are similar. It's a ridiculously easy way to ride a particular sonic groove.

Genius An even easier way to create a Genius playlist is to play the song you want to use as the basis of the playlist, press and hold the Home button to display Siri, and then say "Play more songs like this."

Here's how to create a Genius playlist:

1. **In the Music app, tap Playlists.** The Music app displays the Playlists screen.

2. **Tap Genius Playlist.** The Music app displays a list of the songs on your iPhone.

3. **Tap the song you want to use as the basis of the Genius playlist.** The Music app gathers the similar tunes on your iPhone, briefly displays a list of them in the Genius Playlist screen, switches to the Now Playing window, and plays the song you chose.

4. **Tap the Back button.** The Music app displays the Genius Playlist screen (see Figure 7.12), which holds the list of songs that are similar to the one you chose in Step 3.

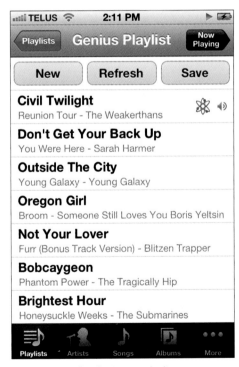

7.12 An example of a Genius playlist.

In the Genius Playlist screen, you can perform the following actions to mess around with your shiny new playlist:

- **Tap Refresh to re-create the playlist.**
- **Tap a song to play it.**
- **Tap Save to save the playlist to the Playlists screen.**
- **Tap New to crank out a new Genius playlist.**

Customizing Your Audio Settings

Audiophiles in the crowd don't get much to fiddle with in the iPhone, but there are a few audio settings to play with. Here's how to get at them:

1. **Press the Home button to get to the Home screen.**

2. **Tap the Settings icon.** The Settings app opens.

3. **Tap the Music icon.** Your iPhone displays the Music settings screen, as shown in Figure 7.13.

Besides the Shake to Shuffle switch discussed earlier, you get six other settings to try:

- **iTunes Match.** If you have an iCloud account and you've shelled out the extra $24.99 per year for the iTunes Match service, tap this switch to On to activate iTunes Match on your iPhone. This means that any songs that you own that aren't available via the iTunes Store will be automatically synced to your iPhone as soon as you upload those songs to iCloud.

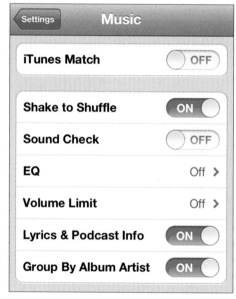

7.13 Use the Music settings screen to muck around with the audio settings.

- **Sound Check.** Every track is recorded at different audio levels, so invariably you get some tracks that are louder than others. With the Sound Check feature, you can set your iPhone to play all of your songs at the same level. This feature only affects the baseline level of the music and doesn't change any of the other levels, so you still get the highs and lows. If you use it, you don't need to worry about having to quickly turn down the volume when a really loud song comes on. To turn on Sound Check, in the Music settings page, tap the Sound Check switch to On.

- **EQ.** This setting controls the built-in equalizer in your iPhone, which is actually a long list of preset frequency levels that affect the audio output. Each preset is designed for a specific type of audio: vocals, talk radio, classical music, rock, hip-hop, and lots more. To set the equalizer, tap EQ and then tap the preset you want to use (or tap None to turn off the equalizer).

- **Volume Limit.** You use this setting to prevent the iPhone volume from being turned up too high and damaging your (or someone else's) hearing. You know, of course, that pumping up the volume while you have your earbuds on is an audio no-no, right? I thought so. However, I also know that when a great tune comes on, it's often a little too tempting to go for 11 on the volume scale. If you can't resist the temptation, use Volume Limit to limit the damage. Tap Volume Limit and then drag the Volume slider to the maximum allowed volume.

- **Lyrics & Podcast Info.** Leave this setting on to see extra info about songs and podcasts when you click the Details button in the Music app. For example, if you add lyrics for a song in iTunes (right-click the song, click Get Info, and then click the Lyrics tab), you see those lyrics in Details view.

- **Group By Album Artist.** Leave this setting on to group the Artists browse button based on the value in the Album Artist field, as opposed to the Artist field. For most albums, these two fields are the same, but some compilation albums use "Various" in the Artist field, and the names of the individual track artists in the Album Artist field. If you were to turn off this switch, you'd end up with all such albums listed under Various in the Artists browse button, which probably isn't what you want.

Genius

If you're setting up an iPhone for a younger person, you should set the Volume Limit. However, what prevents the young whippersnapper from setting a higher limit? To prevent this, in the Volume Limit screen, tap Lock Limit Volume. In the Set Code screen, tap out a four-digit code, and then tap the code again to confirm. This disables the Volume slider in the Volume Limit screen.

How Do I Max Out the iPhone Photo and Video Features?

Your iPhone is a perk-filled device, to be sure, and one of the best of those

perks is that the iPhone moonlights as a digital media player. Not only do

you have the music, podcasts, and audiobooks that I talk about in Chapter 7,

but you also have movies, TV shows, videos, photos, and even YouTube right

there in the palm of your hand. So when you're tired of calling, researching,

e-mailing, scheduling, and other serious iPhone pursuits, you can kick back

with a photo slide show or a video to relax. However, your iPhone is capable

of more than just playing and viewing media. It's actually loaded with cool

features that enable you to create and manipulate photos and videos, and

use those files to enhance other parts of your digital life. This chapter is your

guide to these features.

Getting More Out of iPhone Photos

Your iPhone comes with a couple of built-in digital cameras that you can use to take pictures while you're running around town. Taking a picture is straightforward. First, on the Home screen, tap Camera. If this is the first time you've opened the Camera app, it will ask if it can use your current location. This is an excellent idea because it tags your photos with your present whereabouts, so be sure to tap OK. When the Camera app appears, make sure the Mode switch (pointed out later in Figure 8.1) is on Camera (to the left) instead of Video (to the right). Now line up your shot and tap either the Camera button (which, again, I point out later in Figure 8.1) or the Volume Up switch, which appears on the top edge of the iPhone when you hold it in the landscape position with the Home button on the left. To view your photo, tap the Camera Roll button, which appears in the lower-left corner of the Camera app screen (see Figure 8.1).

Genius When your iPhone is locked, you can get to the Camera app in seconds flat by double-clicking the Home button and then tapping the Camera icon that appears in the Lock screen.

While using the cameras may be simple, what you can do with photos on your iPhone is pretty cool. You can e-mail photos to friends, take a photo and assign it to a contact, or make a slide show with music in the background. The large screen on your iPhone makes it the perfect portable photo album. No more whipping out wallet shots of your kids. Now you can show people your iPhone photo album!

To get to your photos, tap the Photos icon in your iPhone Home screen to display the Albums screen, which lists your photo albums. Tap an album to see its pictures, and then tap the picture you want to check out.

Understanding the iPhone camera features

Before getting to the Photos app, I should take a second here to talk about the coolest camera features found in the iPhone:

- **Rear- and front-facing cameras.** The iPhone 4S comes with two cameras: an 8-mega-pixel camera on the back for regular shots, and a 0.3-megapixel camera on the front for taking self-portraits. In the Camera app, tap the Switch Camera icon (pointed out in Figure 8.1) to switch between the front and rear cameras.

- **Autofocus.** The iPhone cameras automatically focus on whatever subject is in the middle of the frame.

- **Tap to focus.** If the subject you want to focus on is not in the middle of the frame, you can tap the subject and the iPhone automatically moves the focus to that object. It also automatically adjusts the white balance and exposure.

- **5X digital zoom.** You can zoom using the iPhone back camera. Pinch two fingers together on the screen to display the Zoom slider, as shown in Figure 8.1. Then, tap and drag the slider right to zoom in, or left to zoom out.

Flash icon   Options   Switch Camera icon

Zoom slider

Camera
Roll button   Camera button   Mode switch

8.1 Tap the screen and then drag the slider to zoom in and out.

- **Automatic macro.** If you're taking a close-up of a flower or something similar, the rear camera has built-in macro capabilities to bring out the detail in such shots.

- **Geotagging.** The iPhone can use its built-in GPS sensor to add location data to each photo, a process called *geotagging*. This means you can organize your photos by location, which is great for vacation snaps and other trip-related photos.

- **LED flash.** The iPhone has a built-in LED flash that sits right beside the rear camera, so you can take pictures at night or in extremely low-light conditions. The LED flash is in Auto mode by default, which means it flashes automatically when the ambient light is low. To control this in the Camera app, tap the Flash icon (pointed out in Figure 8.1), and then tap On (to use the flash with every shot), Off (to never use the flash), or Auto.

- **Backside illumination sensor.** This rear sensor can tell when you're shooting in low-light conditions and adjust the camera settings to compensate.

Taking High Dynamic Range photos

Your iPhone usually takes a pretty decent picture, but it works best when the ambient light isn't too extreme — that is, not too dark or too light. In particular, your iPhone has trouble taking good photos in places where the light conditions cause a wide variation in tone. The best example is an outdoor scene on a bright, sunny day, where some parts of your subject are bathed in sunlight and others are mired in shade. This large contrast between bright and dark elements is called a *High Dynamic Range (HDR),* and your iPhone — indeed, *any* digital camera — won't do well in these scenarios. Depending on where you focus the shot, you usually end up with either the sunlit elements overexposed and washed out or the shaded elements underexposed and murky. Either way, you lose crucial details and the photo just doesn't look right.

Fortunately, your iPhone comes with a feature called HDR that can often compensate for these problems and actually produce beautiful, detailed photos of high-contrast scenes. The HDR feature works by taking not one, not two, but *three* photos of the scene: one underexposed to capture the high-contrast areas of the scene, one overexposed to capture the low-contrast areas, and one with normal exposure. The iPhone then blends all three shots into a finished photo that — theoretically, at least — combines the best parts of each shot. No, I'm sorry to say that it doesn't work perfectly every time, but I think you'll be pleasantly surprised at how often it *does* work.

Before you get started with HDR, you need to make a decision. As I mentioned earlier, HDR takes three photos: underexposed, overexposed, and normal. By default, HDR saves the composite version that combines all three exposures, as well as the normal exposure photo. Keeping the normal exposure shot is a good idea because that photo is sometimes better than the composite version. If you don't want to clutter your iPhone Camera Roll with extra pictures — or if later you find that the normal exposure shot is rarely (or never) superior to the composite version — then you can configure HDR not to save the normal exposure.

Genius In the Camera Roll, how do you know which photo is the HDR version and which is the normal exposure? Display the photo and tap the screen. If the photo is the HDR version, you see HDR in the upper-left corner of the screen.

Follow these steps:

1. **On your iPhone Home screen, tap Settings.** The Settings app appears.

2. **Tap Photos.** The Photos screen appears.

3. **In the HDR section, tap the Keep Normal Photo switch to Off.**

Note Because the HDR feature has to take three consecutive shots, it takes a few seconds for the operation to complete. Therefore, try to keep the iPhone as steady as possible while the *Saving HDR* message appears on the screen.

To take an HDR shot, open the Camera app, tap Options, tap the HDR switch to On, and then take your shot. Figure 8.2 shows a high dynamic range scene shot with normal exposure, and Figure 8.3 shows the HDR version of the same scene.

8.2 A high dynamic range scene captured with normal exposure.

8.3 The HDR version of the same scene shown in Figure 8.2.

Scrolling, rotating, zooming, and panning photos

You can do quite a lot with your photos once they are in your iPhone, and it isn't your normal photo browsing experience. You aren't just a passive viewer because you actually have some control over what you see and how the pictures are presented.

You can use the following techniques to navigate and manipulate your photos:

- **Scroll.** You move forward or backward through your photos by flicking. Flick from the right to left to view the next photo; flick left to right to view the previous shot. Alternatively, tap the screen, and then tap the Previous and Next buttons to navigate your photos.

- **Rotate.** When a landscape shot shows up on your iPhone, it gets letterboxed at the top (that is, you see black space above and below the image). To get a better view, rotate the screen into the landscape position and the photo rotates right along with it, filling the entire screen. When you come upon a photo with a portrait orientation, rotate the iPhone back to the upright position for best viewing.

- **Zoom.** Zooming magnifies the shot that's on the screen. There are two methods to do this:

  - **Double-tap the area of the photo on which you want to zoom in.** The iPhone doubles the size of the portion you tapped. Double-tap again to return the photo to its original size.

  - **Spread and pinch.** To zoom in, spread two fingers apart over the area you want magnified. To zoom back out, pinch two fingers together.

- **Pan.** After you zoom in on the photo, you may find that the iPhone didn't zoom in exactly where you wanted or you may just want to see another part of the photo. Drag your finger across the screen to move the photo along with your finger — an action known as *panning*.

Note   You can scroll to another photo if you're zoomed in, but it takes a lot more work to get there because the iPhone thinks you're trying to pan. For faster scrolling, return the photo to its normal size and then scroll.

Adding an existing photo to a contact

You can assign a photo from one of your albums to any of your contacts. This is one of my favorite iPhone features because when the person calls you, her smiling mug appears on your screen. Now that's caller ID! There are two ways to assign a photo to a contact: straight from a photo album or via the Contacts app.

First, here's how you assign a photo from a photo album:

1. **Tap Photos in the Home screen.** The Photos screen appears.

2. **Tap the photo album that has the image you want to use.**

3. **Tap the photo you want to use.** Your iPhone opens the photo.

4. **Tap the image to reveal the controls.**

5. **Tap the Actions icon.** This is the icon with the arrow on the left side of the menu bar. (If you don't see the menu bar, tap the screen.) iPhone displays a list of actions you can perform.

6. **Tap Assign To Contact.** A list of all of your contacts appears.

7. **Tap the contact you want to associate with the photo.** The Move and Scale screen appears.

8. **Drag the image so that it's positioned on the screen the way you want.**

9. **Pinch or spread your fingers over the image to set the zoom level you want.**

10. **Tap Set Photo.** iPhone assigns the photo to the contact and returns you to your photo album.

Taking a contact's photo

If you don't have a picture of a contact handy, that's not a problem because you can take advantage of the rear camera on your iPhone and snap his image the next time you get together. You can do this using either the Camera app or via the Contacts app.

To assign a photo from the Camera app, follow these steps:

1. **In the Home screen, tap the Camera icon to enter the Camera app.** A shutter appears on the screen.

2. **If necessary, tap the Switch Camera icon to activate the rear camera.**

3. **Frame the person on your screen and say "Okay, say iPhooooone."**

4. **Tap the Camera button at the bottom of the screen (or the Volume Up button, if that's easier) to snap the picture.**

5. **Tap the Camera Roll icon.** This opens the Camera Roll screen.

6. **Tap the photo you just took.** Your iPhone opens the photo and reveals the photo controls.

7. **Tap the Actions icon.** Your iPhone displays a list of actions you can perform.

8. **Tap Assign To Contact.** A list of all of your contacts is displayed.

9. **Tap the contact you want to associate with the photo.** The Move and Scale screen appears.

10. **Drag the image so that it's positioned on the screen the way you want.**

11. **Pinch or spread your fingers over the image to set the zoom level you want.**

12. **Tap Set Photo.** Your iPhone assigns the photo to the contact and returns you to the photo.

To assign a photo using the Contacts app, follow these steps:

1. **On the Home screen, tap the Contacts icon.** The Contacts app appears.

2. **Tap the contact to whom you want to assign a photo.** Your iPhone displays the contact's Info screen.

3. **Tap Edit to put the contact into Edit mode.**

4. **Tap Add Photo.** Your iPhone displays a list of photo options.

5. **Tap Take Photo.** This opens the Camera app.

6. **If necessary, tap the Switch Camera icon to activate the rear camera.**

7. **Frame the person on the screen, and then tap the Camera button (or the Volume Up button) to take the photo.** The Move and Scale screen appears.

8. **Drag the image so that it's positioned on the screen the way you want.**

9. **Pinch or spread your fingers over the image to set the zoom level you want.**

10. **Tap Use Photo.** Your iPhone assigns the photo to the contact and returns you to the Info screen.

11. **Tap Done.** Your iPhone exits Edit mode.

Enhancing a photo

Don't worry if you have a photo that's too bright in some spots or if the color is washed out in others — the Photos app comes with an Enhance tool that can automatically adjust the color and brightness. Here's how to use it:

1. **In the Photos app, open the photo you want to fix.**

2. **Tap the photo to display the controls.**

3. **Tap Edit.** The Photos app displays its editing tools at the bottom of the screen.

4. **Tap Enhance (the magic wand icon in the menu bar).** The Photos app adjusts the color and brightness.

5. **Tap Save.** The Photos app saves your changes.

Removing red-eye

When you use a flash to take a picture of one or more people, in some cases the flash may reflect off the subjects' retinas. The result is the common phenomenon of red-eye, where each person's pupils appear red instead of black. Some cameras come with a red-eye reduction feature, which is usually a double flash: one to make the pupils contract before the shot and then another for the actual picture.

If you have a photo on your iPhone where one or more people have red-eye due to the camera flash, you can use the Photos app to remove it and give your subjects a more natural look. Here's how:

1. **In the Photos app, open the photo that contains the red-eye you want to remove.**

2. **Tap the photo to display the controls.**

3. **Tap Edit.** The Photos app displays its editing tools.

4. **Tap Red-Eye (in the menu bar, it's the icon consisting of a red circle with a white line through it).**

5. **Tap the red-eye that you want to remove.** The Photos app removes the red-eye.

6. **Repeat Step 5 until you've removed all the red-eye in the photo.**

7. **Tap Apply.** The Photos app applies the changes to the photo.

Cropping and straightening

If you have a photo containing elements that you do not want or need to see, you can often cut them out. This is called *cropping* and you can use the Photos app to do this. When you crop a photo, you specify a rectangular area of it that you want to keep. The Photos app then discards everything outside of the rectangle. Cropping is a useful skill because it can help you give focus to the true subject of a photo. Cropping is also useful for removing extraneous elements that appear on or near the edges of a photo.

As you probably know from hard-won experience, getting an iPhone camera perfectly level when you take a shot is very difficult. It requires lots of practice and a steady hand. Despite your best efforts, you might still end up with a photo that is not quite level. To fix this problem, you can also use the Photos app to rotate the photo clockwise or counterclockwise so that the subject appears straight.

Follow these steps to crop and straighten a photo:

1. **In the Photos app, open the photo that you want to edit.**
2. **Tap the photo to display the controls.**
3. **Tap Edit.** The Photos app displays its editing tools.
4. **Tap Crop (the icon on the far-right side of the menu bar).** The Photos app displays a grid for cropping and straightening, as shown in Figure 8.4.
5. **Tap and drag a corner of the grid to set the area you want to keep.**
6. **To straighten the photo, place two fingers on the screen and rotate them clockwise or counterclockwise until the image is level.**
7. **Tap Crop.** The Photos app applies the changes to the photo.

8.4 Tap Crop to display the cropping and straightening tools.

Genius

The fastest way to crop some photos is to tell the Photos app the dimensions you want to use for the resulting photo. Tap Constrain, and then tap either a specific shape (Original or Square) or a specific ratio, such as 5 × 7 inches or 8 × 10 inches. You then drag the photo (not the grid!) so the portion you want to keep is within the grid.

Note

Although the Crop feature enables you to rotate a photo to straighten it, it doesn't let you rotate a photo 90 degrees, say, from portrait to landscape. To do this, display the photo, tap the screen, and then tap the Rotate icon (the curved arrow on the left side of the menu bar) until the photo is in the orientation you want.

Sending a photo via e-mail

More often than you'd think, it really comes in handy to be able to e-mail photos from your iPhone. This is particularly true if it's a photo you've just taken with one of the iPhone cameras, because then you can share the photo pronto, without having to trudge back to your computer. You also have the option of e-mailing an existing photo in one of your iPhone photo albums.

Here are the steps to follow to take a photo with one of the iPhone cameras and then e-mail it:

1. **On the Home screen, tap Camera.** The Camera screen appears.

2. **Line up your subject and tap the Camera button to take the picture.**

3. **Tap the Camera Roll button.** The Camera Roll photo album appears.

4. **Tap the photo you just took.** A preview of the photo appears.

5. **Tap the Actions icon.** Your iPhone displays a list of actions you can perform.

6. **Tap Email Photo.** The New Message screen appears and your iPhone embeds the photo in the body of the message.

7. **Choose your message recipient and enter a Subject line.**

8. **Tap Send.** If the photo is large, your iPhone asks whether you want to scale the image to a smaller size.

9. **If you want to send the photo as is, tap Actual Size.** Otherwise, tap either Small or Medium to create a scaled-down version of the photo. Your iPhone sends the message and returns you to the photo.

If you have an existing image in one of your iPhone photo albums that you'd prefer to e-mail, follow these steps:

1. **On the Home screen, tap Photos.** The Photo Albums screen appears.

2. **Tap the photo album that has the image you want to send.**

3. **Tap the photo you want to send.** Your iPhone opens the photo.

4. **Tap the Actions icon.** Your iPhone displays a list of actions you can perform.

5. **Tap Email Photo.** In the New Message screen that is displayed, the photo appears in the body of the message.

6. **Choose your message recipient and enter a Subject line.**

7. **Tap Send.** If the photo is large, your iPhone asks whether you want to scale the image to a smaller size.

8. **If you want to send the photo as is, tap Actual Size.** Otherwise, tap either Small or Medium to create a scaled-down version of the photo. Your iPhone sends the message and returns you to the photo.

Note

To send a photo via e-mail, you must have a default e-mail account set up on your iPhone. See Chapter 5 for information about setting up a default e-mail account.

Texting a photo

The new Messages app sends text messages outside of your cellular provider's messaging system. This means that you can use the Messages app to send unlimited (yes, that's right: *unlimited*) text messages via Wi-Fi or 3G to other people using iOS devices, including iPads, iPod touches, and other iPhones. You can also send a photo in a text message. Here are the steps to follow:

1. **On the Home screen, tap Messages.** The Messages screen appears.

2. **Tap New Message.**

3. **Select your recipient.**

4. **Tap the Photo icon, which appears to the left of the text box.**

5. **Select or take a photo.**

- If you want to send a photo already on your iPhone, tap Choose Existing, locate and tap the photo, and then tap Choose. Your iPhone embeds the photo in the new message, as shown in Figure 8.5.

- If you want to take a new photo, tap Take Photo or Video, take the shot, and then tap Use.

6. **Type your message text.**

7. **Tap Send.** Your iPhone sends the message with the photo attached.

Sending a photo to your Flickr account

If you have a Flickr account, you can send photos from your iPhone by e-mail. Flickr gives you an e-mail address specifically to do this. When you want to upload a photo to Flickr, all

8.5 You can use the Messages app to text a photo.

you do is attach it to an e-mail as described earlier in the chapter. Then, enter the address given by Flickr into the address field. You can find out the address to use by visiting www.flickr.com/account/uploadbyemail.

Tweeting a photo

If you set up your Twitter account (or accounts) on your iPhone (see Chapter 1), you can use it to tweet a sweet photo to your followers. Here's how it works:

1. **In the Photos app, open the photo you want to tweet.**

2. **Tap the Actions icon.**

3. **Tap Tweet.** The Photos app displays the Tweet dialog.

4. **If you added more than one account to the iPhone Twitter settings, tap the user-name in the From section and then tap the name of the account you want to use to send the tweet.**

5. **Type your tweet text in the large text box.**

6. **If you want to include your present whereabouts as part of the tweet, tap Add Location.**

7. **Tap Send.** Your iPhone posts the photo as a tweet.

Saving a photo from a text message

If someone sends you a nice photo in a text message, you might want to save it to your iPhone so you can check it out whenever you want, assign it to a contact, sync it to your computer, and so on. Follow these steps to save a photo from a text message:

1. **On the Home screen, tap Messages.** The Messages screen appears.

2. **Tap the conversation that contains the photo message.** The Messages app opens the conversation screen.

3. **Tap the photo.** Your iPhone opens the photo for viewing.

4. **Tap the Actions icon in the lower-left corner of the screen.** The Actions options appear.

5. **Tap Save Image.** Your iPhone saves the image to the Camera Roll.

Creating a custom photo slide show

Okay, the basic slide show is pretty neat, but your iPhone also offers a few settings for creating custom slide shows. Here's how to display them on your iPhone:

1. **On the Home screen, tap the Settings icon.** The Settings app opens.

2. **Tap the Photos icon.** Your iPhone displays the Photos screen.

You get three settings to configure your custom slide show:

- **Play Each Slide For.** You use this setting to set the amount of time that each photo appears on-screen. Tap Play Each Slide For, and then tap a time: 2 Seconds, 3 Seconds (this is the default), 5 Seconds, 10 Seconds, or 20 Seconds.

- **Repeat.** This setting determines whether the slide show repeats from the beginning after the last photo is displayed. To turn this setting on, tap the Repeat switch to On.

- **Shuffle.** You use this setting to display the album photos in random order. To turn this setting on, tap the Shuffle switch to On.

Playing a slide show with background music

Here's is a little bonus that the iPhone throws your way. Yes, you can wow them back home by running a custom slide show, but you can positively make their jaws hit the floor when you add a music soundtrack to the show! They'll be cheering in the aisles.

Here's how you do it:

1. **Tap the Photos icon.** The Photos app appears.
2. **Open the photo album you want to use.**
3. **Tap the first photo you want to see in the slide show.**
4. **Tap Play.** The Photos app displays the Slideshow Options screen.
5. **Tap the Play Music switch to On.**
6. **Tap Music.** Your iPhone opens the Music app and displays the Songs list.
7. **Use the Music app to select the song you want to play.**
8. **Tap Start Slideshow.** Your iPhone starts the slide show and the music.

Note   The Photos app stops playing the slide show when the music ends, which is a bit annoying. If you have lots of photos, you might prefer to play an entire album or playlist while the show is running. To do that, first open the Music app and start playing the album or playlist. Then switch to the Photos app and run the slide show with the Play Music switch set to Off.

Creating a photo album

Normally you'd use your computer to organize your photos into albums prior to syncing them to your iPhone. However, if you have been taking a lot of pictures on your iPhone and your computer is nowhere in sight, you don't have to wait to organize your pics. The iOS 5 version of the Photos app enables you to create your own photo albums right on your iPhone. These albums aren't transferred to your computer when you sync, but they're handy if you need to organize your photos quickly. Here's what you do:

1. **In the Photos app, tap Albums.** The Albums screen appears.

2. **Tap Edit.** The Photos app opens the Albums section for editing.

3. **Tap Add.** The Photos app prompts you for an album name.

4. **Type the name and then tap Save.** You return to the Albums screen.

5. **Open an album and tap each image that you want to include in your new album.** A check mark appears next to each photo you select.

6. **Tap Done.** The Photos app creates the new album and adds it to the Albums screen.

Note To remove a custom album you no longer need, tap Albums, tap Edit, tap the red Delete icon to the left of the custom album, and then tap the Delete button that appears.

Deleting a photo

If you mess up a photo using one of the iPhone cameras, you should delete it before people think you have shoddy camera skills (because we all know it was the phone's fault, right?).

You might think that deleting a photo would be a straightforward proposition. Nope, not even close. That's because your iPhone differentiates between two types of photos:

- Photos that you add to the iPhone via syncing with iTunes.

- Photos that you create directly on the iPhone by using the cameras; taking a screenshot; saving a photo from an e-mail, text message, or web page; and so on.

Synced photos *can't* be deleted directly via the iPhone, but photos you create on the iPhone *can* be deleted. Clear as mud, I know.

To delete a photo, follow these steps:

1. **Tap Photos in the Home screen.**

2. **Tap the photo album that has the image you want to blow away.**

3. **Tap the doomed photo.** Your iPhone opens it.

4. **Tap the image to reveal the controls.**

5. **Tap the Trash icon.** The Trash icon is on the right side of the menu bar. (If you don't see the menu bar, tap the screen.) Your iPhone asks you to confirm the deletion.

6. **Tap Delete Photo.** Your iPhone tosses the photo into the trash, wipes its hands, and displays the previous photo in the album.

Genius

What happens if you have duplicate synced photos on your iPhone if you can't delete the copies? The way you fix that is to connect the iPhone to your computer, click the iPhone in iTunes, click the Photos tab, uncheck Sync Photos, and then click Apply. This removes all the synced photos from the iPhone. You then recheck Sync Photos and click Apply. You should end up with no duplicates on the iPhone.

Getting More Out of iPhone Video Features

The iPhone is a visual medium (it uses a touchscreen after all). The large screen makes it a perfect portable media device. The Videos app organizes and plays back videos that you import from your computer. Your commute (okay, your nondriving commute) doesn't have to be boring any more. Just put in your headphones and start an episode of your favorite show.

Playing iPhone videos on your TV

You can carry a bunch of videos with you on your iPhone, so why shouldn't you be able to play them on a TV if you want? Well, you can. You have to buy another cord, but that's the only investment you have to make to watch iPhone videos right on your TV.

To hook your iPhone up to your TV, you have three choices:

- **Apple Digital AV Adapter.** This $39 cable has a 30-pin connector on one end that connects to the iPhone or an Apple Universal Dock. The other end has another 30-pin connector so you can connect your iPhone to a power outlet and an HDMI port that enables you to make a connection to the corresponding HDMI input on your HDTV.

- **Apple Component AV cable.** This $39 cable plugs into the iPhone or Apple Universal Dock connector on one end and the component inputs on your TV at the other.

- **Apple Composite AV cable.** This $39 cable plugs into the iPhone or Apple Universal Dock connector on one end and the composite inputs on your TV at the other.

The cable you choose depends on the type of TV you have. Older sets have composite inputs, more recent TVs have component inputs, while the latest sets have at least one HDMI port.

After connecting your cables, set your TV to the input and play your videos as you normally would.

Streaming iPhone video to Apple TV

If you have an Apple TV that supports AirPlay, you can use AirPlay to stream a video from your iPhone to your TV. Here's how it works:

1. **Make sure your Apple TV is turned on.**

2. **On your iPhone, start the video you want to stream.**

3. **Tap the screen to display the controls.**

4. **Tap the Output button, which appears to the right of the Next button.** Your iPhone displays a menu of output choices, as shown in Figure 8.6.

5. **Tap the name of your Apple TV device.** Your iPhone streams the video to that device, and hence to your TV.

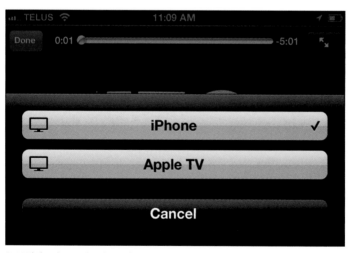

8.6 While playing back a video, tap the screen and then tap the Output button to display different output choices that allow you to stream the video to your Apple TV.

Mirroring the iPhone screen on your TV

In iOS 5 running on an iPhone 4S, you can set up a *mirrored* display. This means that what you see on your iPhone is also displayed on your TV in HD. One way to do this is to use the Apple Digital AV Adapter to connect your iPhone to your TV's HDMI port. However, iOS 5 also offers wireless AirPlay mirroring through Apple TV. As long as you have a second-generation Apple TV (and it has been updated with the latest software), you can use AirPlay mirroring not only to send videos to your TV, but also photos, slide shows, websites, apps, games, and anything else you can display on your iPhone 4S.

Follow these steps to start mirroring the iPhone screen on your TV:

1. **Turn on your Apple TV device.**

2. **On your iPhone, double-click the Home button to display the multitasking bar.**

3. **In the multitasking bar, swipe right to reveal the playback controls, and then swipe right again to reveal the volume control.**

4. **Tap the AirPlay button, which appears to the right of the volume control.** Your iPhone displays a menu of output choices.

5. **Tap the name of your Apple TV device.**

6. **Tap the Mirroring switch to On and then tap Done.** Your iPhone streams the screen to Apple TV and indicates that AirPlay is active by displaying the AirPlay icon in the status bar. Note, too, that the status bar appears blue to indicate that mirroring is on.

Watching videos from a shared iTunes library

If you have iTunes Home Sharing activated on your computer, you can use your iPhone to tap in to that library and play its video content. I showed you how to activate iTunes Home Sharing in Chapter 7. Assuming that's done, your next task is to configure your iPhone Videos app with the same Home Sharing Apple ID and password. (If you already did this using the Music settings, as I described in Chapter 7, then you can skip the steps that follow.) Follow these steps:

1. **On your iPhone Home screen, tap Settings.** The Settings app appears.

2. **Tap Video to open the Video screen.**

3. **In the Home Sharing section, use the Apple ID and Password boxes to type the same account information that you used to set up Home Sharing in iTunes.**

Now open the Videos app on your iPhone and then tap Shared. As you can see in Figure 8.7, the Videos app displays icons for the available shared libraries. Tap the library you want to access, and the Videos app displays that library's video content instead of your iPhone videos.

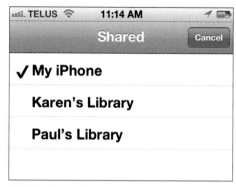

8.7 With Home Sharing configured, tap Shared to see a list of the available shared libraries.

Converting a video file to iPhone format

Your iPhone is happy to play video, but only certain formats are compatible with it. Here's the list:

- **H.264 video.** Up to 1080p, 30 frames per second, High Profile level 4.1 with AAC-LC audio up to 160 Kbps, 48 kHz, stereo audio in M4V, MP4, and MOV file formats.

- **MPEG-4 video.** Up to 2.5 Mbps, 640 × 480 pixels, 30 frames per second. Simple Profile with AAC-LC audio up to 160 Kbps, 48 kHz, stereo audio in M4V, MP4, and MOV file formats.

- **Motion JPEG video.** Up to 35 Mbps, 1280 × 720 pixels, 30 frames per second, audio in u-law PCM stereo audio using the AVI file format.

If you have a video file that doesn't match any of these formats, you might think you're out of luck. Nope. You can use iTunes to convert that video to an MPEG-4 file that's iPhone friendly. Here's how:

1. **If the video file isn't already in iTunes, choose File ⇨ Add to Library, or press ⌘+O.** The Add To Library dialog appears. If the file is already in iTunes, skip to Step 3.

2. **Locate and choose your video file, and then click Open.** iTunes copies the file into the library, which may take a while depending on the size of the video file. Usually, iTunes adds the video to the Movies section of the library.

3. **In iTunes, click your movie.**

4. **Choose Advanced ⇨ Create iPod or iPhone Version.** iTunes begins converting the video to the MPEG-4 format. This might take some time for even a relatively small video. When the conversion is complete, a copy of the original video appears in the iTunes Library.

Because the converted video has the same name as the original, you should probably rename one of them so you can tell them apart when you sync your iPhone. If you're not sure which file is which, right-click one of the videos and then click Get Info. In the Summary tab, read the Kind value. The iPhone-friendly file has a Kind setting of MPEG-4 video file.

Recording video with an iPhone camera

If sometime in the first half of 2009 you polled people using the original iPhone or the iPhone 3G to find out the most important feature missing from their phone, I guarantee you the most popular choice would be video recording. Any smartphone worthy of the name should do all the things you need it to do during the course of your busy life, and one of the things you probably want to do is record events, happenings, moments, or just whatever's going on. Sure, a picture is worth the proverbial thousand words, but at 30 frames per second, a video is worth a lot more than that.

Caution The high-definition (HD) video recording capabilities of the iPhone 4 and 4S are so welcome that you might start shooting everything in sight. Be my guest! However, just be aware that your iPhone churns through disk space at the rapid rate of 10 Mbps, which means each minute of video carves out nearly 80MB of disk real estate.

So it was applause all around when Apple announced that the iPhone 3GS would indeed come with video recording capabilities. Woohoo! Apple upped the ante with the iPhone 4, which not only recorded in 720p HD video, but also supported tap-to-focus and could use the LED flash in low-light situations. In the iPhone 4S, video recording is even better with full 1080p HD recording and a new video stabilization feature that helps to reduce shaky shots.

And, this being an iPhone and all, it's no surprise that recording a video is almost criminally easy. Here's what you do:

1. **On the Home screen, tap the Camera button.** The Camera screen appears.

2. **Flick the Mode switch in the lower-right corner from Camera to Video.**

3. **Tap the screen to focus the video, if necessary.**

4. **Tap the Flash icon, and then tap On, Off, or Auto.**

5. **Tap the Switch Camera icon if you want to use the front camera rather than the rear camera.**

6. **Tap the Record button.** Your iPhone starts recording video and displays the total recording time in the upper-right corner of the screen.

7. **When you're done, tap the Record button again to stop the recording.** Your iPhone saves the video to the Camera Roll.

Genius

If you have an AirPlay-friendly Apple TV, you can stream your recorded iPhone videos to your TV. Make sure your Apple TV device is on, open the video on your iPhone, and then tap the Output button (the rectangle with the upward-pointing arrow in the menu bar). In the menu that appears, tap Apple TV, and away you go.

Editing recorded video

Okay, being able to record video at the tap of a button is pretty cool, but your iPhone tops that by also letting you perform basic editing chores right on the phone. (Insert sound of jaw hitting floor here.) It's nothing fancy — basically, you can trim video from the beginning and end of the file — but it sure beats having to first sync the video to your computer, and then fire up iMovie or some other video-editing software.

Here's how to edit a video right on your iPhone:

1. **Open the Camera Roll album:**
   - **Camera app.** Tap the Camera Roll button in the lower-left corner of the screen.
   - **Photos app.** Display the Albums screen and then tap Camera Roll.

2. **Tap the video you want to edit.**

Note

Video thumbnails show a video camera icon in the lower-left corner and the duration of the video in the lower-right corner.

3. **Tap anywhere to display the on-screen controls.** If the video is playing, tap Pause to stop the playback. You see a timeline of the video along the top of the screen.

4. **Tap and drag the left edge of the timeline to set the starting point of the video.**

Genius If you need more precision when trimming the timeline, tap and hold either the start trim control or the end trim control. Your iPhone expands the timeline to show more frames, which enables you to make more precise edits.

5. **Tap and drag the right edge of the timeline to set the ending point of the video.** The trimmed timeline appears surrounded by orange, as shown in Figure 8.8.

6. **Tap Play to ensure you've set the start and end points correctly.** If not, repeat Steps 4 and 5 to adjust the timeline as needed.

7. **Tap Trim.** Your iPhone trims the video and then saves your work.

Sending a video via e-mail

If you want to share your newly shot and edited video with someone, you can e-mail it by following these steps:

1. **Open the Camera Roll album:**

   - **Camera app.** Tap the Camera Roll button in the lower-left corner of the screen.

   - **Photos app.** Display the Albums screen and then tap Camera Roll.

2. **Tap the video you want to send.**

3. **Tap the Actions icon in the lower-left corner.** The Share options appear.

4. **Tap Email Video.** Your iPhone creates a new e-mail message that includes your video as an MPEG-4 video file attachment.

5. **Fill in the rest of your message and send it.**

8.8 Use the video timeline to set the start and end points of the video footage you want to keep.

Note

If your video is too long to send via e-mail, your iPhone lets you know and asks if you want to send a shorter version. If so, tap OK, use the trim control to shorten the clip, and then tap Email.

Texting a video

To pass along your video in a text message, follow these steps:

1. **Open the Camera Roll album:**

   - **Camera app.** Tap the Camera Roll button in the lower-left corner of the screen.

   - **Photos app.** Display the Albums screen and then tap Camera Roll.

2. **Tap the video you want to send.**

3. **Tap the Actions icon in the lower-left corner.** The Share options pop up.

4. **Tap Message.** Your iPhone displays the New Message screen and includes your video as an MPEG-4 video file.

5. **Select the recipient, and then tap Send.**

Note

If your video is too long to send via text message, your iPhone lets you know and asks if you want to send a shorter version. If so, tap OK, use the trim control to shorten the clip, and then tap Send.

Uploading recorded video to YouTube

Of course, you want to be able to instantly record something because you can then upload that video to YouTube and share it with the world. Your iPhone is happy to help here, too, as shown by the following steps:

1. **Open the Camera Roll album:**

   - **Camera app.** Tap the Camera Roll button in the lower-left corner of the screen.

   - **Photos app.** Display the Albums screen and then tap Camera Roll.

2. **Tap the video you want to share.**

3. **Tap the Action icon in the lower-left corner.** The Share options appear.

4. **Tap Send to YouTube.** Your iPhone compresses the video and prompts you to log in to your YouTube account.

5. **Enter your YouTube username and password, and then tap Sign In.** The Publish Video screen appears.

6. **Tap a title, description, and tags for your video, and then choose a category.**

7. **If you want to upload an HD version of the video, tap HD.** HD versions of iPhone videos are more than three times larger than standard-definition versions, so uploading them takes longer.

8. **Tap Publish.** Your iPhone publishes the video to your YouTube account. This may take several minutes, depending on the size of the video. When the video is published, you see a dialog with a few options.

9. **Tap one of the following options:**

   - **View on YouTube.** Tap this option to cue up the video on YouTube.

   - **Tell a Friend.** Tap this option to send an e-mail message that includes a link to the video on YouTube.

   - **Close.** Tap this option to return to the video.

Customizing your iPhone video settings

Your iPhone offers a few video-related settings that you can try on for size. Follow these steps to use them:

1. **Press the Home button.** The Home screen appears.

2. **Tap the Settings icon.** The Settings app opens.

3. **Tap the Video icon.** Your iPhone displays the Video settings screen.

Besides the Home Sharing options that I mentioned in the preceding section, you get two settings with which to meddle:

- **Start Playing.** This setting controls what your iPhone does when you stop and restart a video. You have two choices: Where Left Off (the default), which picks up the video from the same point where you stopped it; and From Beginning, which always restarts the video from scratch. Tap Start Playing, and then tap the setting you prefer.

- **Closed Captioning.** This setting toggles support for closed captioning on and off, when it's available. To turn on this feature, tap the Closed Captioning switch to On.

Editing Video with iMovie for iPhone

Earlier I showed you the built-in editing feature that comes with the iPhone, which essentially boils down to being able to trim video clips. That's pretty handy, but proper video editing requires features such as adding transitions and titles, changing the theme, and adding a music track. Ah, you might be saying to yourself, all I have to do is sync my videos to my computer, and then use video-editing software, such as iMovie on the Mac to do all that.

Well, yes, you can certainly do that, but what if your computer is nowhere in sight? If it's just you, your iPhone, and some cool-but-not-ready-for-primetime video, you can go well beyond the native iPhone video-editing capabilities by purchasing the iMovie for iPhone app, which is available from the App Store for $4.99. With iMovie for iPhone, you can perform many of the same tasks that you can using the full-fledged iMovie application, such as importing live or recorded videos and photos, trimming clips, adding transitions, applying a Ken Burns effect to a photo, adding titles and music tracks, applying themes, and much more.

Creating a new iMovie project

Assuming you've already purchased and installed the iMovie for iPhone app, to get started with it (which, for efficiency's sake, I just call iMovie from here on), tap the iMovie icon. In the Projects screen that appears, follow these steps to get a new iMovie project off the ground:

1. **Tap the Add (+) button.** iMovie displays the Add Project screen.
2. **Select a project theme.**
3. **If you want to include the theme's default music in your project, tap the Theme Music switch to On.**
4. **Tap Done.** iMovie saves your new project and adds it to the Projects list.

At this point, iMovie prompts you to insert or record media. I show you how this works later in this chapter.

Opening a project for editing

For the rest of this chapter, you'll be working within a specific project, so go ahead and use the Projects list to tap the one with which you want to work. You end up in the iMovie project editing environment. Figure 8.9 shows an example of the editing environment for a project that already has clips and other media imported.

There are three main elements in the iMovie editing environment:

- **Timeline.** This is the strip along the bottom of the screen. It displays your video clips, photos, transitions, and music track.

- **Viewer.** This is the larger pane that takes up most of the top half of the window. It shows your video when you play it and when you scroll through the timeline.

- **Toolbars.** These appear to the left and right of (or, in portrait mode, above and below) the Viewer. There are six buttons (pointed out in Figure 8.9): Projects, which returns you to the Projects screen; Record Narration, which enables you to record a voiceover track for the video; Import, which you use to import existing videos, photos, and music; Settings, which lets you set various project options; Record, which you use to import videos or photos shot with an iPhone camera; and Play, which plays your movie.

Projects — Settings

Record Narration — Record

Import — Play

8.9 You see a screen similar to this when you open a video for editing in iMovie.

Importing media into your project

With your new project on the go, your first task is to import media into it. With iMovie, you can import four kinds of media: recorded video, existing video, photos, and music (which I cover later in this chapter).

215

Importing a video from an iPhone camera

You can record whatever is happening around you and import it directly into your iMovie project using one of the built-in iPhone cameras. Here's how you do it:

1. **Open your iMovie project.**
2. **Scroll through the timeline to the location where you want the video to appear.**
3. **Tap the Record icon.** Your iPhone switches to the Camera app, which activates the Video mode switch.
4. **Tap the Switch Camera icon to choose to a different camera, if necessary.**
5. **Tap the screen to focus the video, if necessary.**
6. **Tap the red Record button.** Your iPhone starts recording video and displays the total recording time in the upper-right corner of the screen.
7. **When you're done, tap the Record button again to stop recording.** iMovie displays a preview of the recorded video.
8. **If the video looks good, tap Use to add it to the timeline.** Otherwise, tap Retake and then reshoot the video.

Importing existing video

If you've already recorded your video or synced one from your computer, you can add it to your project timeline. Here are the steps to follow:

1. **Open your iMovie project.**
2. **Scroll through the timeline to the location where you want the video to appear.**
3. **Tap the Import icon.** iMovie displays the importing screen.
4. **Tap Video.** iMovie displays the Video screen, which includes thumbnails of the available videos on your iPhone.
5. **Scroll through the videos until you find the one you want to import.**
6. **Tap the video.** iMovie adds it to the timeline.

Importing a photo from the camera

You can take a still image and import it directly into your iMovie project using one of the built-in cameras on your iPhone. Here's how you do it:

1. **Open your iMovie project.**
2. **Scroll through the timeline to the location where you want the video to appear.**

3. **Tap the Record icon.** Your iPhone switches to the camera.

4. **Flick the Mode switch in the lower-right corner from Video to Camera.**

5. **Tap the screen to focus the photo, if necessary.**

6. **Tap the Shutter button.** Your iPhone takes the photo and displays a preview of the result.

7. **If the photo looks good, tap Use to add it to the timeline.** Otherwise, tap Retake and then reshoot the photo.

Importing an existing photo

You can also import a photo to your project, which iMovie automatically animates by applying a Ken Burns effect (which is a pan-and-zoom effect popularized by filmmaker Ken Burns). Follow these steps to add a photo to your project:

1. **Open your iMovie project.**

2. **Scroll through the timeline to the location where you want the photo to appear.**

3. **Tap the Import icon.** iMovie displays the importing screen.

4. **Tap Photos.** iMovie displays the Photos screen.

5. **Tap the album that contains the photo you want to import.** iMovie displays thumbnails of the album's photos.

6. **Tap the photo.** iMovie adds the photo to the timeline.

Working with video clips

iMovie gives you a surprisingly complete collection of video-editing tools that enable you to move and trim clips, change transitions, work with a photo's Ken Burns effect, and add clip titles.

Moving a clip

If a clip doesn't appear where you want it, follow these steps to move it to the position you prefer:

1. **Tap and hold the middle of the clip you want to move.**

2. **Drag the clip left or right through the timeline.**

3. **Drop the clip when you reach the location you want.** iMovie moves the clip.

Trimming a clip

If an imported video clip includes footage at the beginning or end (or both) that you don't want to include in your movie, you can trim those unwanted scenes. Here are the steps to follow:

1. **Tap the clip you want to trim.** iMovie displays the trim controls, as shown in Figure 8.10.

2:04.5

8.10 Tap a clip to display the trimming tools.

Genius

For more precise trimming, spread your fingers on the clip to expand it in the time-line. If you go too far, pinch the clip to shrink it.

2. **Tap and drag the left trim control to set the starting point of the clip.**

3. **Tap and drag the right trim control to set the ending point of the clip.**

Changing the transition between two clips

iMovie makes transitions a no-brainer because it adds them automatically between any two clips when you add videos or photos to the timeline. It also defines different transitions for each theme applied to a project. (I show you how to change themes a bit later.) If you don't like the theme transitions, you can switch to a Cross Dissolve transition (where the end of one clip dissolves into the beginning of the next), or you can turn off the transition altogether. You can also vary the length of the transition.

Here are the steps to follow:

1. **Double-tap the transition you want to change.** iMovie displays the Transition Settings window, shown in Figure 8.11.

2. **Tap the transition you want: Theme, Cross Dissolve, or None.**

None	**0.5s**
Cross Dissolve	1.0s
Theme	**1.5s**
	2.0s

8.11 Double-tap the transition to open the Transition Settings window.

3. **Tap the length of the transition in seconds.**

4. **Tap Done.** iMovie saves the transition settings.

Adjusting a photo's Ken Burns effect

I mentioned earlier that when you import a photo, iMovie automatically applies a Ken Burns effect, which pans and zooms the photo. You can control the panning and zooming by following these steps:

1. **Tap the photo you want to edit.** iMovie selects the photo and displays the Ken Burns effect tools, as shown in Figure 8.12.

8.12 Tap the photo to display the Ken Burns effect tools.

219

2. **Set the start of the pan by dragging the photo to the starting position you prefer.**

3. **Set the opening zoom level by pinching or spreading on the photo.**

4. **Tap Start.**

5. **Set the end of the pan by dragging the photo to the ending position you prefer.**

6. **Set the closing zoom level by pinching or spreading on the photo.**

7. **If you want to return to the start settings, tap End and repeat Steps 2 and 3.**

8. **Tap Done.** iMovie saves the settings.

Adding a title to a clip

You can get your movie off to a proper start by adding a title to your opening clip. iMovie offers a number of title styles that you can choose from, and it automatically adds the video location (picked up from the geolocation data supplied by the iPhone cameras) as the subtitle.

Follow these steps to add a title to any clip:

1. **Double-tap the clip with which you want to work.** iMovie displays the Clip Settings screen.

2. **Tap Title Style.** iMovie opens the Title Style screen.

3. **Tap the title style you're adding: Opening, Middle, or Ending.**

4. **Tap inside the Title Text Here text box.** iMovie displays the Edit Title screen.

5. **Type the title and tap Done to return to the Title Style screen.**

6. **Tap Done.** iMovie adds the title to the clip.

Removing a clip

If you add a clip accidentally or decide a clip is no longer needed, you can use either of the following techniques to remove it from your project:

- Double-tap the clip to open the Clip Settings screen, and then tap Delete.
- Tap and drag the clip up and off the timeline. When you release the clip, iMovie deletes it.

Working with your project

Your iMovie project is coming along nicely, with its trimmed clips, transitions, Ken Burns effects, and titles. What else can iMovie do? Three things, actually: add music, change the theme, and export your project to a movie file.

Adding a music track

What would a video be without a music track playing in the background? Boring, that's what! Fortunately, iMovie lets you add either a song from your iTunes Library or an audio track from the project's current theme. Here's how it works:

1. **Tap the Import icon.** iMovie displays the import screen.

2. **Tap Audio.** iMovie displays the Audio screen.

3. **Tap the music category you want to use.** To use an audio track from the project's theme, tap Theme Music; otherwise, tap an iTunes music category, such as Playlists, Albums, or Artists.

4. **Navigate the music until you locate the track you want to add.** For example, if you selected the Artists category, you'd need to select an artist and then an album.

5. **Tap the track.** iMovie adds the track to the bottom of the timeline, as shown in Figure 8.13.

8.13 After you select a song or audio track, iMovie displays the track as a green strip at the bottom of the timeline.

Changing the project theme

The secret to easy iMovie-making is the project theme. As you've seen, the project theme enables you to automatically apply clip transitions, title styles, and music tracks to give your movie a cohesive and consistent feel. iMovie ships with five built-in themes, so you can pick the one that best complements your movie subject.

Follow these steps to change the project theme:

1. **Open your iMovie project.**

2. **Tap the Settings icon.** iMovie displays the Project Settings screen, as shown in Figure 8.14.

3. **Tap the theme you want to use.**

4. **If you want to use the music tracks that come with the theme, tap the Theme Music switch to On.**

5. **If your movie is longer than the project audio, but you don't want the audio to keep repeating for the duration of the movie, tap the Loop Background Music switch to Off.**

6. **Tap Done.** iMovie saves your settings and updates the project with the new theme.

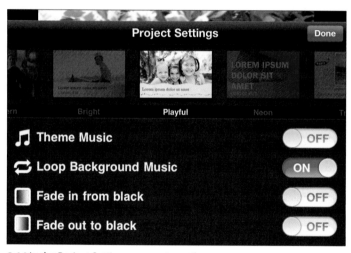

8.14 In the Project Settings screen, tap a theme.

Naming your project

Your movie just isn't complete without a snappy title, so follow these steps to name your movie:

1. **If you have your project open in the editing environment, tap Projects to return to the Projects screen.**

2. **Select the project you want to name.**

3. **Tap inside the marquee.** iMovie opens the title for editing.

4. **Tap the movie title.**

5. **Tap Done.**

Exporting your project

With your clips imported and trimmed, your transitions and titles in place, your music added and your theme applied, your movie is finally ready for prime time. Although you can play the movie within the editing environment (by tapping the Play button in the upper toolbar), you won't really be able to show it off until you export it to a movie file. iMovie gives you three choices: HD (720p), Large (540p), or Medium (360p).

Follow these steps to export your project to the Camera Roll:

1. **If you have your project open in the editing environment, tap Projects to return to the Projects screen.**

2. **Select the project you want to export.**

3. **Tap the Export icon (the rectangle with the right-pointing arrow).** iMovie displays a list of sharing options.

4. **Tap Camera Roll.** iMovie asks you to select an export size, as shown in Figure 8.15.

5. **Tap the size you want.** iMovie exports the project to a movie file, which it then stores in Camera Roll on your iPhone.

8.15 Tap the Export icon, tap Camera Roll, and then choose the video size you want.

How Can I Use My iPhone to Manage Contacts and Appointments?

The iPhone has never just been about the technology. Yes, it looks stylish, has enough bells and whistles to cause deafness, and it just works. iPhone users don't know or care about things like antennae, flash drives, memory chips, and whatever else Apple somehow managed to cram into that tiny case. These things don't matter because iPhone has always been about helping you get things done and making your life better, more creative, and more efficient. And, as you'll see in this chapter, your iPhone can also go a long way toward making your life — particularly your contacts and your calendar — more organized.

Managing Your Contacts

One of the paradoxes of modern life is that as contact information becomes more important, you store less and less of it in the easiest database system of all — your memory. Instead of memorizing phone numbers like you used to, you now store your contact info electronically. When you think about it, this isn't exactly surprising. It's not just a landline phone number that you have to remember for each person anymore, but also a cell number, e-mail and website addresses, a Twitter username, a physical address, and more. That's a lot to remember, so it makes sense to go the electronic route. And for the iPhone, *electronic* means the Contacts app, which seems basic enough but is actually loaded with useful features that can help you get organized and get the most out of the contact management side of your life.

Creating a new contact

I showed you how to sync your computer's contacts program (such as Address Book on Mac or Windows or the Outlook Contacts folder) in Chapter 6. That's by far the easiest way to populate your iPhone Contacts app with a crowd of people, but it might not include everyone in your posse. If someone's missing and you're not around your computer, you can add that person directly to your iPhone Contacts.

Begin by creating a contact with just the basic info: first name, last name, and company name. In subsequent sections, I show you how to add data such as phone numbers and e-mail addresses. Here are the steps to follow:

1. **In the Home screen, tap the Contacts icon.** In a bit of a head scratcher, Apple has secreted the Contacts app on the second Home screen inside the Utilities folder. Your iPhone opens the All Contacts screen. If you are in the Phone app, you can also tap the Contacts icon.

2. **Tap the Plus (+) button at the top-right corner of the screen.** The New Contact screen appears, as shown in Figure 9.1.

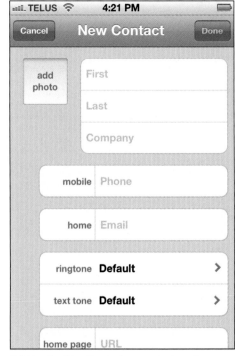

9.1 Use the New Contact screen to type the person's name and company name.

3. **Tap the First box and then type the person's first name.** If you're jotting down the contact data for a company or some other inanimate object, skip to Step 5.

4. **Tap the Last box and then type the person's surname.**

5. **If you want to note where the person works (or if you're adding a business to your Contacts app), tap the Company box and type the company name.**

6. **Tap Done.** Your iPhone saves the new contact and returns you to the All Contacts screen.

Editing an existing contact

Now that your new contact is off to a flying start, you can go ahead and fill in details, such as phone numbers, addresses (e-mail, web, and real world), and anything else you can think of (or have the patience to enter into your iPhone; it can be a lot of tapping!). The next few sections take you through the steps for each type of data. When you're done, be sure to tap Done to preserve all your hard work.

Note See Chapter 8 to get the scoop on sprucing up your contact with a photo.

Here are the steps required to open an existing contact for editing:

1. **In the Home screen, tap the Contacts icon.** The All Contacts screen appears.

2. **Tap the contact you want to edit.**

3. **Tap Edit.** Your iPhone displays the contact's data in the Info screen.

4. **Make your changes, as described in the next few sections.**

5. **Tap Done.** Your iPhone saves your work and returns you to the All Contacts screen.

Assigning phone numbers to a contact

Your iPhone is, of course, a phone, so it's only right and natural to use it to call your contact. Sure, but which number? Work? Home? Cell? Fortunately, there's no need to choose just one, because your iPhone is happy to store all these numbers, plus a few more if need be.

Here are the steps to follow to add one or more phone numbers for a contact:

1. **With the contact's data open for editing, tap inside the Phone field.** Your iPhone displays a numeric keypad, as shown in Figure 9.2.

2. **Type the phone number with area code first.** Your iPhone helpfully adds extra stuff like parentheses around the area code and the dash.

3. **Examine the label box to see if the default label is the one you want.** If it is, skip to Step 5; if it's not, tap the label box to open the Label screen.

4. **Tap the label that best applies to the phone number you're adding (your iPhone automatically sends you back to the Info screen after you tap), such as mobile, iPhone, home, or work.**

5. **Repeat Steps 1 to 4 to add any other numbers you want to store for this contact.** Note that each time you add a number, Contacts creates a new phone field below the current field, and you tap inside the new field to add the new number.

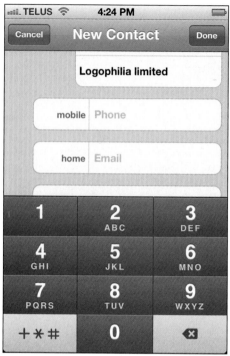

9.2 Tap inside the Phone field and use the numeric keypad to assign a phone number to your contact.

Genius

Some numbers — such as those used by long-distance calling cards — require a pause in mid-dial to wait for the system to do something. To tell your iPhone to pause for two seconds while dialing, tap the +*# key, and then tap the Pause key. The iPhone inserts a comma (,) to indicate the pause location.

Assigning e-mail addresses to a contact

It makes sense that you might want to add a phone number or three for a contact, but would you ever need to enter multiple e-mail addresses? Well, sure you would! Most people have at least a couple of addresses — usually for home and work — and some type-A e-mailers have a dozen or more. Life is too short to enter that many e-mail addresses, but you need at least the important ones if you want to use your iPhone Mail app to send a note to your contacts.

Follow these steps to add one or more e-mail addresses for a contact:

1. **With the contact's data open for editing, tap inside the Email field.** Your iPhone displays the keyboard.

2. **Type the person's e-mail address.**

3. **Check out the label box to see if the default label is the one you want.** If it is, skip to Step 5; if it's not, tap the label box to open the Label screen.

4. **Tap the label that best applies to the e-mail address you're inserting (your iPhone automatically sends you back to the Info screen after you tap), such as home or work.**

5. **Repeat Steps 1 to 4 to add other e-mail addresses for this contact, as you see fit.** Note that each time you add an e-mail address, Contacts creates a new Email field below the current one. You tap inside the new field to add the new address.

Assigning web addresses to a contact

Who on earth doesn't have a website these days? It could be a humble home page, a blog, a Tumblr page, a home business site, or someone's corporate website. Some busy web beavers may even have all five! Whatever web home a person has, it's a good idea to toss the address into her contact data because then you can simply tap it and your iPhone (assuming it can see the Internet from here) immediately fires up Safari and takes you to the site. Does your pal have multiple websites? No sweat: your iPhone is happy to take you to all of them.

Genius

To save some wear and tear on your tapping finger, don't bother adding the http:// stuff at the beginning of the address. Your iPhone adds those characters automatically anytime you type an address to visit a site. Same with the www prefix. So if the full address is http://www.wordspy.com, you need only type wordspy.com.

You can add one or more web addresses for a contact by making your way through these steps:

1. **With the contact's data open for editing, tap inside the URL field.** Your iPhone displays the keyboard, as shown in Figure 9.3. Note the . (period) and .com keys in the on-screen keyboard, which come in very handy.

2. **Type the person's web address.**

3. **Examine the label box to see if the default label is the one you want.** If it is, skip to Step 5; if it's not, tap the label box to open the Label screen.

4. **Tap the label that best applies to the web address you're inserting (your iPhone automatically sends you back to the Info screen after you tap), such as home page or work.**

5. **Repeat Steps 1 to 4 to add other web addresses for this contact.** Note that each time you add a web address, Contacts creates a new URL field below the current one and you tap inside the new field to add the new URL.

Assigning social network data to a contact

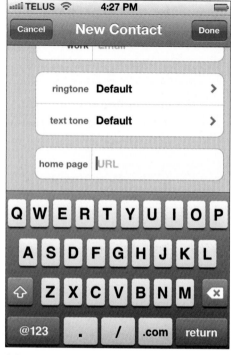

9.3 Tap inside the URL field to type a web address for your contact.

These days, many of us are far more likely to contact friends, family, and colleagues via social networks, such as Twitter, Facebook, and LinkedIn, than we are through more traditional methods like e-mail. The Contacts app in iOS 5 reflects this new reality by enabling you to save social network data for each contact, including data for Twitter, Facebook, LinkedIn, Flickr, and MySpace. Here are the steps to follow to add one or more social network details to a contact:

1. **With the contact's data open for editing, tap Add Field to open the Add Field dialog.**

2. **Tap Twitter.** Yes, you need to tap Twitter even if you are entering data for some other social network. Your iPhone is quirky that way.

3. **If you want to use a different social network, tap the Twitter label to see a list of social networks, as shown in Figure 9.4.**

4. **Tap the label that suits the social network data you're entering, such as Facebook or Flickr.** The Contacts app adds the new label.

5. **Tap inside the field and then tap the person's username for the chosen social network.** Note that as soon as you tap at least one character, Contacts adds a new social network field.

6. **If necessary, use the new social network field to add another social network, repeating as needed.**

Assigning physical addresses to a contact

With all this talk about cell numbers, e-mail addresses, and web addresses, it's easy to forget that people actually live and work somewhere. You may have plenty of contact information in which the location of that somewhere doesn't much matter. But, if you

9.4 Tap Twitter to see the social networks supported by the Contacts app.

ever need to get from here to there, taking the time to insert a contact's physical address really pays off. Why? Because you need only tap the address and your iPhone displays a Google map that shows you the precise location. From there you can get directions, see a satellite map of the area, and more. (I talk about all this great map stuff in Chapter 10.)

Tapping out a full address is a bit of work, but as the following steps show, it's not exactly root-canalishly painful:

1. **With the contact's data open for editing, tap inside the Add New Address field.** Your iPhone displays the address fields, as shown in Figure 9.5.

2. **Tap the first Street field and then type the person's street address.**

3. **If necessary, tap the second Street field, and type even more of the person's street address.**

4. **Tap the City field and type the person's city.**

5. **Tap the State field and type the person's state.** Depending on what you later select for the country, this field might have a different name, such as Province.

6. **Tap the ZIP field and type the ZIP code.** Again, depending on what you later select for the country, this field might have a different name, such as Postal Code.

7. **Tap the Country field to open the Country screen, and then tap the contact's country.**

8. **Examine the label box to see if the default label is the one you want.** If it is, skip to Step 10; if it's not, tap the label box to open the Label screen.

9. **Tap the label that best applies to the physical address you're inserting (your iPhone automatically sends you back to the Info screen after you tap), such as home or work.**

10. **Repeat Steps 1 to 9 to add other addresses for this contact.**

9.5 Tap Add New Address to display the fields shown here so you can tap out your contact's physical coordinates.

Creating a custom label

When you fill out contact data, your iPhone insists that you apply a label to each tidbit, such as home, work, and mobile. If none of the predefined labels fit, you can always just slap on the generic *other* label. However, this seems so, well, dull. If you've got a phone number or address that you can't shoehorn into any of the prefab labels, get creative and make one up. Here's how:

1. **With the contact's data open for editing, tap the label beside the field in which you want to work.** The Label screen appears.

2. **Tap Add Custom Label.** Scroll to the bottom of the screen to see this command. The Custom Label screen appears.

3. **Type the custom label.**

4. **Tap Save.** Your iPhone returns you to the screen for the field you were editing and applies the new label.

5. **Edit the field data if necessary.**

6. **Tap Done.** Your iPhone saves the contact data as well as your custom label.

Conveniently, you can apply your custom label to any type of contact data. For example, if you create a label named college, you can apply that label to a phone number, e-mail address, web address, or physical address.

If a custom label wears out its welcome, follow these steps to delete it:

1. **With the contact's data open for editing, tap any label.** The Label screen appears.

2. **Tap Edit.** Your iPhone puts the Label screen into Edit mode.

3. **Tap the Delete icon to the left of the custom label you want to remove.** Your iPhone displays a Delete button to the right of the label.

4. **Tap Delete.** Your iPhone deletes the custom label.

5. **Tap Done.** Your iPhone exits Edit mode.

6. **Tap Cancel.** Your iPhone returns you to the Info screen.

Adding extra fields to a contact

The New Contact screen (which appears when you add a contact) and the Info screen (which appears when you edit an existing contact) display only the fields you need for basic contact info. However, these screens lack quite a few common fields. For example, you might need to specify a contact's prefix (such as Dr. or Professor), suffix (such as Jr., Sr., or III), or job title.

Thankfully, your iPhone is merely hiding these and other useful fields. There are 15 hidden fields that you can add to any contact (see Figure 9.6):

- Prefix
- Phonetic First Name
- Phonetic Last Name
- Middle
- Suffix

- Nickname
- Job Title
- Department
- Twitter
- Profile
- Instant Message
- Birthday
- Date
- Related People
- Notes

The iPhone is only too happy to let you add as many of these extra fields as you want. Here are the steps involved:

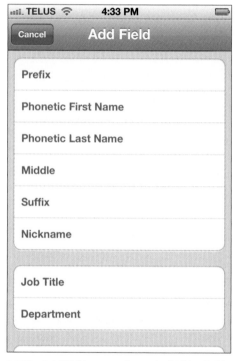

1. **With the contact's data open for editing, tap Add Field.** The Add Field screen appears, as shown in Figure 9.6.

2. **Tap the field that you want to add.** Your iPhone adds the field to the contact's data.

3. **Type the field data.**

4. **Tap Done.** Your iPhone saves the new info.

9.6 The Add Field screen shows the hidden fields that you can add to any contact.

Keeping track of birthdays and anniversaries

Do you have trouble remembering birthdays? If so, then I feel your pain because I, too, used to be pathetically bad at keeping birthdays straight — and it's no wonder. These days, you not only have to keep track of birthdays for your family and friends, but you also increasingly have to remember birthdays for staff, colleagues, and clients, as well. It's too much! My secret is that I simply gave up and outsourced the job to my iPhone Contacts app, which has a hidden field that you can use to store birth dates.

To add the Birthday field to a contact, follow these steps:

1. **With the contact's data open for editing, tap Add Field.** Your iPhone opens the Add Field screen.

2. **Tap Birthday.** The Contacts app adds the birthday field to the contact's data and its nifty scroll wheels appear, as shown in Figure 9.7.

3. **Scroll the left wheel to set the month for the birth date.**

4. **Scroll the middle wheel to set the day of the month for the birth date.**

5. **Scroll the right wheel to set the year for the birth date.**

6. **Tap Done.** Your iPhone saves the birthday info and displays it on the contact's Info screen.

9.7 Use the fun scroll wheels to set a contact's birth date or anniversary.

Everyone has a birthday, naturally, but lots of people have anniversaries, too. It could be a wedding date, a quit-smoking date, or the date that someone started working at the company. Whatever the occasion, you can add it to the contact info so that it's staring you in the face as a friendly reminder each time you open that contact.

Follow these steps to include an anniversary with a contact:

1. **With the contact's data open for editing, tap Add Field.** The Add Field screen appears.

2. **Tap Date.** The Contacts app adds an anniversary field to the contact and displays the scroll wheels, as shown previously in Figure 9.7.

3. **Scroll the left wheel to set the month for the anniversary.**

4. **Scroll the middle wheel to set the day of the month for the anniversary.**

5. **Scroll the right wheel to set the year for the anniversary.**

6. **The label box should already show the anniversary label, but if not, tap the label box, and then tap anniversary.**

7. **Tap Done.** The iPhone saves the anniversary and displays it on the contact's Info screen.

Note

Although you can only add one birthday to a contact (not surprisingly), you are free to add multiple anniversaries. Open the contact's data for editing and tap the empty Date field that appears below the most recent date you entered.

Creating a new contact from an electronic business card

Entering a person's contact data by hand is a tedious bit of business at the best of times, so it helps if you can find a faster way to do it. If you can cajole a contact into sending his contact data electronically, then you can add it with just a couple of taps. What do I mean when I talk about sending contact data electronically? Long ago, the world's contact-management gurus came up with a standard file format for contact data — the vCard. It's a kind of digital business card that exists as a separate file. People can pass this data along by attaching their (or someone else's) card to an e-mail message.

If you get a message with contact data, you see an icon for the VCF file, as shown in Figure 9.8.

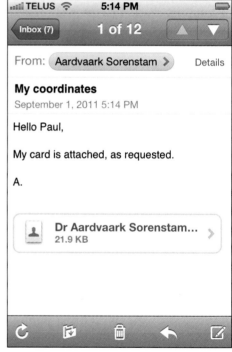

9.8 If your iPhone receives an e-mail message with an attached vCard, an icon for the file appears in the message body.

To get this data into your Contacts app, follow these steps:

1. **In the Home screen, tap Mail to open the Mail app.**

2. **Tap the message that contains the vCard attachment.**

3. **Tap the icon for the vCard file.** Your iPhone opens the vCard.

4. **Tap Create New Contact.** If the person is already in your Contacts app, but the vCard contains new data, tap Add to Existing Contact and then tap the contact.

Managing contacts with Siri voice commands

If you have an iPhone 4S, the Siri voice recognition app enables you to locate and query your contacts using simple voice commands. To get started, tap and hold the Home button (or press and hold the Mic button of the iPhone headphones, or the equivalent button on a Bluetooth headset) until Siri appears.

To display one or more contacts, use the following techniques within Siri:

- **Displaying a specific contact.** Say "Show (or Display or Find) *first last*," where *first* and *last* are the person's first and last names as given in the Contacts list; you can also just say the person's name. If the contact is a business, say "Show (or Display or Find) *company*," where *company* is the business name as given in your Contacts list; you can also just say the company name.

- **Displaying a contact who has a relationship with you.** Say "Show (or Display or Find) *relationship*," where *relationship* is the connection you've defined (such as sister or father).

- **Displaying a contact with a unique first name.** Say "Show (or Display or Find) *first*," where *first* is the person's first name as given in your Contacts list.

- **Displaying multiple contacts who have some information in common.** Say "Find people *criteria*," where *criteria* defines the common data. Examples: "Find people named Stevens" or "Find people who live in New York."

To query your contacts, you use the following general syntax:

Question contact info?

Here, *question* can be "What is" (for general data), "When is" (for dates), or "Who is" (for people); *contact* specifies the name (or relationship) of the contact; and *info* specifies the type of data you want to retrieve (such as "birthday" or "home phone number"). Here are some examples:

- "What is Paul Sellar's mobile phone number?"
- "When is my sister's anniversary?"
- "What is David Cutrere's address?"
- "Who is Kyra's husband?"

Tracking Your Appointments

When you meet someone and ask, "How are you?" the most common reply these days is a short one: "Busy!" We're all as busy as can be these days, and that places-to-go, people-to-see feeling is everywhere. All the more reason to keep your affairs in order, and that includes your appointments. Your iPhone comes with a Calendar app that you can use to create items called *events*, which represent your appointments, vacations, trips, meetings, and anything else that can be scheduled. Calendar acts as a kind of electronic personal assistant, leaving your brain free to concentrate on more important things.

Adding an event to your calendar

I showed you how to sync your computer's calendar application (such as iCal on the Mac, or the Outlook Calendar folder) in Chapter 6, and that's the easiest way to fill your iPhone with your events. However, something always comes up when you're running around, so you need to know how to add an event directly to your iPhone Calendar.

Here are the steps to follow:

1. **In the Home screen, tap the Calendar icon.** The Calendar app appears.

2. **Tap Month and then tap the date on which the event occurs.** If the event happens in a different month, use the arrow keys (to the right and left of the month and year) to navigate to the month you want.

3. **Tap the + button at the top-right corner of the screen.** The Add Event screen appears, as shown in Figure 9.9.

4. **The cursor starts off in the Title box, so enter a title for the event.**

5. **Tap the Location box and type the location of the event.**

6. **Tap the Starts/Ends/Time Zone box.** The Start & End screen appears, as shown in Figure 9.10.

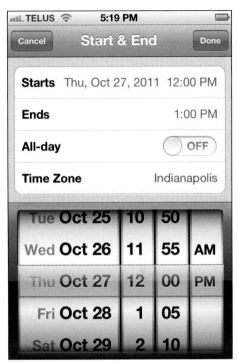

9.9 Use the Add Event screen to create your event.

9.10 Use the Start & End screen to set your event times.

7. **Tap Starts and then use the scroll wheels to set the date and time that your event begins.**

8. **Tap Ends and then use the scroll wheels to set the date and time that your event finishes.**

9. **Tap Done.** The Calendar app saves your info and returns you to the Add Event screen.

10. **If you have multiple calendars, tap Calendar, and then tap the one in which you want this event to appear.**

11. **Tap Done.** The Calendar app saves your info and returns you to the Add Event screen.

12. **Tap Done.** The Calendar app adds the event to the calendar.

When you add an event, Calendar displays a dot underneath the day as a visual reminder that you have something going on that day. Tap the day, and Calendar displays a list of all the events you have scheduled, as shown in Figure 9.11. If you have multiple calendars and you want to see all your events, tap Calendars and then tap All to open the All Calendars screen.

If you want to see the duration of each event, tap the date and then tap Day. Calendar switches to Day view and shows your events as blocks, as you can see in Figure 9.12.

9.11 Tap a date in Calendar to see all the events you have scheduled on that day.

9.12 Tap Day to switch to Day view and see your events as blocks of time.

Editing an existing event

Whether you've scheduled an event by hand or synced it from your computer, the event details might change: a new time, a new location, and so on. Whatever the change, you need to edit the event to keep your schedule accurate.

Here are the steps to follow to edit an existing event:

1. **In the Home screen, tap the Calendar icon.** The Calendar app appears.

2. **Tap the date that contains the event you want to edit.**

3. **Tap the event.** You can do this in either Month or Day view. Calendar displays the event info.

4. **Tap Edit.** Your iPhone displays the event data in the Edit screen.

5. **Make your changes to the event.**

6. **Tap Done.** Your iPhone saves your changes and returns you to the event details.

Setting up a repeating event

One of the truly great timesavers in Calendar is the repeat feature. It enables you to set up a single event and then get Calendar to automatically repeat it at a regular interval. For example, if you set up an event for a Friday, you can also set Calendar to automatically repeat it every Friday. You can continue repeating events indefinitely or end them on a specific date.

Follow these steps to configure an existing event to repeat:

1. **In Calendar, tap the date that contains the event you want to edit.**

2. **Tap the event.** Calendar opens the event info.

3. **Tap Edit.** Calendar displays the event data in the Edit screen.

4. **Tap Repeat.** The Repeat screen appears, as shown in Figure 9.13.

5. **Tap the repeat interval you want to use.**

6. **Tap Done to return to the Edit screen.**

7. **Tap End Repeat.** The End Repeat screen appears, as shown in Figure 9.14.

8. **You have two choices here:**

9.13 Use the Repeat screen to decide how often you want your event to recur.

- **Set the event to stop repeating on a particular day.** Use the scroll wheels to set the day, month, and year that you want the final event to occur. Then, tap Done to return to the Edit screen.

- **Set the event to repeat indefinitely.** Tap Repeat Forever. Calendar returns you to the Edit screen.

9. **Tap Done.** Calendar saves the repeat data and returns you to the event details.

9.14 Use the End Repeat screen to decide how long you want the event to repeat.

Converting an event to an all-day event

Some events don't really have specific times that you can pin down. These include birthdays, anniversaries, sales meetings, trade shows, conferences, and vacations. What all these types of events have in common is that they last all day: in the case of birthdays and anniversaries, literally so; in the case of trade shows and the like, "all day" refers to the entire workday.

Why is this important? Well, suppose you schedule a trade show as a regular event that lasts from 9 a.m. to 5 p.m. When you examine that day in Calendar, you see a big fat block that covers the entire day. If you also want to schedule meetings that occur at the trade show, Calendar lets you do that, but it displays these new events on top of the existing trade show event. This makes the schedule hard to read, so you might miss a meeting.

To solve this problem, you can configure the trade show as an all-day event. Calendar clears it from the regular schedule and displays the event separately near the top of the Day view. Here are the steps to follow:

1. **In Calendar, tap the date that contains the event you want to edit.**

2. **Tap the event.** Calendar opens the event info.

3. **Tap Edit.** Calendar switches to the Edit screen.

4. **Tap Starts/Ends.** The Start & End screen appears.

5. **Tap the All-day switch to On.**

6. **Tap Done to return to the Edit screen.**

7. **Tap Done.** Calendar saves the event and returns you to the event details.

Figure 9.15 shows Calendar in Day view with an all-day event added.

Adding an alert to an event

One of the truly useful secrets of stress-free productivity in the modern world is what I call the set-it-and-forget-it school of scheduling. That is, you set up an event electronically and then get the same technology to remind you when the event occurs. That way, your mind doesn't have to waste energy fretting about missing the event because you know your technology has your back.

9.15 All-day events appear in the all-day section near the top of the Day view screen.

Caution
If you flick the Ring/Silent switch on the side of the iPhone to the Silent setting, remember that you won't hear the Calendar alert chirps. When the alert runs, your iPhone still vibrates and you still see the alert message on-screen.

With your iPhone, the technology of choice for doing this is Calendar and its alert feature. When you add an alert to an event, Calendar automatically displays a reminder of the event, which is a Notification Center banner that pops up on the screen. Your iPhone also vibrates and sounds a few beeps to get your attention. You can choose when the alert triggers (such as a specified number of minutes, hours, or days before the event), and you can even set up a second alert just to be on the safe side.

Follow these steps to set an alert for an event:

1. **In Calendar, tap the date that contains the event you want to edit.**

2. **Tap the event.** Calendar opens the event info.

3. **Tap Edit.** Calendar displays the event data in the Edit screen.

4. **Tap Alert.** The Event Alert screen appears, as shown in Figure 9.16.

5. **Tap the number of minutes, hours, or days before the event you want to see the alert.** If you're editing an all-day event, you can set the alert at 9 a.m. on the day of the event or one day before, two days before, or a week before the event.

243

Genius   You can disable the alert chirps if you find them annoying. On the Home screen, tap Settings, tap Sounds, tap the Calendar Alerts, and then tap None.

6. **Tap Done to return to the Edit screen.**

7. **To set up a backup alert, tap Second Alert.** Tap the number of minutes, hours, or days before the event you want to see the second alert, and then tap Done.

8. **Tap Done.** Calendar saves your alert choices and returns you to the event details.

Figure 9.17 shows an example of a banner alert. The alert closes by itself after a few seconds, but before that you can tap the alert to see the details.

Setting a birthday or anniversary alert

If someone you know has a birthday coming up, you certainly don't want to forget. As I covered earlier in this chapter, you can use the Contacts app to add a Birthday field for someone. This works great if you actually look at the contact. If you don't, though, you're toast. The best way to remember is to get your iPhone to do the remembering for you.

Follow these steps to set up an alert about a birthday (or anniversary, or some other important date):

1. **In Calendar, tap the date on which the birthday occurs.**

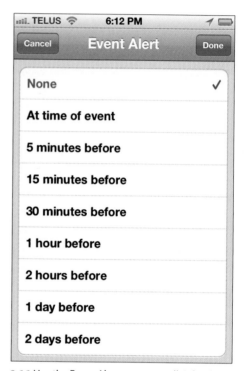

9.16 Use the Event Alert screen to tell Calendar when to remind you about your event.

9.17 Your iPhone displays an alert similar to this to remind you of an upcoming event.

2. **Tap the + button at the top-right corner of the screen.** The Add Event screen appears.

3. **Tap the Title box and type a title for the event ("Karen's Birthday," for example).**

4. **Tap Starts/Ends/Time Zone, tap the All-day switch to On, use the scroll wheels to choose the birthday, and then tap Done.**

5. **Tap Repeat, tap Every Year, and then tap Done.**

6. **Tap Alert, tap the On date of event option, and then tap Done.**

7. **Tap Second Alert, tap the 2 days before option, and then tap Done.** This gives you a couple of days' notice so you can go out and shop for a card and a present!

8. **Tap Done.** Calendar saves the event and you have another load off your mind.

Controlling events with Siri voice commands

On the iPhone 4S, the Siri personal assistant offers a number of voice commands for creating, editing, and querying your events.

To tell Siri to schedule an event, you use the following general syntax:

Schedule what with *who* at *when*.

Here, *schedule* can be any of the following:

- "Schedule"
- "Meet"
- "Set up a meeting"
- "New appointment"

The *what* part of the command (which is optional) determines the topic of the event, so it could be something like "lunch" or "budget review" or "dentist"; you can also precede this part with "about" (for example, "about expenses"). The *who* part of the command specifies the person you're meeting with, if anyone, so it can be a contact name or a relationship (such as "my husband" or "Dad"). The *when* part of the command sets the time and date of the event; the time portion can be a specific time such as "3" (meaning 3 p.m.) or "8 a.m.," or "noon"; the date portion can be "today" or "tomorrow," a day in the current week (such as "Tuesday" or "Friday"), a relative day (such as "next Monday"), or a specific date (such as "August 23rd").

Here are some examples:

- "Schedule lunch with Karen tomorrow at noon."
- "Meet with my sister Friday at 4."
- "Set up a meeting about budgeting next Tuesday at 10 a.m."
- "New appointment with Sarah Currid on March 15 at 2:30."

You can also use Siri to modify existing events. For example, you can change the event time by using the verbs "Reschedule" or "Move":

- "Reschedule my meeting with Sarah Currid to 3:30."
- "Move my noon appointment to 1:30."

You can also use the verb "Add" to include another person in a meeting, and the verb "Cancel" to remove a meeting from your schedule:

- "Add Charles Aster to the budgeting meeting."
- "Cancel my lunch with Karen."

Finally, you can query your events to see what's coming up. Here are some examples:

- "When is my next appointment?"
- "When is my meeting with Sarah Currid?"
- "What is on my calendar tomorrow?"
- "What does the rest of my day look like?"

Displaying a list of your upcoming events

The Month view in Calendar indicates dates that have scheduled events by displaying a teensy dot under the day number. So now you know you have something scheduled on those days, but the dots don't convey any more information than that. To see the scheduled events, you have to tap each day. Way too much work! A better way is to have Calendar do the work for you by displaying a list of what's scheduled over the next few days. Here's how:

1. **In the Home screen, tap the Calendar icon.** The Calendar screen displays.
2. **Tap the List button.** Calendar displays a list of your upcoming events, as shown in Figure 9.18. Tap an event to see its details.

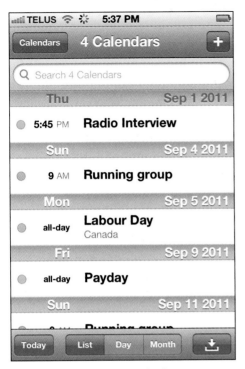

Handling Microsoft Exchange meeting requests

If you've set up a Microsoft Exchange account in your iPhone, there's a good chance you're already using its push features. That is, the Exchange Server automatically sends incoming e-mail messages to your iPhone, as well as new and changed contacts and calendar data. If someone back at headquarters adds your name to a scheduled meeting, Exchange generates an automatic meeting request, which is an e-mail message that tells you about the meeting and asks if you want to attend.

9.18 Tap the List button in Calendar to see what's ahead on your schedule.

Note

If you don't see the Inbox tray icon, then you need to turn on syncing for your Exchange calendar. I show you how to do this in Chapter 5.

How will you know? Tap Calendar in the Home screen and then examine the bottom-right corner of the screen. The menu bar icon that looks like an Inbox tray will have a red dot with a number inside telling you how many meeting requests you have waiting for you, as shown in Figure 9.19.

It's best to handle such requests as soon as you can, so here's what you do:

1. **Tap the Inbox-like icon in the bottom-right corner of the screen.** Calendar displays your pending meeting requests.

2. **Tap the meeting request to which you want to respond.** Calendar displays the meeting details, as shown in Figure 9.20.

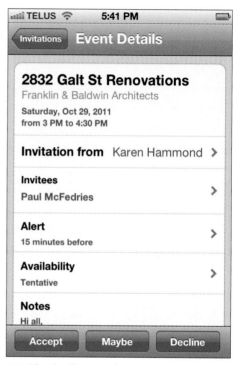

9.19 The meeting requests icon in Calendar shows you how many Exchange meeting requests you have.

9.20 The details screen for an Exchange meeting request.

Note Meeting requests show up as events in your calendar and you can recognize them thanks to their gray background. Another way to open the meeting details is to tap the meeting request in your calendar.

3. **Tap your response:**

- **Accept.** Tap this button to confirm that you can attend the meeting.
- **Maybe.** Tap this button if you're not sure and will decide later.
- **Decline.** Tap this button to confirm that you can't attend the meeting.

Subscribing to a calendar

If you know someone who has published a calendar, you might want to keep track of it within your iPhone Calendar app. You can do that by subscribing to the published calendar. iPhone sets up the published calendar as a separate item in the Calendar app, so you can easily switch between your own calendars and the published calendar.

To pull this off, you need to know the address of the published calendar. This address usually takes the following form: *server*.com/*calendar*.ics. Here, *server*.com is the address of the calendar server and *calendar*.ics is the name of the iCalendar file (almost always preceded by a folder location).

For calendars published to iCloud, the address always looks like this: ical.icloud.com/*member*/*calendar*.ics. Here, *member* is the iCloud member name of the person who published the calendar and *calendar* is the name of the file. Here's an example address:

ical.icloud.com/aardvarksorenstam/aardvark.ics

Follow these steps to subscribe to a published calendar:

1. **On the Home screen, tap Settings.** The Settings app appears.

2. **Tap Mail, Contacts, Calendars.** The Mail, Contacts, Calendars screen appears.

3. **Tap Add Account.** The Add Account screen appears.

4. **Tap Other.** Your iPhone displays the Other screen.

5. **Tap Add Subscribed Calendar.** You see the Subscription screen, as shown in Figure 9.21.

6. **Type the calendar address in the Server text box.**

7. **Tap Next.** Your iPhone connects to the calendar.

8. **Tap Save.** Your iPhone adds an account for the subscribed calendar.

To view the subscribed calendar, tap Calendar on the Home screen to open the Calendar app, and then click Calendars to open the Calendars screen. Your new calendar appears in the Subscribed section, as shown in Figure 9.22. Tap the calendar to view its events.

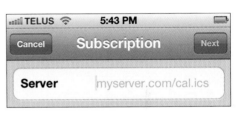

9.21 Use the Subscription screen to specify the address of the calendar to which you want to subscribe.

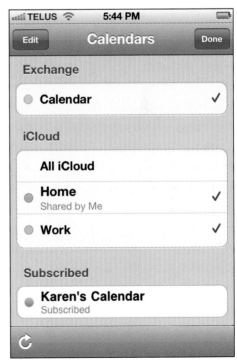

9.22 Your calendar subscriptions appear in the Subscribed section of the Calendars screen.

Creating Reminders

The Calendar app is an excellent tool for tracking appointments, meetings, and other events. By adding an alert to an event, you get a digital tap on the shoulder to remind you when and where your presence is required.

However, our days are littered with tasks that could be called subevents. These are things that need to be done at a certain point during your day, but don't rise to the level of full-fledged events: returning a call, taking the laundry out of the dryer, turning off the sprinkler. If you need to be reminded to perform such a subevent, it seems like overkill to crank out an event using the Calendar app.

Fortunately, iOS 5 offers a better solution: the Reminders app. You use this app to create *reminders*, which are simple nudges that tell you to do something, to be somewhere, or whatever. These nudges come in the form of Notification Center banners that appear on your screen at a time you specify or when your iPhone reaches a particular location. If you have an iCloud account, you can sync your reminders between your iPhone, your Mac, your iPad, and any other supported device.

Setting a reminder for a specific time

Here are the steps to follow to set up a reminder that alerts you at a specific time:

1. **On the iPhone Home screen, tap Reminders.** The Reminders app appears.

2. **Flick right or left to choose the list you want to use to store the reminder.**

3. **Tap the plus sign (+) in the upper-right corner of the screen.** The Reminders app creates a new reminder.

4. **Type the reminder text and then tap Done.**

5. **Tap the reminder.** The Details screen appears.

6. **Tap Remind Me.** The Remind Me screen appears.

7. **Tap the On a Day switch to On.**

8. **Tap the date that appears, and then use the scroll wheels to set the date and time of the reminder.**

9. **Tap Done.**

10. **Tap Show More to expand the Details dialog, as shown in Figure 9.23.**

11. **Use the Repeat setting to set up a repeat interval for the reminder.**

12. **Use the Priority setting to assign a priority to the reminder: None, Low, Medium, or High.**

13. **Use the Notes text box to add some background text or other information about the reminder.**

14. **Tap Done.**

Setting a reminder for a specific location

Getting an alert at a specific time is the standard way of working with reminders, but the Reminders app supports a second type of criterion: location. That is, when you specify a particular location for a reminder, the app sets up a *geo-fence* — a kind of virtual border — around that location. When your iPhone crosses that geo-fence, the associated reminder appears on your screen. So, for example, if you're on your way to a meeting with a client, you could create a reminder that includes notes about the meeting or the client, and then specify the meeting location as the Remind Me criterion.

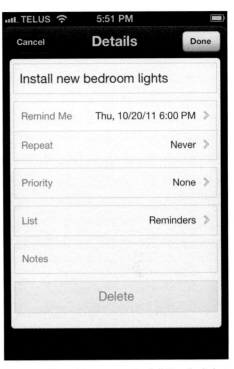

9.23 Tap Show More to see the full Details dialog options.

Here's how it works:

1. **On the iPhone Home screen, tap Reminders.** The Reminders app appears.

2. **Flick right or left to select the list you want to use to store the reminder.**

3. **Tap the plus sign (+) in the upper-right corner of the screen.** The Reminders app creates a new reminder.

4. **Type the reminder text and then tap Done.**

5. **Tap the reminder.** The Details dialog appears.

6. **Tap Remind Me.** The Remind Me dialog appears.

7. **Tap the At a Location switch to On.** If your iPhone asks whether the Reminders app can use your location, tap OK.

251

8. **To choose a location other than your current address, tap Current Location, tap Choose Address, and then specify the location you want to use.**

9. **To have the reminder appear when your iPhone first comes within range of the location, tap When I Arrive.** If you prefer to see the reminder when your iPhone goes out of range of the location, tap When I Leave instead.

10. **Follow Steps 10 to 14 from the previous section to fill in the reminder details.**

Setting reminders with Siri voice commands

iPhone 4S users can also create reminders via voice using the new Siri app. Time-based reminders use the following general syntax:

Remind me to *action* at *when*.

Here, *action* is the task you want to be reminded to perform, and *when* is the date and time you want to be reminded (as described earlier in the chapter when I discussed creating calendar events using Siri). Here are some examples:

- "Remind me to call my wife at 5."
- "Remind me to pick up Greg at the airport tomorrow at noon."
- "Remind me to bring lunch."

Location-based reminders use the following general syntax:

Remind me to *action* when I *location*.

Again, *action* is the task you want to be reminded to perform; *location* is the place around which you want the geo-fence set up (including either "get to" or "leave," depending on whether you want to be reminded coming or going). Some examples:

- "Remind me to pick up milk when I leave here."
- "Remind me to call my husband when I get to La Guardia airport."
- "Remind me to call my sister when I get home."
- "Remind me to grab my sample case when I arrive at Acme Limited."

For the last of these, you can assume that "Acme Limited" is a company name defined (with an address) in your Contacts list.

How Do I Use My iPhone to Navigate My World?

Dedicated GPS devices have become gasp-inducingly popular over the past few years because it's not easy finding your way around in a strange city or an unfamiliar part of town. The old way — deciphering hastily scribbled directions or scratching your head over a possibly out-of-date map — was just too hard and error prone, so having a device tell you where to go (so to speak) was a no-brainer. However, dedicated devices, whether they're music players, eBook readers, or GPS receivers, are going the way of the dodo. They're being replaced by multifunction devices that can play music, read books, and display maps. In this chapter, you take advantage of the multi-function prowess of your iPhone to learn about the amazingly useful Maps app and the almost too-cool Compass app.

and B, the questions often come thick and fast: "Where am I now?" "Which turn do I take?" "What's the traffic like on the highway?" "Can I even get there from here?" Fortunately, the answers to those and similar questions are now just a few finger taps away. That's because your iPhone comes loaded not only with a way-cool Maps app (brought to you by the good folks at Google) but also a GPS receiver. Now your iPhone knows exactly where it is (and so, by extension, do you) and it can help you get where you want to go.

To get the Maps app on the job, tap the Maps icon in the iPhone Home screen. Figure 10.1 shows the Maps screen.

Viewing your destination

When you want to locate a destination using Maps, the most straightforward method is to search for it:

1. **Tap inside the Search box at the top of the screen.**

2. **Type the name, address, or a keyword or phrase that describes your destination.**

3. **In the on-screen keyboard, tap Search.** The Maps app locates the destination, moves the map to that area, and drops a pin on the destination, as shown in Figure 10.2.

10.1 Use the iPhone Maps app to navigate your world.

Now that you have your destination pin-pointed (literally), you can read the map to find your way by looking for street names, local landmarks, nearby major intersections, and so on. (You also can use the Maps app to get specific directions; I show you how that works later in this chapter.) However, it's always hard to transfer the abstractions of a map to the real-world vista you see outside your car window (or whatever) when you're close to the destination.

Fortunately, Maps can bridge that gap. If Google Street View is available in that area, you see a red icon on the left side of the destination pushpin. Tap that icon, and Maps immediately shows you the destination in all its Street View glory, as shown in Figure 10.3. To get your bearings, flick the screen left or right to get a full 360-degree view of the area surrounding your destination.

10.2 When you search for a destination, Maps displays a pin to mark its location on the map.

10.3 Tap the Google Street View icon to see a real-world representation of your destination.

Displaying your current location

When you arrive at an unfamiliar shopping mall and you need to get your bearings, your first instinct might be to seek out the nearest mall map and look for the inevitable *You are here* marker. This gives you a sense of your current location with respect to the rest of the mall, so locating Pottery Barn shouldn't be all that hard.

When you arrive at an unfamiliar part of town or a new city, have you ever wished you had something that could provide you with that same *You are here* reference point? If so, you're in luck because you have exactly that waiting for you right in your iPhone. Tap the Tracking icon in the Maps app menu bar, as pointed out in Figure 10.4. (If this is the first time you've used the Tracking icon, Maps asks for permission to use your current location, so be sure to tap OK.)

That's it! Your iPhone examines GPS coordinates, Wi-Fi hot spots, and nearby cellular towers to plot your current position. When it completes the necessary processing and triangulating, your iPhone displays a map of your current city, zooms in on your current area, and then adds a blue dot to the map to pinpoint your current location, as shown in Figure 10.4. Amazingly, if you happen to be in a car, taxi, or other moving vehicle, the blue dot moves in real time.

Tracking icon

10.4 Tap the Tracking icon to see your precise location as a blue dot on a map.

Genius

Knowing where you are is a good thing, but it's even better to know what's nearby. For example, suppose you're in a new city and you're dying for a cup of coffee. Tap Search in the menu bar, tap the Search box, type coffee (or perhaps café or espresso, depending on what you're looking for), and then tap Search. The Maps app drops a bunch of pins that correspond to nearby locations that match your search. Tap a pin to see the name, and tap the blue More Info icon to see the location's phone number, address, and website.

Displaying a map of a contact's location

In the old days (that is, a few years ago), if you had a contact located in an unfamiliar part of town or even in another city altogether, visiting that person required a phone call or e-mail asking for directions. You'd then write down the instructions, get written directions via e-mail, or perhaps even get a crudely drawn map faxed to you. Those days, fortunately, are long gone thanks to a myriad of online resources that can show you where a particular address is located and even give you driving directions to get there from here (wherever *here* may be).

Even better, your iPhone takes it one step further and integrates with Google Maps to generate a map of a contact's location based on the person's contact address. So as long as you've tapped in (or synced) a contact's physical address, you can see where he or she is located on the map.

To display a map of a contact's location, follow these steps:

1. **In the Home screen, tap the Contacts icon.** The Contacts app appears.

2. **Tap the contact you want to work with.** Your iPhone displays the contact's data.

3. **Tap the address you want to map.** Your iPhone switches to the Maps app and drops a pushpin on the contact's location.

Note   You can also display a map of a contact's location by using the Maps app. In the menu bar, tap the Bookmarks icon (it's on the right side of the Search box). Tap Contacts, and then tap the contact you want to map. The Maps app maps the contact's address.

Saving a location as a bookmark for easier access

If you know the address of the location you want to map, you can add a pushpin for that location by opening the Maps app and running a search on the address. That is, you tap Search in the menu bar, tap the Search box, type the address, and then tap the Search button.

That's no big deal for one-time-only searches, but what about a location you refer to frequently? Typing that address over and over gets old in a hurry, I assure you. You can save time and tapping by telling the Maps app to save that location on its Bookmarks list, which means you can access the location usually with just a few taps.

Follow these steps to add a location to the Maps app's Bookmarks list:

1. **Search for the location you want to save.** The Maps app marks the location with a pushpin and displays the name or address of the location in a banner above the pushpin.

2. **Tap the blue More Info icon in the banner.** The Maps app displays the Info screen with details about the location:

   - **If the location is in your Contacts list, you see the contact's data.**
   - **If the location is a business or institution, you see the address as well as other data such as the organization's phone number and web address.**
   - **For all other locations, you see just the address.**

3. **Tap Add to Bookmarks.** The Maps app displays the Add Bookmarks screen.

4. **Edit the name of the bookmark if you want to, and then tap Save.** The Maps app adds the location to the Bookmarks list.

To map a bookmarked location, follow these steps:

1. **Tap the Bookmark icon in the menu bar.** The Maps app opens the Bookmarks screen.

2. **Tap Bookmarks in the menu bar.** The Maps app displays your list of bookmarked locations, as shown in Figure 10.5.

3. **Tap the location you want to map.** The Maps app displays the appropriate map and adds a pushpin for the location.

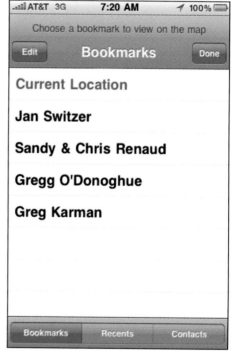

10.5 You can access frequently used locations with just a few taps by saving them as bookmarks.

Genius

The Bookmarks screen also comes with a Recents button in the menu bar. Tap this button to see your last few searches, locations entered, and driving directions requested. To get the Maps app to run any item again, just tap it.

Specifying a location when you don't know the exact address

Sometimes you have only a vague notion of where you want to go. In a new city, for example, you might decide to head downtown and then see if there are any good coffee shops or restaurants. That's fine, but how do you get downtown from your hotel in the suburbs? Your iPhone can give you directions, but it needs to know the endpoint of your journey, and that's precisely the information you don't have. Sounds like a conundrum, for sure, but there's a way to work around it. You can drop a pin on the map in the approximate area where you want to go. The Maps app can then give you directions to the dropped pin.

Here are the steps to follow to drop a pin on a map:

1. **In the Maps app, display a map of the city you want to work with:**

   - **If you're in the city now, tap the Tracking icon in the lower-left corner of the screen.**

   - **If you're not in the city, tap Search, tap the Search box, type the name of the city (and perhaps also the name of the state or province), and then tap the Search button.**

2. **Use finger flicks to pan the map to the approximate location you want to use as your destination.**

3. **Tap the Actions icon in the lower-right corner of the screen.** The Maps app displays a list of actions.

4. **Tap Drop Pin.** The Maps app drops a purple pin in the middle of the current map.

5. **Drag the purple pin to the location you want.** The Maps app creates a temporary bookmark called Dropped Pin that you can use when you ask the iPhone for directions (as described next).

Getting directions to a location

One possible navigation scenario with your iPhone Maps app is to specify a destination (using a contact, an address search, a dropped pin, or a bookmark) and then tap the Tracking icon. This gives you a map that shows both your destination and your current location. You can then eyeball the streets to see how to get from here to there. Depending on how far away the destination is, you may need to zoom out — by pinching the screen or by tapping the screen with two fingers — to see both locations on the map.

Eyeball the streets? Hah, how primitive! Your iPhone Maps app can bring you into the twenty-first century not only by showing you a route to the destination but also by providing you with the distance and time it should take and by giving you street-by-street, turn-by-turn instructions. It's one of the sweetest features of your iPhone, and it works like so:

1. **Use the Maps app to add a pushpin for your journey's destination.** Use whatever method works best for you: the Contacts list, an address search, a dropped pin, or a bookmark.

2. **Tap Directions in the menu bar.** The Maps app opens the Directions screen. As shown in Figure 10.6, you should see Current Location in the Start box and your destination address in the End box.

Swap icon ——

10.6 Use the Directions screen to specify the start and end points of your trip, and to swap them.

3. **If you want to use a starting point other than your current location, tap the Start box and then type the address of the location you want to use.**

4. **Tap Route.** The Maps app figures out the best route and then displays it on the map in the Overview screen, which also shows the trip distance and approximate time.

5. **Tap the icon for the type of directions you want: Car, Transit, or Walking.** The Maps app adjusts the route accordingly.

6. **Tap Start.** The Maps app displays the directions for the first leg of the journey.

7. **Tap the Next (right arrow) key.** You see the directions for the next leg of the journey. Repeat to see the directions for each leg. You can also tap the Previous (left arrow) key to go back.

Note Instead of seeing the directions one step at a time, you might prefer to see them all at once. Tap the Actions icon in the lower-right corner of the screen, and then tap List.

Showing alternate routes

When you map a journey to a location, the main route is shown on the map using a thick blue line, as shown in Figure 10.7. However, if you look carefully at the directions screen shown in Figure 10.7, you'll notice that (in this case) two other routes are shown using lighter blue lines. These routes are labeled Route 2 and Route 3; they're alternate routes suggested by the Maps app. So, for example, if you happen to know that Route 1 goes through a construction zone or is particularly busy at this time of day, tap an alternate route that avoids the congestion.

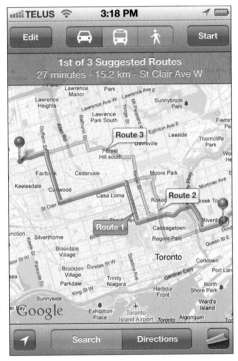

10.7 The iOS 5 version of Maps gives you multiple routes to your destination.

Getting live traffic information

Okay, it's pretty darn amazing that your iPhone can tell you precisely where you are and precisely how to get somewhere else. However, in most cities it's the getting somewhere else part that's the problem. Why? One word: traffic. The Maps app might tell you the trip should take ten minutes, but that could easily turn into a half hour or more if you run into a traffic jam.

That's life in the big city, right? Maybe not. If you're on a highway in a major U.S. city, the Maps app can most likely supply you with — wait for it — real-time traffic conditions! This is really an amazing tool that can help you avoid traffic messes and find alternative routes to your destination.

To see the traffic data, tap the Actions icon in the lower-right corner of the screen, and then tap Show Traffic. As you can see in Figure 10.8, the Maps app uses four colors to illustrate the traffic flow:

10.8 For most U.S. metropolitan highways, the color of the route tells you the current speed of traffic.

- **Green.** Routes where the traffic is moving at 50 miles per hour or faster.
- **Yellow.** Routes where the traffic is moving between 25 and 50 mph.
- **Red.** Routes where the traffic is moving at 25 mph or slower.
- **Gray.** Routes that currently have no traffic data.

Now you don't have to worry about finding a news radio station and waiting for the traffic report. You can get real-time traffic information whenever you need it.

Controlling Maps with Siri voice commands

If you have an iPhone 4S, you can use the Siri app to control Maps with straightforward voice commands. You can display a location, get directions, and even display traffic information. Tap and hold the Home button (or press and hold the Mic button of the iPhone headphones, or the equivalent button on a Bluetooth headset) until Siri appears.

To display a location in Maps via Siri, say "Show *location*" (or "Map *location*" or "Find *location*" or "Where is *location*"), where *location* is an address, name, or a Maps bookmark. Similarly, to get directions from Siri, say "Directions to *location*," where *location* is an address, name, or a Maps bookmark. To see the current traffic conditions, say "Traffic *location*," where *location* can be a specific place or someplace local, such as "around here" or "nearby." To get your current location, you can say "Where am I?" or "Show my current location."

Genius

Siri generally ignores extra terms you say that aren't relevant to the task at hand. So you can say something like "Give me directions to Hoover Dam" and Siri won't miss a beat. Also, the location you specify can be based on Contacts data; for example, you can say "Show my wife's work" or "Directions to my sister's home."

Configuring Location Services

On your iPhone, *location services* refers to the features and technologies that provide apps and system tools with access to location data. This is a handy thing, but it's also something that you need to keep under your control because your location data, particularly your current location, is fundamentally private and shouldn't be given out willy-nilly. Fortunately, your iPhone comes with a few tools for controlling and configuring location services.

Controlling app access to GPS

When you open an app that comes with a GPS component, the app displays a dialog like the one shown in Figure 10.9 to ask your permission to use the GPS hardware in your iPhone to determine your current location. Tap Don't Allow if you think that your current location is none of the app's business, or tap OK if that's just fine with you.

However, after you make your decision, you might change your mind. For example, if you deny your location to an app, that app might lack some crucial functionality. Similarly, if you allow an app to use your location, you might have second thoughts about compromising your privacy.

Whatever the reason, you can control an app's access to GPS by following these steps:

1. **In your iPhone Home screen, tap Settings.** The Settings app appears.
2. **Tap Location Services.** The Location Services screen appears, as shown in Figure 10.10.

10.9 When you first launch a GPS-aware app, it asks your permission to use your current location.

10.10 Use the Location Services screen to control which apps have access to your location.

3. **Configure app access to GPS as follows:**

- If you want to deny your current location to all apps, tap the Location Services switch to Off.

- If you want to deny your current location to specific apps, for each app tap the switch to Off.

Enabling or disabling system location services

Your iPhone also provides location services to various internal system services that perform tasks, such as calibrating the iPhone compass, setting the time zone, and serving up iAds that change depending on location data. If you don't want your iPhone providing any of these services, you can turn them off this way:

1. **On the Home screen, tap Settings.**
   The Settings app appears.

2. **Tap Location Services.** The Location Services screen appears.

3. **Tap System Services.** The Settings app displays the System Services screen, as shown in Figure 10.11.

4. **For any system service that you don't want to provide access to location data, tap its switch to Off.**

Sharing Map Data

If you want to show someone where you live, where you work, or where you want to meet, you could just send the address, but that's so last century. The more modern way is to send your friend a digital map that shows the location. With your iPhone this is a snap — you can send a map via e-mail or text message, or post a map on Twitter.

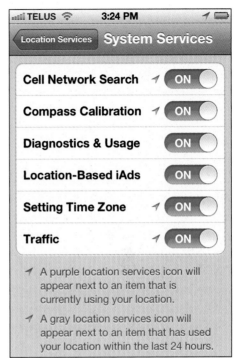

10.11 Use the System Services screen to control which system tools have access to your location.

Here are the steps to follow:

1. **Use the Maps app to add a pushpin for the location you want to send.** Use whatever method works best for you: the Contacts list, an address search, a dropped pin, or a bookmark. If you want to send your current location, display it and then tap the blue dot.

2. **Tap the blue More Info icon.** Maps displays the Info screen for the location.

3. **Tap Share Location.** Maps displays a list of ways to share the map.

4. **Tap the method you want to use to share the map: Email, Message, or Tweet.** The Maps app creates a new e-mail message, text message, or tweet that includes a Google Maps link to the location.

5. **Fill in the rest of your message or tweet, and send it.**

Getting Your Bearings with the Compass App

Your iPhone is loaded with fancy equipment, perhaps the most famous of which is the accelerometer, which enables the iPhone to sense when its orientation changes. (It's the accelerometer that makes so many of the iPhone games so addictive.) Your iPhone also comes with an internal gadget called a magnetometer, which is a device that measures the direction and intensity of a magnetic field. That sounds a bit esoteric, but having data about the magnetic field means that the iPhone can orient itself with respect to direction. It is, in short, a compass!

With the iPhone acting as a compass, you can do two things:

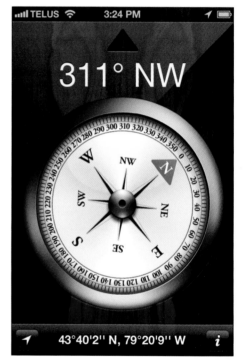

- **Orient a map.** In Maps, tap the Tracking icon to see your current location, and then tap the Tracking icon a second time. Your iPhone orients the map so that it matches the direction you're facing. Nice!

- **Get your bearings.** On the Home screen, tap the Utilities Folder, tap Compass, and, if your iPhone asks whether Compass can use your current location, tap OK. This launches the Compass app, which, as you can see in Figure 10.12, bears an uncanny resemblance to a real compass. Also like a real compass, the app always points north (true north or magnetic north — tap the *i* button in the bottom-right corner to choose which), so you always know which way you're going.

10.12 The Compass app uses the iPhone magnetometer to show you which way you're going.

How Do I Manage My eBook Library?

Physical books are an awesome invention: they're portable, easy to use, and fully showoffable, whether being read on the subway or sitting on a book-shelf at home. Physical books aren't going away anytime soon, but the age of electronic books — eBooks — is upon us. The Amazon Kindle lit a fire under the eBook category, but it's clunky to use and tied to Amazon. Apple filled in these gaps by offering iBooks, an app that's easy to use and supports an open eBook format. The iPhone screen is a bit on the small side, but the Retina display renders text sharply and clearly, so reading books on the iPhone isn't a chore. This chapter introduces you to eBooks on the iPhone.

Installing the iBooks App

In this chapter, I concentrate on iBooks, which is Apple's eReader app. However, it's important to stress right off the bat that you're not restricted to using iBooks for reading eBooks on your iPhone. Tons of great eBook apps are available (I mention a few of them at the end of this chapter; see the section on reading other eBooks on your iPhone), so feel free to use any or all of them in addition to (or even instead of) iBooks.

Unlike most of the other apps I talk about in this book, iBooks isn't part of the default iPhone app collection. Instead, you have to install it (it's free) from the App Store. When you first launch the App Store, it might ask if you want to download iBooks automatically. If so, go ahead and download it, and then feel free to skip the steps that follow. If not, or if you earlier chose not to download iBooks, then follow these steps to get the app onto your iPhone:

1. **On the Home screen, tap App Store.** Your iPhone opens the App Store.

2. **Tap Search to open the Search page.**

3. **Tap inside the Search box to display the keyboard, type iBooks, and then tap Search.** The search results appear.

4. **Tap the iBooks app.** The app's Info screen appears.

5. **Tap the Free icon.** The Free icon changes to the Install icon.

6. **Tap Install.** The App Store asks for your iTunes account password.

7. **Type your password, and tap OK.** The App Store downloads and installs the app, and an iBooks icon appears on the Home screen.

8. **When the installation is complete, tap the iBooks icon to launch the app.** iBooks asks if you want to sync your eBook bookmarks, notes, and collections with your iTunes account, as shown in Figure 11.1. Syncing is a good idea if you plan to use iBooks on other devices, such as an iPad or iPod touch.

9. **Tap Sync.** Tap Don't Sync if you don't need this functionality.

Getting Your Head around eBook Formats

11.1 When you first launch iBooks, the app asks if you want to sync your bookmarks, notes, and collections.

If there was one reason why eBooks took a long time to take off (in the same way that, say, digital music now rules the planet), it was because the eBook world started out as hopelessly, head-achingly confusing. At its worst, at least two dozen (yes, two *dozen!*) eBook formats were available, and new formats jumped on the eBook bandwagon with distressing frequency. That was bad enough, but it got worse when you considered that some of these formats required a specific eReading device or program. For example, the Kindle eBook format required either the Kindle eReader or the Kindle app; similarly, the Microsoft LIT format required the Microsoft Reader program. Finally, things turned positively chaotic when you realized that some formats came with built-in restrictions that prevented you from reading eBooks in other devices or programs or from sharing eBooks with other people.

What the eBook world needed was the simplicity and clarity that comes with having a near-universal eBook format (such as the MP3 format in music). Well I'm happy to report that one format has emerged from the fray: EPUB. This is a free and open eBook standard created by the International Digital Publishing Forum (IDPF; see www.idpf.org). EPUB files, which use the .epub extension, are supported by most eReader programs and by most eReader devices (with the Amazon Kindle being the very noticeable exception). EPUB is leading the way not only because it's free and non-proprietary, but also because it offers quite a few cool features:

- Text is resizable, so you can select the size that's most comfortable for you.

- The layout and formatting of the text are handled by Cascading Style Sheets (CSS), which is an open and well-known standard that makes it easy to alter the look of the text, including changing the font.

- Text is *reflowable,* which means that when you change the text size or the font, the text wraps naturally on the screen to accommodate the new character sizes (as opposed to some eBook formats that simply zoom in or out of the text).

- A single eBook can have alternative versions of the book in the same file.

- eBooks can include high-resolution images right on the page.

- Publishers can protect book content by adding *digital rights management* (DRM) support. DRM refers to any technology that restricts the usage of content to prevent piracy. Of course, depending on where you fall in the "information wants to be free" spectrum, DRM may not be cool and may not even be considered a feature.

So the first bit of good news is that the iBooks app supports the EPUB format, so all the features in the previous list are available in the iBooks app.

Note
For the record, I should also mention that you can use the iBooks app to read books in three other formats: plain text, HTML, and PDF.

The next bit of good news is that iBooks' support for EPUB means that a vast universe of public domain books is available to you. On its own, Google ebookstore (http://books.google.com/ebooks) offers over a *million* public domain eBooks. Several other excellent EPUB sites exist on the web, and I tell you about them (as well as how to get them onto your iPhone) a bit later in this chapter.

By definition, public domain eBooks are DRM-free, and you can use them in any way you see fit. However, lots of the EPUB books you'll find come with DRM restrictions. In the case of iBooks, the DRM scheme of choice is called FairPlay. This is the DRM technology that Apple used on iTunes for many years. Apple phased out DRM on music a while ago, but still uses it for other content, such as movies, TV shows, and audiobooks.

FairPlay means that many of the eBooks you download through iBooks face the following restrictions:

- You can access your books on a maximum of five computers, each of which must be authorized with your iTunes Store account info.
- You can read your eBooks only on your iPhone, iPad, iPod touch, or a computer that has iTunes installed.

It's crucial to note here two restrictions you'll trip over with DRM-encrusted eBooks:

- FairPlay eBooks do *not* work on other eReader devices that support the EPUB format, including the Sony Reader and the Barnes & Noble Nook.
- EPUB-format books that come wrapped in some other DRM scheme do not work on your iPhone.

However, remember that DRM is an optional add-on to the EPUB format. Although it's expected that most publishers will bolt FairPlay DRM onto books they sell in the iBookstore, it's not required, so you should be able to find DRM-free eBooks in the iBookstore (and elsewhere).

Note If you have an Amazon Kindle, I'm afraid it uses a proprietary eBook format, so Kindle eBooks won't transfer to the iBooks app (or any other eReader). However, Amazon does offer a Kindle app for the iPhone. You can use it to download and read any Kindle book, even those you purchased earlier.

Syncing eBooks via iCloud

If you purchase an eBook on your iPad or on your Mac or PC, getting that book onto your iPhone requires a lot of connecting and syncing, which seems a tad primitive in this modern age. However, if you have an iCloud account, you can configure it to automatically download any new eBook purchases directly to your iPhone, all without a cable or your computer's iTunes application in sight.

Here's how to set this up:

1. **On your iPhone, tap Settings in the Home screen.** The Settings app appears.
2. **Tap Store.**
3. **If you haven't signed in to the iTunes Store, tap Sign In and then enter your iCloud username and password.**

4. **Tap the Books switch to On, as shown in Figure 11.2.**

5. **If you want iCloud to sync eBooks even when you have a cellular-only connection, tap the Use Cellular Data switch to On.**

Now, each time you purchase an eBook via iTunes on another device, that book is sent automatically to the iBooks library on your iPhone, usually within a few seconds.

Managing Your iBooks Library

The iBooks app comes with a virtual wood bookcase, as shown in Figure 11.3. It's a nice bit of eye candy, for sure, but is certainly no more than that because the real point is to fill that bookcase with your favorite digital reading material. So your first task is to add a few titles to the bookcase, and the next few sections show you how to do just that.

11.2 In the Store settings, tap the Books switch to On to sync eBooks via iCloud.

11.3 The iBooks Bookshelf is designed to mimic a real bookcase.

Browsing books in the iBookstore

What if you're out and about with your iPhone, you've got a bit of time to kill, and you decide to start a book? That's no problem, because iBooks has a direct link to Apple's book marketplace, the iBookstore. Your iPhone can establish a wireless connection to the iBookstore anywhere you have Wi-Fi access or a cellular signal (ideally, at least 3G for faster downloads). You can browse and search the books, read reviews, and purchase any book you want (or grab a title from the large collection of free books). The eBook downloads to your iPhone and adds itself to the iBooks book-case. You can start reading within seconds!

What about the selection? When Apple announced the iPhone and the iBooks app, it also announced that five major publishers would be stocking the iBookstore: Hachette, HarperCollins, Macmillan, Penguin, and Simon & Schuster. Since then, a number of other publishers have been added, including Random House, the last of the major publishers to sign on. So, along with all those free eBooks, you can rest assured that the iBookstore has an impressive selection.

To access the iBookstore, follow these steps:

1. **Display the iBooks Bookshelf.**

   - **If you haven't loaded the app yet, tap the iBooks icon to open the iBooks app.**

   - **If you're in the iBooks app and reading a book, tap the screen to display the controls.** Then, tap Bookshelf.

2. **Tap the Store icon.**

As you can see in Figure 11.4, your iPhone organizes the iBookstore similar to the App Store. That is, you get five browse buttons in the menu bar: Featured, Charts, Browse, Search, and Purchased. You use these buttons to navigate the iBookstore.

Here's a summary of what each browse but-ton does for you:

11.4 Use the browse buttons in the iBookstore menu bar to locate and manage eBooks for your iPhone.

- **Featured.** Tap this button to display a list of books picked by the iBookstore editors. The list shows each book's cover, title, author, category, star rating, number of reviews, and price. Tap Categories to browse books by subject.

- **Charts.** Tap this button to see a collection of charts, including the Top Paid books and the Top Free books.

- **Browse.** Tap this button to browse through the bookstore using an alphabetical list of author names, also divided into the Top Paid and the Top Free lists. You can also tap Categories to browse the iBookstore by subject.

- **Search.** Tap this button to run a search on the iBookstore.

- **Purchased.** Tap this button to see a list of the books you've downloaded.

Note

Tap a book to get more detailed information about it. The Info screen that appears is divided into two sections. The top section shows standard book data, such as the title, author, cover, publisher, and number of pages; the bottom section gives you a description of the book, user ratings for the book, a list of related books, and a link to other books by the same author.

Adding a PDF attachment to your library

If you receive an e-mail with an attached PDF file, you can open the attachment right from the Mail app. However, the iBooks app now supports PDFs, so if you'd prefer to read the PDF in the friendly confines of iBooks (where you can search the PDF and bookmark your current location), you need to transfer it to your iBooks Library. Here's how it's done:

1. **In the Mail app, open the message that contains the PDF attachment.**

2. **Tap and hold the PDF attachment.** Mail displays a menu of commands.

3. **Tap Open in "iBooks".** Your iPhone opens the iBooks app and displays the PDF.

Working with collections

The latest version of iBooks now supports both eBooks and PDF documents. In a welcome burst of common sense, the iBooks programmers decided not to combine eBooks and PDFs on the same part of the Bookshelf. Instead, iBooks now supports separate Library sections called collections, and it comes with two default collections: one for eBooks (called Books) and one for PDF documents (called PDFs).

You can use the following techniques to work with your iBooks collections:

- **Switching to another collection.** Tap the name of the current collection at the top of the Bookshelf and then tap the name of the collection you want to use.

- **Creating a new collection.** Tap the name of the current collection at the top of the Bookshelf, tap New, type the name of your collection (such as Fiction or Nonfiction), and then tap Done.

- **Moving an item to a different collection.** Tap the Edit button, tap the item you want to move, and then tap the Move button. In the list of collections that appears, tap the collection you want to use as the item's new iBooks home.

- **Deleting a collection.** Tap the name of the current collection at the top of the Bookshelf and tap Edit. Next, tap the red Delete button beside the collection you want to remove and then tap Delete. If the collection isn't currently empty, tap Remove when iBooks asks you to confirm. For a nonempty collection, iBooks returns the items to their original locations (for example, eBooks to the Books collection).

Adding other EPUB eBooks to your library

With the ascendance of the EPUB format, publishers and book packagers are tripping over each other to make their titles EPUB friendly. As a result, the web is awash in EPUB books, so you don't have to get all the eBook content on your iPhone from the iBookstore. Here's a short list of some sites where you can download EPUB files to your computer:

- **BooksOnBoard: www.booksonboard.com.** This site offers a variety of eBooks, although most aren't compatible with iBooks, thanks to DRM. To find non-DRM titles, go to the Advanced Search page and select the Adobe EPUB check box.

- **epubBooks: www.epubbooks.com.** This is a terrific site for all things related to the EPUB format, and it offers a wide selection of public domain EPUB books.

- **eBooks.com: www.ebooks.com.** This site has a variety of books in various eBook formats, although most won't work in the iBooks app because most of the EPUB books use the DRM scheme from Adobe. However, you can go to the Search Options page and search for the "Unencrypted EPUB" file format to see the iBooks-friendly titles that are offered.

- **Feedbooks: www.feedbooks.com.** This site offers public domain titles in several formats, including EPUB.

- **Google ebookstore: http://books.google.com/ebooks.** This site offers more than a million public domain titles, many of which are free, plus lots of current releases that you can buy. However, note that as of this writing, the Google ebookstore is only available in the United States.

- **ManyBooks: http://manybooks.net.** This site offers a nice collection of free eBooks in a huge variety of formats. When you download a book, be sure to choose the EPUB (.epub) format in the Select Format drop-down list.

- **Smashwords: www.smashwords.com.** This intriguing site offers titles by independent and self-published authors. All eBooks are DRM free, and each book is available in the EPUB format.

- **Snee: www.snee.com/epubkidsbooks.** This site offers a lot of children's picture books in the EPUB format.

After you download an EPUB title to your computer, follow these steps to import the book into iTunes:

1. **In iTunes for the Mac, choose File ➪ Add to Library or press ⌘+O.** In iTunes for Windows, choose File ➪ Add File to Library or press Ctrl+O. The Add to Library dialog appears.

2. **Locate and click the EPUB file you downloaded.**

3. **In iTunes for the Mac, click Choose.** In iTunes for Windows, click Open. iTunes adds the eBook to the Books section of the library.

Editing the iBooks Bookshelf

When you add a book to the iBooks Bookshelf, the app clears a space for the new title on the left side of the top shelf of the bookcase. The rest of the books are shuffled to the right and down.

This is a sensible way to go about things if you read each book as you download it because it means the iBooks Bookshelf displays your books in the order you read them. Of course, life isn't always that orderly, and you might end up reading your eBooks more haphazardly. This means that the order in which the books appear in the Bookshelf won't reflect the order in which you read them.

Similarly, you may have one or more books in your iBooks Bookshelf that you refer to frequently for reference, or because you're reading them piecemeal (such as a book of poetry or a collection of short stories). In that case, it would be better to have such books near the top of the bookcase where they're slightly easier to find and open.

For these and similar Bookshelf maintenance chores, iBooks lets you shuffle the books around to get them into the order you prefer. Here's how it works:

1. **Display the iBooks Bookshelf.**

   - **If you haven't loaded the app yet, tap the iBooks icon to open the iBooks app.**

   - **If you're in the iBooks app and reading a book, tap the screen to display the controls and then tap Bookshelf.**

2. **Tap Edit.** iBooks opens the Bookshelf for editing, as shown in Figure 11.5.

3. **Tap and drag the book covers to the bookcase positions you prefer.**

4. **If you want to remove a book from your library, tap Edit, tap the book's cover, tap Delete, and then tap Delete when iBooks asks you to confirm.**

11.5 With the Bookshelf open for editing, you can move and remove books.

5. **Tap Done.** iBooks closes the Bookshelf for editing.

Creating a custom eBook cover

If you've obtained any free books from the iBookstore, or if you've downloaded public domain books to iTunes, you'll no doubt have noticed that many (or, really, most) of these books use generic covers. That's no big deal for a book or two, but it can get monotonous if you have many such books in your iBooks library (as well as making it hard to find the book you want). To work around this, you can create custom book covers from your own photos.

Your first task is to convert a photo (or any image) to something that's usable as a book cover. This involves loading the image into your favorite image-editing program and then doing three things:

- **Crop the image so that it's 420 pixels wide and 600 pixels tall.**

- **Use the text tool in the image-editing program to add the book title to the image.**

- **Save the image as a JPEG file.** If the image is already a JPEG, be sure to save it under a different name so you don't overwrite the original file.

Now you're ready to use the new image as a book cover, which you do by importing the cover image into iTunes on your computer:

1. **In iTunes, click the Books category.** iTunes displays your eBooks.

2. **Right-click the book you want to customize, and then click Get Info.** iTunes displays the book's Info dialog.

3. **Click the Artwork tab.** This tab includes a large box for the book cover image.

4. **Use Finder (on a Mac) or Explorer (on a Windows PC) to locate the new cover image.** On a Mac, you can also locate the image in iPhoto.

5. **Click the new image and drop it inside the large box in the Artwork tab.**

6. **Click OK.** iTunes applies the new image as the book's cover.

Reading eBooks with the iBooks App

If you're a book lover like me and you have your iBooks Bookshelf groaning under the weight of all your eBooks, you may want to spend some time just looking at all the covers. Or not. If it's the latter, then it's time to get some reading done. The next few sections show you how to control eBooks and modify the display for the best reading experience.

Controlling eBooks on the reading screen

When you're ready to start reading a book using iBooks, getting started couldn't be simpler:

1. **Display the iBooks Bookshelf.**

   - **If you haven't loaded the app yet, tap the iBooks icon to open the iBooks app.**

   - **If you're in the iBooks app and reading a book, tap the screen to display the controls and then tap Library.**

2. **Tap the book you want to read.** iBooks opens it.

Here's a list of techniques you can use to control an eBook while reading it:

- To flip to the next page, tap the right side of the screen.

- To flip to the previous page, tap the left side of the screen.

- To "manually" turn a page, flick the page with your finger. Flick left to turn to the next page; flick right to turn to the previous page.

- To access the iBooks controls, tap the middle of the screen. To hide the controls, tap the middle of the screen again.

- To access the book's Table of Contents, display the controls and tap the Contents icon, pointed out in Figure 11.6. You can then tap an item in the Table of Contents to jump to that section of the book.

- To go to a different page in the book, display the controls and tap a dot at the bottom of the screen.

- To search the book, display the controls and tap the Search icon in the upper-right corner. Type your search text and tap Search. In the search results that appear, tap a result to display that part of the book.

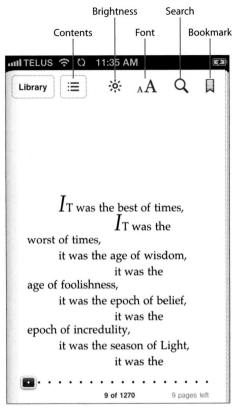

11.6 Tap the middle of the screen to display the controls.

- To return to the iBooks Bookshelf, display the controls and tap Library in the upper-left corner.

Formatting eBook text

I mentioned near the top of the show that the EPUB format supports multiple text sizes and multiple fonts, and that the text reflows seamlessly to accommodate the new text size. The iBooks app takes advantage of these EPUB features, as shown here:

1. **While reading an eBook, tap the middle of the screen to display the controls.**

2. **Tap the Font icon, pointed out earlier in Figure 11.6.** iBooks displays the Font options, as shown in Figure 11.7.

3. **Tap the larger "A" to increase the text size.** Tap the smaller "A" to reduce the size.

4. **Tap Fonts.** iBooks displays a list of fonts.

5. **Tap the font you want to use.** iBooks reformats the eBook for the new font.

6. **If you want to read with a sepia-colored background, tap the Sepia switch to On.**

7. **Tap the middle of the screen to hide the controls.**

Adding a bookmark

Reading an eBook with the iBooks app is so pleasurable that you may not want to stop! However, you have to eat at some point, so when it's time to set your book aside, mark your spot with a bookmark:

1. **Display the page where you want to set your bookmark.**

2. **Tap the page.** iBooks displays its controls.

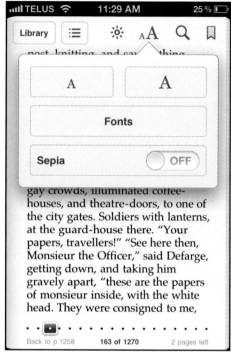

11.7 Tap the Font icon and then tap Fonts to see a list of those that are available.

3. **Tap the Bookmark icon, pointed out earlier in Figure 11.6.** iBooks saves your spot by creating a bookmark at the location you chose.

To return to your place, follow these steps:

1. **Tap the page.** iBooks displays the reading controls.

2. **Tap the Contents icon.** iBooks displays the table of contents.

3. **Tap the Bookmarks tab.** iBooks offers up a list of the saved bookmarks.

4. **Tap the bookmark.** iBooks returns you to the bookmarked page.

Looking up a word in the dictionary

While you peruse an eBook, you may come across an unfamiliar word. You can look it up using any of the umpteen online dictionaries, but there's no need for that with iBooks:

1. **Tap and hold the word that has you furrowing your brow.** iBooks displays a set of options.

2. **Tap Dictionary.** The first time you do this, iBooks tells you that it needs to download a dictionary.

3. **Tap Download.** iBooks loads the dictionary, looks up the word, and then displays its definition.

4. **Tap Done to close the definition.**

Highlighting text

If you come across a word, phrase, sentence, paragraph, or section of text that strikes your fancy, there's a good chance you'll want to return to that text later on. The easiest way to do that is to highlight the text. This not only makes the text stick out from the surrounding prose by displaying it with a yellow background, but iBooks also bookmarks it so you can quickly find it again. To do so, use the same steps described earlier for returning to a bookmark.

Follow these steps to highlight text with iBooks:

1. **Tap and hold a word in the text you want to highlight.** iBooks selects the word and displays a set of options. If the word is all you want to highlight, skip to Step 3.

2. **Use the selection controls to expand the selection to include all the text you want to highlight.**

3. **Tap Highlight.** iBooks adds a yellow background to the text and creates a bookmark for it (see Figure 11.8).

Genius

If the yellow highlight background doesn't do it for you, you can change the color. Tap the highlight, tap Colors, and then tap the color you prefer.

Adding a note

Sometimes when you're reading a book, you feel an irresistible urge to provide your own two cents' worth. With a paper book, you can grab the nearest writing implement and jot a margin note, but that's not going to work too well with an eBook. Fortunately, the iBooks programmers have taken pity on inveterate margin writers and provided a Note feature that lets you add your own comments and asides. Even better, iBooks also creates a bookmark for each note, so you can quickly find your additions.

Follow these steps to create a note with iBooks:

1. **Tap and hold a word in the text you want to comment on.** iBooks selects the word and displays a set of options. If the word is all you want to work with, skip to Step 3.

2. **Use the selection controls to expand the selection to include all the text you want to use.**

3. **Tap Note.** iBooks displays a text box that looks like a sticky note.

4. **Type your note.**

5. **Tap Done.** As shown in Figure 11.8, iBooks adds a yellow background to the text, displays a note icon in the margin, and bookmarks it.

> **TELUS** 11:46 AM
>
> Library
>
> of this day's disfig- urement—and I hear him tell the child my story, with a tender and a faltering voice. "It is a far, far better thing that I do, than I have ever done; it is a far, far better rest that I go to than I have ever known."
>
> Back to p.1268   **1257 of 1270**   Last page

11.8 You can highlight passages and add notes to your eBooks.

Reading Other eBooks

In this chapter, I focus on the iBooks app, mostly because it's an excellent app that's optimized for the iPhone and integrates seamlessly with iTunes. But the iPhone is arguably the best eReader available today, so it seems a shame to ignore the massive universe of eBooks that aren't iBooks-compatible. If you want to turn your iPhone into an ultimate eReader that's capable of reading practically *any* eBook in practically *any* format, then just head for the App Store and install the appropriate eReader apps.

A complete list of eReader apps would extend for pages, so I'll just hit the highlights here:

- **Barnes & Noble NOOK for iPhone.** If you don't have the NOOK (the Barnes & Noble eReading device), you can still read Barnes & Noble eBooks by installing the company's NOOK for iPhone app, which supports the EPUB format protected by the Adobe DRM scheme.

- **eReader.** This app supports the eReader format.

- **iSilo.** This app (which costs $9.99) supports the iSilo and Palm Doc formats.

- **Kindle.** The Amazon Kindle app is the way to go if you want to read Kindle eBooks on your iPhone.

- **Kobo.** This app is supplied by the same folks who make the Kobo eReader, and it supports both EPUB books and PDF documents.

- **Stanza.** This powerful app supports an amazing variety of eBook formats, including EPUB (protected by Adobe DRM), eReader, and Mobipocket.

Reading Magazines with Newsstand

Magazine publishers have been coming up with all kinds of innovative new tools and techniques that make reading a digital version of a magazine a more interactive and media-rich experience than reading the print version.

If there's a problem with iPhone-based magazines, it's that you have to manage a different app for each magazine, which gets clumsy once you have more than a half dozen or so magazine apps scattered around your Home screens. You can try plopping all your magazine apps into a single folder, but then it makes it hard to see the icon badges that tell you a new issue is available.

To solve these kinds of problems, iOS 5 introduces Newsstand, an app specifically designed to manage magazines. Newsstand is really a special folder, and when you tap it, you see a replica of a magazine shelf (see Figure 11.9). For magazine apps that know how to work with Newsstand, (in the App Store, open the Newsstand category) when you install such an app, it loads the most recent issue in the Newsstand, which lets you browse your available issues in a single spot. As I write this, a number of magazine publishers have signed on to support Newsstand, including Condé Nast (*Wired*, the *New Yorker*, *Vanity Fair*, and many more), National Geographic, Hearst, Bloomberg, and Disney. Newsstand also supports newspaper subscriptions, so expect to see the likes of the *New York Times* and other major newspapers.

11.9 Use the Newsstand app to organize your iPhone magazine subscriptions.

How Do I Keep My Life in Sync with iCloud?

Understanding iCloud

These days, the primary source of online chaos and confusion is the ongoing proliferation of services and sites that demand your time and attention. What started with web-based e-mail has grown to a website, a blog, a photo-sharing site, online bookmarks, and perhaps a few social networking sites, just to consume those last few precious moments of leisure time. You might be sitting in a chair, but you're getting run ragged anyway!

A great way to simplify your online life is to get a free iCloud account. You get a one-stop web shop that includes e-mail, an address book, a calendar, and 5GB of online file storage. (If you want more storage, you can get an extra 10GB for $20 a year, an extra 20GB for $40 a year, or an extra 50GB for $100 a year.)

The web applications that make up iCloud — Mail, Contacts, Calendar, Find My iPhone, and iWork — are certainly useful and are surprisingly functional for online applications. However, the big news with iCloud is the "cloud" part of the name. This means that your data, particularly your e-mail accounts, contacts, calendars, and bookmarks, is stored on a bunch of icloud.com networked servers that Apple collectively calls the cloud. When you sign in to your iCloud account at icloud.com, you use the web applications to interact with that data.

That's pretty mundane stuff, right? What's revolutionary here is that you can let the cloud know about all the other devices in your life: your Mac, your home computer, your work PC, your notebook, your iPad, and, of course, your iPhone. If you sign in to your iCloud account and, say, add a new appointment, the cloud takes that appointment and immediately sends the data to all your devices. Fire up your Mac, open iCal, and the appointment's there; switch to your Windows PC, click the Outlook Calendar folder, and the appointment's there; tap Calendar on your iPhone Home screen and, yup, the appointment's there, too.

This works if you change data on any of your devices. Move an e-mail message to another folder on your Mac, and the same message is moved to the same folder on the other devices and on your iCloud account; modify a contact on your Windows PC, and the changes also propagate everywhere else. In each case, the new or changed data is sent to the cloud, which then sends the data to each device, usually in a matter of seconds.

With iCloud, you never have to worry about entering the same information into all of your devices. With iCloud, you won't miss an important meeting because you forgot to enter it into the calendar on your work computer. With iCloud, you can never forget data when you're traveling because you have up-to-the-moment data with you at all times. iCloud practically organizes your life for you; all you have to do is show up.

Note If you've used e-mail, contacts, and calendars in a company that runs Microsoft Exchange Server, then you're no doubt used to push technology because Exchange has done that for a while through ActiveSync (a feature that your iPhone supports, by the way). iCloud push is a step up, however, because you don't need a behemoth corporate server to make it happen. Apple calls iCloud "Exchange for the rest of us."

Understanding iCloud Device Support

iCloud promises to simplify your online life, but the first step to that simpler existence is to configure iCloud on all the devices that you want to keep in sync. The next few sections show you how to configure iCloud on various devices, but it's important to understand exactly which devices can do the iCloud thing. Here's a summary:

- **iPhone (3GS or later), iPad, and iPod touch (3rd or 4th generation).** iCloud works with any of these devices as long as they're running version 5.0 or later of iOS.

- **Mac.** You must be running Mac OS X Lion (10.7.2) or later. To access the iCloud web applications, you need either Safari 5 or later, Firefox 5 or later, or Chrome 12 or later.

- **Windows Vista.** Any Vista version works with iCloud (as long as you've installed Service Pack 2 or later). To access the iCloud web applications, you need Internet Explorer 8 or later, Safari 5 or later, Firefox 5 or later, or Chrome 12 or later. For push e-mail, contacts, and calendars, you need Outlook 2007 or later.

- **Windows 7.** Any Windows 7 version works with iCloud. To access the iCloud web applications, you need Internet Explorer 8 or later, Safari 5 or later, Firefox 5 or later, or Chrome 12 or later. For push e-mail, contacts, and calendars, you need Outlook 2007 or later.

Configuring iCloud on Your iPhone

iCloud is designed particularly with the iPhone in mind, because it's when you're on the town or on the road that you need data pushed to you. To ensure your iPhone works seamlessly with your iCloud data, you need to add your iCloud account and configure the iCloud sync settings on your iPhone.

Setting up your iCloud account on your iPhone

Start by setting up your iCloud account on your iPhone:

1. **On the Home screen, tap Settings.** Your iPhone opens the Settings app.

2. **Tap Mail, Contacts, Calendars.** The Mail, Contacts, Calendars screen appears.

3. **Tap Add Account.** The Add Account screen appears.

4. **Tap the iCloud logo.** Your iPhone displays the iCloud screen, as shown in Figure 12.1.

5. **Tap the Apple ID text box and enter your iCloud e-mail address.**

6. **Tap the Password text box and enter your iCloud password.**

7. **Tap Next.** Your iPhone verifies the account info and then asks if you want to allow iCloud to use your location.

8. **Tap OK.** Allowing iCloud to use your location enables you to use the Find My iPhone feature, which I discuss in Chapter 1. Your iPhone displays a different iCloud screen, as shown in Figure 12.2.

9. **For each type of data you want pushed to your iPhone, tap the corresponding switch to On.**

10. **If after tapping a switch to On, your iPhone asks if you want to merge previous synced data with your iCloud data, tap Merge.**

11. **Tap Save.** Your iPhone returns you to the Mail settings screen with your iCloud account added to the Accounts list.

12.1 Use the iCloud screen to configure your iCloud account on your iPhone.

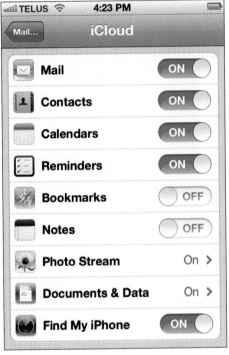

12.2 Use this iCloud screen to specify the types of data you want iCloud to push to your iPhone.

Setting up iCloud synchronization on your iPhone

No matter where you are, iCloud ensures that your e-mail messages, contacts, and calendars get pushed to your iPhone and remain fully synced with all your other devices. Your iPhone comes with this push feature turned on, but if you want to double-check this or if you want to turn off push to concentrate on something else, you can configure the setting by following these steps:

1. **In the Home Screen, tap Settings.** The Settings app appears.

2. **Tap Mail, Contacts, Calendars.** The Mail, Contacts, Calendars screen appears.

3. **Tap Fetch New Data.** Your iPhone displays the Fetch New Data screen, as shown in Figure 12.3.

12.3 Use the Fetch New Data screen to configure iCloud synchronization on your iPhone.

4. **If you want iCloud data sent to you automatically, tap the Push switch to On.** Otherwise, tap Push to Off.

5. **If you turned push off, tap the frequency with which your iPhone should fetch new data: Every 15 Minutes, Every 30 Minutes, Hourly, or Manually.**

Configuring iCloud on Your Mac

If you want to keep your Mac in sync with the iCloud push services, you need to add your iCloud account to the Mail application and configure iCloud synchronization on your Mac.

Setting up an iCloud account on your Mac

Here are the steps to follow to get your iCloud account into the Mail application:

1. **In the Dock, click the Mail icon.** The Mail application appears.

2. **Choose Mail ⇨ Preferences to open the Mail preferences.**

293

3. **Click the Accounts tab.**

4. **Click +.** Mail displays the Add Account dialog.

5. **Type your name in the Full Name text box.**

6. **Type your iCloud e-mail address in the Email Address text box.**

7. **Type your iCloud password in the Password text box.**

8. **Click Create.** Mail verifies the account info and displays the Account Summary screen.

9. **Select the check box beside each type of data you want to set up.**

10. **Click Create.** Mail returns you to the Accounts tab with the iCloud account added to the Accounts list.

Setting up iCloud synchronization on your Mac

Macs were made to sync with iCloud, so this process should be a no-brainer. To ensure that is the case, you need to configure your Mac to make sure iCloud sync is activated and that your e-mail accounts, contacts, and calendars are part of the sync process. Follow these steps to set your preferences:

1. **Click the System Preferences icon in the Dock.** Your Mac opens the System Preferences window.

2. **In the Internet & Wireless section, click the iCloud icon.** The first time you do this, your Mac prompts you to sign in to iCloud.

3. **Type your iCloud e-mail address and password, and then click Sign In.** If this is the first time you've launched the iCloud preferences, you run through a few dialogs to set your initial preferences. When that's done, you end up at the iCloud preferences window.

4. **Select the check box beside each data item you want to sync with your iCloud account, particularly the following push-related items (see Figure 12.4):**

   - **Bookmarks**
   - **Calendars**
   - **Contacts**
   - **Mail & Notes**
   - **Photo Stream**

5. **Click the Close button.** Your Mac is now ready for iCloud syncing.

12.4 Select the check box beside each item you want to sync.

Configuring iCloud on Your Windows PC

iCloud is happy to push data to your Windows PC. However, unlike with a Mac, your Windows machine wouldn't know iCloud if it tripped over it. To get Windows hip to the iCloud thing, you need to do two things:

- **Download and install the latest version of iTunes.**
- **Download and install the iCloud Control Panel for Windows, which you can find at http://support.apple.com/kb/DL1455.**

With that done, you can now configure iCloud to work with your Windows PC by following these steps:

1. **On the Windows PC that you want to configure to work with iCloud, choose Start ⇨ Control Panel to open the Control Panel window.**

2. **Double-click the iCloud icon.** If you don't see this icon, first open the Network and Internet category. The iCloud Preferences window appears.

3. **Use the Member Name text box to type your iCloud address.**

295

4. **Use the Password text box to type your iCloud password.**

5. **Click Sign In.** Windows signs in to your account and then displays the iCloud control panel, as shown in Figure 12.5.

12.5 Use the iCloud control panel to set up your Windows PC to work with iCloud.

6. **Select the check box beside each type of data you want to sync.**

7. **Click Apply.**

How Do I Fix My iPhone?

The good news about iPhone problems — whether they're problems with iPhone software or with the actual iPhone — is that they're relatively rare. On the hardware side, although the iPhone is a sophisticated device that's really a small computer (not just a fancy phone), it's far less complex than a full-blown computer, and so far less likely to go south on you. On the software side (and to a lesser extent on the accessories side), app developers (and accessory manufacturers) only have to build their products to work with a single device made by a single company. This really simplifies things, and the result is fewer problems. Not, however, zero problems. Even the iPhone sometimes behaves strangely or not at all. This chapter gives you some general troubleshooting techniques for iPhone woes and also tackles a few specific problems.

General Techniques for Troubleshooting Your iPhone

If your iPhone is behaving oddly or erratically, it's possible that a specific component inside the phone is the cause. In that case, you don't have much choice but to ship your iPhone back to Apple for repairs. Fortunately, however, most glitches are temporary and can often be fixed by using one or more of the following techniques:

- **Restart your iPhone.** By far the most common solution to an iPhone problem is to shut it down and then restart it. By rebooting the iPhone, you reload the entire system, which is often enough to solve many problems. You restart your iPhone by pressing and holding the Sleep/Wake button for a few seconds until you see the Slide to Power Off screen (at which point you can release the button). Drag the Slide to Power Off slider to the right to start the shutdown. When the screen goes completely black, your iPhone is off. To restart, press and hold the Sleep/Wake button until you see the Apple logo and then release the button.

- **Reboot your iPhone hardware.** When you restart your iPhone by pressing and holding Sleep/Wake for a while, what you're really doing is rebooting the system software. If that still doesn't solve the problem, you might need to reboot the iPhone hardware as well. To do that, press and hold down the Sleep/Wake and Home buttons. Keep them pressed until you see the Apple logo (it takes about eight seconds or so), which indicates a successful restart.

Genius

The hardware reboot is also the way to go if your iPhone is *really* stuck and holding down just the Sleep/Wake button doesn't do anything.

- **Recharge your iPhone.** It's possible that your iPhone just has a battery that's completely discharged. Connect your iPhone to your computer or to the dock. If it powers up and you see the battery logo (this might take a few seconds), then it's charging just fine and will be back on its feet in a while.

- **Shut down a stuck app.** If your iPhone is frozen because an app has gone haywire, you can usually get it back in the saddle by forcing the app to quit. Press and hold the Sleep/Wake button until you see the Slide to power off screen; then press and hold the Home button for about six seconds. Your iPhone shuts down the app and returns you to the Home screen. If an app is frozen but your iPhone still works fine otherwise, double-click the Home button to display the multitasking bar, press and hold the Home button until you see the app icons jiggling, tap the red Delete icon that appears in the upper-left corner of the stuck app's icon, and then click Home.

- **Check for iPhone software updates.** If Apple knows about the problem you're having, it will fix it and then make the patch available in a software update. I tell you how to update your iPhone a bit later in this chapter.

- **Check for app updates.** It's possible that a bug in an app is causing your woes. On the Home screen, tap App Store, and then tap Updates to see if any updates are available. If so, tap each app and tap the Update button to make it so. If you have quite a few updates ready, an easier route is to tap the Updates icon and then tap Update All to process all the updates automatically.

- **Erase and restore your content and settings.** This may seem like drastic advice, but it's possible to use iTunes to perform a complete backup of everything on your iPhone. You can then reset the iPhone to its original, pristine state, and then restore the backup. I show you how to back up your iPhone in Chapter 1, and I explain the rather lengthy restore process later in this chapter.

- **Reset your settings.** Sometimes your iPhone's settings become corrupted. In that case, you can fix the problem by restoring iPhone to its original settings. If iTunes doesn't recognize your iPhone, then the restore option is out. However, you can still reset the settings on the iPhone. Tap Settings in the Home screen, tap General, tap Reset, and then tap Reset All Settings. When your iPhone asks you to confirm, tap Reset All Settings.

Genius

If resetting your iPhone doesn't get the job done, it could be some recalcitrant bit of content that's causing the problem. In that case, tap Settings in the Home screen, tap General, tap Reset, and then tap Erase All Content and Settings. When your iPhone asks you to confirm, tap Erase iPhone.

Troubleshooting connected devices

There are only a few ways that you can connect devices to your iPhone: using the headset jack, the dock connector, or Bluetooth. Although the number of devices you can connect is relatively limited, that doesn't mean you might never have problems with those devices.

If you're having trouble with a device attached to your iPhone, the good news is that a fair chunk of those problems have a relatively limited set of causes. You may be able to get the device back on its feet by attempting a few tried-and-true remedies. If it's not immediately obvious what the problem is, then your hardware troubleshooting routine should always start with these very basic techniques:

- **Check connections, power switches, and so on.** Some of the most common (and most embarrassing) causes of hardware problems are the simple physical things, so make sure that a device is turned on and check that cable connections are secure. For example, if you can't access the Internet through the Wi-Fi connection on your iPhone, make sure your network's router is turned on. Also make sure that the cable between your router and the ISP's modem is properly connected.

- **Replace the batteries.** Wireless devices such as headsets really chew through batteries, so if such a device is working intermittently (or not at all), always try replacing the batteries to see if that solves the problem.

- **Turn the device off and then on again.** You *power cycle* a device by turning it off, waiting a few seconds for its innards to stop spinning, and then turning it back on. You'd be amazed how often this simple procedure can get a device back up and running. For a device that doesn't have an On/Off switch, try either unplugging it from the power outlet or removing and replacing the batteries.

- **Reset the device's default settings.** If you can configure a device, then perhaps some new setting is causing the problem. If you recently made a change, try returning the setting back to its original value. If that doesn't do the trick, most configurable devices have some kind of Restore Default Settings option that enables you to quickly return them to their factory settings.

- **Upgrade the device's firmware.** Some devices come with *firmware* — a small program that runs inside the device and controls its internal functions. For example, all routers have firmware. Check with the manufacturer to see if a new version exists. If it does, download the new version and then see the device's manual to learn how to upgrade the firmware.

Updating software

The iPhone software should check for available updates from time to time when you connect it to your computer, provided the computer has an Internet connection. This is another good reason to sync your iPhone regularly. The problem is, you might hear about an important update that adds a feature you're really looking forward to or perhaps fixes a gaping security hole. What do you do if iTunes isn't scheduled to check for an update for a few days?

In that case, you take matters into your own hands and check for updates yourself.

In iOS 5, you can now check for updates right on your iPhone. Here's how:

1. **On the Home screen, tap Settings.** The Settings app appears.

2. **Tap General.** Your iPhone displays the General options screen.

3. **Tap Software Update.** Your iPhone begins checking for available updates. If you see the message "Your software is up to date," then you can move on to bigger and better things.

4. **If an update is available, tap Download and Install.** Your iPhone downloads the update and then proceeds with the installation, which takes a few minutes.

Here's the iTunes route:

1. **Connect your iPhone to your computer.** iTunes opens and connects to your iPhone.

2. **Click your iPhone in the Devices list.**

3. **Click the Summary tab.**

4. **Click Check for Update.** iTunes connects to the Apple servers to see if any iPhone updates are available. If an update exists, you see the iPhone Software Update dialog, which offers a description of the update.

5. **Click Next.** iTunes displays the Software License Agreement.

6. **Click Agree.** iTunes downloads the software update and installs it.

Restoring data and settings

Sometimes your iPhone goes down for the count because its settings have become corrupted. In that case, you can attempt to fix the problem by restoring your iPhone to its original settings. The best way to go about this is to use the Restore feature in iTunes because that enables you to make a backup of your settings. However, it does mean that your iPhone must be able to connect to your computer and be visible in iTunes.

If that's not the case, see the instructions for resetting in Chapter 1. Otherwise, follow these steps to restore your iPhone:

1. **Connect your iPhone to your computer.**

2. **In iTunes, click your iPhone in the Devices list.**

3. **Click Sync.** This ensures that iTunes backs up your iPhone and has copies of all the data from your iPhone.

Caution If you have confidential or sensitive data on your iPhone, that data becomes part of the backup files and could be viewed by some snoop. To prevent this, select the Summary tab's Encrypt iPhone backup check box, and then use the Set password dialog to specify your decryption password. Then right-click your iPhone in the Devices list and click Back Up.

4. **Click the Summary tab.**

5. **Click Restore.** iTunes asks you to confirm you want to restore.

6. **Click Restore.** iTunes downloads the software and restores the original software and settings. When your iPhone restarts, iTunes connects to it and displays the Set Up Your iPhone screen, as shown in Figure 13.1.

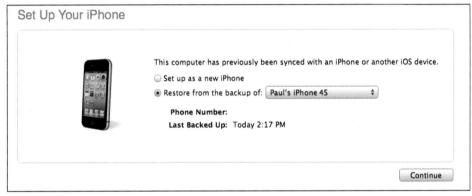

13.1 When your factory-fresh iPhone restarts, use iTunes to restore your settings and data.

7. **Select the Restore from the backup of option.**

8. **If you happen to have more than one iPhone backed up, use the list to choose yours.**

9. **Click Continue.** iTunes restores your backed-up data, restarts your iPhone, and syncs it.

10. **Go through the tabs and check the sync settings to make sure they're set up the way you want.**

11. **If you made any changes to the settings, click Apply.** Doing this ensures that your iPhone has all of its data restored.

Putting your iPhone in Device Firmware Upgrade mode

In some rare cases, your iPhone goes utterly haywire, where not only does iTunes not recognize the device, but even completely resetting it doesn't solve the problem. (This sort of scenario occurs most often if you've tried something naughty, such as jailbreaking your iPhone.) If this happens, you can still recover everything, but you have to do it using a special hardware mode called Device Firmware Upgrade (DFU). This mode essentially bypasses the current OS installed on the phone (which is good because in this scenario your current OS is toast) and tells iTunes to install a factory-fresh version of the OS. You can then restore your stuff as described in the previous section.

Follow these steps to put your iPhone into DFU mode:

1. **Turn off your iPhone.**

2. **Connect your iPhone to your Mac or Windows PC.**

3. **Launch iTunes.**

4. **Press and hold down the Sleep/Wake and Home buttons for exactly ten seconds.**

5. **After ten seconds, release the Sleep/Wake button, but continue to hold down the Home button for another ten seconds.**

6. **After ten seconds, release the Home button.** iTunes now recognizes your iPhone and displays the dialog shown in Figure 13.2.

7. **Click OK.**

8. **Click Restore.** iTunes asks you to confirm, as shown in Figure 13.3.

9. **Click Restore and Update.** iTunes restores your iPhone to the factory state.

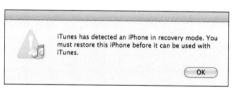

13.2 When you boot your iPhone in DFU mode, iTunes recognizes the phone and displays this dialog to remind you to restore it.

13.3 iTunes asks you to confirm that you want to revert to the iPhone factory settings.

Genius

If you need to exit DFU mode before restoring your iPhone, hold down the Sleep/ Wake and Home buttons for ten seconds. If that doesn't work for some reason, or if you find your iPhone is stuck in DFU mode, then you need to download and install a program called QuickPwn from blog.iphone-dev.org. Disconnect your iPhone, run QuickPwn, and wait until it prompts you to connect. Connect your phone and then follow the instructions that QuickPwn provides.

Taking Care of the iPhone Battery

Your iPhone comes with a large lithium-ion battery. Apple claims that the iPhone 4S gives you up to 200 hours of standby time, eight hours of talk time on a 3G network (14 hours on an EDGE network), 6 hours of Internet use on a 3G connection (9 hours using Wi-Fi), 40 hours of audio playback, and 10 hours of video playback. Those are all impressive times, although you should count on getting less in the real world.

The biggest downside to the iPhone battery is that it's not, in Apple parlance, *user-installable*. If your battery dies, you have no choice but to return it to Apple to get it replaced. This is all the more reason to take care of your battery and try to maximize its life.

Tracking battery use

Your iPhone doesn't give a ton of battery data, but you can monitor both the total usage time (this includes all activities: calling, surfing, playing media, and so on) and standby time (time when your iPhone was in Sleep mode). Here's how:

1. **On the Home screen, tap Settings.** The Settings app appears.

2. **Tap General.** Your iPhone displays the General options screen.

3. **Tap Usage.** Your iPhone displays the Usage screen.

4. **Tap the Battery Percentage switch to On.** Your iPhone shows you the percentage of battery life left in the status bar beside the Battery icon, as shown in Figure 13.4.

13.4 In the iPhone Usage screen, turn on the Battery Percentage option to monitor battery life in the iPhone status bar.

Note

If you don't want to clutter the status bar with the battery percentage, you can examine the Usage and Standby values that appear in the Usage screen instead. As your battery runs down, check the Usage screen periodically to get a sense of your iPhone battery use.

Tips for extending battery life

Reducing battery consumption as much as possible on the iPhone not only extends the time between charges but also extends the overall life of your battery. Here are a few suggestions:

- **Dim the screen.** The touchscreen drains a lot of battery power, so dimming it reduces the amount of power used. On the Home screen, tap Settings, tap Brightness, and then drag the slider to the left to dim the screen.

- **Cycle the battery.** All lithium-based batteries slowly lose their charging capacity over time. If you can run your iPhone on batteries for four hours today, later on you'll only be able to run it for three hours on a full charge. You can't stop this process, but you can delay it significantly by periodically cycling the iPhone battery. *Cycling* — also called *reconditioning* or *recalibrating* — a battery means letting it completely discharge and then fully recharging it again. To maintain optimal performance, you should cycle your iPhone battery every one or two months.

Note

Paradoxically, the less you use your iPhone, the *more* often you should cycle its battery. If you often go several days or a week or two (I can't imagine!) without using your iPhone, then you should cycle its battery at least once a month.

- **Slow the auto-check on your e-mail.** Having your e-mail frequently poll the server for new messages eats up your battery. Set it to check every hour, or, ideally, set it to Manual check if you can. To do this, tap Settings; tap Mail, Contacts, Calendars; tap Fetch New Data; and then tap either Hourly or Manual.

Sending in Your iPhone for Repairs

To have your iPhone repaired, you can either take it to an Apple Store or send it in. Visit www.apple.com/support and follow the prompts to find out how to send in your iPhone for repairs. Remember that the memory comes back wiped, so be sure to sync with iTunes, if you can. Also, don't forget to remove your SIM card before you send it in.

Turn off push. If you have an iCloud account, consider turning off the push feature to save battery power. Tap Settings; tap Mail, Contacts, Calendars; and then tap Fetch New Data. In the Fetch New Data screen, tap the Push switch to Off and tap Manually in the Fetch section (see Figure 13.5).

Minimize your tasks. If you won't be able to charge your iPhone for a while, avoid background chores, such as playing music, or secondary chores, such as organizing your contacts. If your only goal is to read all your e-mail, stick to that until it's done because you don't know how much time you have.

Put your iPhone into Sleep mode by hand, if necessary. If you are interrupted — for example, the pizza delivery guy shows up on time — don't wait for your iPhone to put itself to sleep

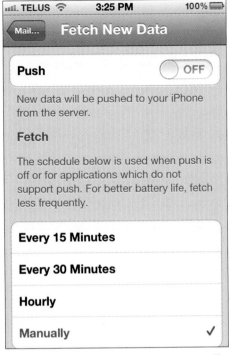

13.5 You can save battery power by turning off the push feature on your iPhone.

because those few minutes use precious battery time. Instead, put your iPhone to sleep manually right away by pressing the Sleep/Wake button.

Avoid temperature extremes. Exposing your iPhone to extremely hot or cold temperatures reduces the long-term effectiveness of the battery. Try to keep your iPhone at a reasonable temperature.

Turn off Wi-Fi if you don't need it. When Wi-Fi is on, it regularly checks for available wireless networks, which drains the battery. If you don't need to connect to a wireless network, turn off Wi-Fi to conserve energy. Tap Settings, tap Wi-Fi, and then tap the Wi-Fi switch to Off.

Turn off 3G if you don't need it. Your iPhone constantly looks for nearby cellular towers to maintain the signal, which can use up battery power in a hurry. If you're surfing on a Wi-Fi network, you don't need 3G, so turn it off. Tap Settings, tap General, tap Network, and then tap the Enable 3G switch to Off.

- **Turn off GPS if you don't need it.** When GPS is on, the receiver exchanges data with the GPS system regularly, which uses up battery power. If you don't need the GPS feature for the time being, turn off the GPS antenna. Tap Settings, tap Location Services, and then tap the Location Services switch to Off.

- **Turn off Bluetooth if you don't need it.** When Bluetooth is running, it constantly checks for nearby Bluetooth devices, and this drains the battery. If you aren't using any Bluetooth devices, turn off Bluetooth to save energy. Tap Settings, tap General, tap Bluetooth, and then tap the Bluetooth switch to Off.

Genius

If you don't need all four of the iPhone antennae for a while, a faster way to turn them off is to switch your iPhone to Airplane mode. Tap Settings and then tap the Airplane Mode switch to On.

Solving Specific Problems

The generic troubleshooting and repair techniques that you've seen so far can solve all kinds of problems. However, there are always specific problems that require specific solutions. The rest of this chapter takes you through a few of the most common of these problems.

Your battery won't charge

If you find that your battery won't charge, here are some possible solutions:

- **If the iPhone is plugged into a computer to charge via the USB port, it may be that the computer has gone into standby.** Waking the computer should solve the problem.

- **The USB port might not be transferring enough power.** For example, the USB ports on most keyboards don't offer much in the way of power. If you have your iPhone plugged into a keyboard USB port, plug it into a USB port on the computer.

- **Attach the USB cable to the USB power adapter, and then plug the adapter into an AC outlet.**

- **Double-check all connections to make sure everything is plugged in properly.**

- **Try an iPod cord if you have one.**

If you can't seem to locate the problem after these steps, you may need to send your iPhone in for service.

You have trouble accessing a Wi-Fi network

Wireless networking adds a whole new set of potential snags to your troubleshooting chores because of problems such as interference and device ranges. Here's a list of a few troubleshooting items that you should check to solve any wireless connectivity problems you're having with your iPhone:

- **Make sure the Wi-Fi antenna is on.** Tap Settings, tap Wi-Fi, and then tap the Wi-Fi switch to On.

- **Make sure the iPhone isn't in Airplane mode.** Tap Settings and then tap the Airplane Mode switch to Off.

- **Check the connection.** The iPhone has a tendency to disconnect from a nearby Wi-Fi network for no apparent reason. Tap Settings. If the Wi-Fi setting shows as Not Connected, tap Wi-Fi, and then tap your network in the list.

- **Renew the lease.** When you connect to a Wi-Fi network, the access point gives your iPhone a Dynamic Host Control Protocol (DHCP) lease that allows it to access the network. You can often solve connectivity problems by renewing that lease. Tap Settings, tap Wi-Fi, and then tap the blue More Info icon to the right of the connected Wi-Fi network. Tap the DHCP tab and then tap the Renew Lease button, shown in Figure 13.6.

- **Reconnect to the network.** You can often solve Wi-Fi network woes by disconnecting from the network and then reconnecting. Tap Settings, tap Wi-Fi, and then tap the blue More Info icon to the right of the connected Wi-Fi network. Tap the Forget this Network button to disconnect, and then reconnect to the same network.

13.6 Open the connected Wi-Fi network settings, and then tap Renew Lease to get a fresh lease on your Wi-Fi life.

- **Reset the network settings on your iPhone.** This removes all stored network data and resets everything to the factory state, which might solve the problem. Tap Settings, tap General, tap Reset, and then tap Reset Network Settings. When your iPhone asks you to confirm, tap Reset Network Settings.

- **Reboot and power cycle devices.** Reset your hardware by performing the following tasks, in order: restart your iPhone, reboot your iPhone hardware, power cycle the wireless access point, and power cycle the broadband modem.

- **Look for interference.** Devices such as baby monitors and cordless phones that use the 2.4 GHz radio frequency (RF) band can play havoc with wireless signals. Try either moving or turning off such devices if they're near your iPhone or wireless access point.

- **Check your range.** If you're getting no signal or a weak signal, your iPhone could be too far away from the access point. You usually can't get much farther than about 115 feet away from an access point before the signal begins to degrade. Either move closer to the access point or, if it has one, turn on the access point's range booster. You could also install a wireless range extender.

- **Update the wireless access point firmware.** The wireless access point firmware is the internal program that the access point uses to perform its various chores. Wireless access point manufacturers frequently update their firmware to fix bugs, so you should see if an updated version of the firmware is available. See your device documentation to learn how this works.

- **Reset the router.** As a last resort, reset the router to its default factory settings (see the device documentation to learn how to do this). Note that if you do this, you need to set up your network from scratch.

Caution You should keep your iPhone and wireless access point well away from microwave ovens, which can jam wireless signals.

iTunes doesn't see your iPhone

When you connect your iPhone to your computer, iTunes should start and you should see the iPhone in the Devices list. If iTunes doesn't start when you connect your iPhone, or if iTunes is already running but the iPhone doesn't appear in the Devices list, it means that iTunes doesn't recognize your iPhone. Here are some possible fixes:

- **Check the connections.** Make sure the USB connector and the dock connector are fully seated.

- **Try a different USB port.** The port you're using might not work, so try another one. If you're using a port on a USB hub, try using one of the computer's built-in USB ports.

- **Restart your iPhone.** Press and hold the Sleep/Wake button for a few seconds until the iPhone shuts down. Press and hold Sleep/Wake again until you see the Apple logo.

- **Restart your computer.** Doing this should reset the computer's USB ports, which might solve the problem.

- **Check your iTunes version.** You need at least iTunes version 10.5 to work with iOS 5.0.

- **Check your operating system version.** On a Mac, your iPhone requires OS X 10.5.8 or later. On a Windows PC, your iPhone requires Windows 7, Windows Vista, or Windows XP Service Pack 2 or later.

iTunes won't sync your iPhone

If iTunes sees your iPhone, but you can't get it to sync, you probably have to adjust some settings. See Chapter 6 for some troubleshooting ideas related to syncing. Another possibility is that your iPhone is currently locked. That's not usually a problem for iTunes, but it sometimes gets confused by a locked iPhone. The easy remedy is to unplug the iPhone, unlock it, and then plug it in again.

You have trouble syncing music or videos

You may run into a problem syncing your music or videos to your iPhone. The most likely culprit here is that your files are in a format that the iPhone can't read, such as WMA, MPEG-1, or MPEG-2. First, convert the files to a format that the iPhone does understand using converter software. Then put them back on iTunes and try to sync again. This should solve the problem.

iPhone-supported audio formats include AAC, Protected AAC, HE-AAC, MP3, Audible (formats 2, 3, and 4, Audible Enhanced Audio, AAX, and AAX+), Apple Lossless, AIFF, and WAV. iPhone-supported video formats include H.264, MPEG-4, and Motion JPEG.

You can't get your iPhone serial number

There are times when you might need the serial number of your iPhone. For example, if you contact Apple support, it asks you for your iPhone serial number.

Under normal circumstances, you follow these steps to get the serial number:

1. **Connect your iPhone to your computer.**

2. **In iTunes, click the iPhone in the Devices list.**

3. **Click the Summary tab.**

4. **Read the serial number, as shown in Figure 13.7.**

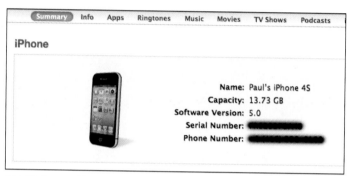

13.7 With your iPhone connected to your computer, use the Summary tab to get your serial number.

If iTunes doesn't recognize your iPhone, you may still be able to get the serial number by following these steps:

1. **Connect your iPhone to your computer.**

2. **In iTunes, choose iTunes ⇨ Preferences.** The iTunes preferences appear.

3. **Click the Devices tab.**

4. **Hover the mouse over a backup of your iPhone.** As you can see in Figure 13.8, iTunes displays a message that includes the phone's serial number.

If you can't boot your phone, if iTunes doesn't recognize your iPhone, or if you don't have a backup of your iPhone, you can still get the serial number. Shut down your iPhone, remove the SIM card tray, and then read the serial number that's printed on the side of the SIM tray.

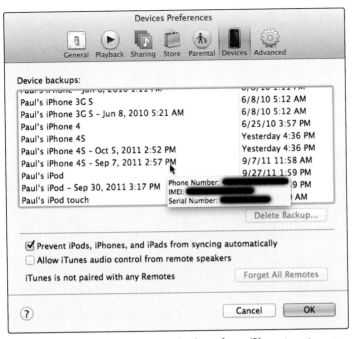

13.8 Hover the mouse pointer over a backup of your iPhone to get your serial number.

An app is taking up a large amount of space

The iPhone is so useful and so much fun, it's easy to forget that it has limitations, especially when it comes to storage. This is particularly true if you have a 16GB model, but even a big 64GB iPhone can fill up in a hurry if you stuff it with movies, TV shows, and tons of magazine subscriptions.

You can tell how much free space your iPhone has left either by connecting it to iTunes or by tapping Settings, then General, and then Usage. In iOS 5, the Usage screen not only shows you how much storage space you have available but also how much space each app is using, as shown in Figure 13.9.

If you see that your iPhone is running low on space, check the apps to see if any of them are taking up more than their fair share of hard drive real estate. If you see a hard drive hog, you have two ways to delete its data and give your iPhone some room to breathe:

- **Third-party apps.** For an app you picked up via the App Store, tap the app, tap Delete App, and then tap Delete App when your iPhone asks you to confirm.

- **Built-in apps.** For an app that came with your iPhone (such as Music or Video), tap the app to display a list of the data it's storing on your iPhone, and then tap Edit. This puts the list in Edit mode, as shown in Figure 13.10. To remove an item, tap the red Delete button to the left of the item, and then tap the Delete button that appears.

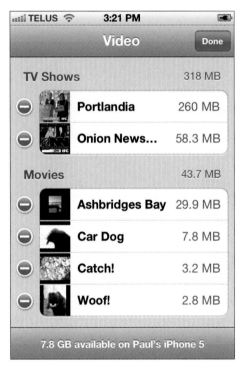

13.9 In iOS 5, the Usage screen tells you how much storage space remains on your iPhone, and how much space each app is taking up.

13.10 In iOS 5, you can free up storage space by deleting individual items from some of the built-in apps.

Glossary

3G A third-generation cellular network that's faster than the old EDGE network and enables you to make calls while also accessing the Internet.

802.11 See *Wi-Fi*.

accelerometer The component inside the iPhone that senses the phone's orientation in space and adjusts the display accordingly (such as switching Safari from portrait view to landscape view).

access point A networking device that enables two or more devices to connect over a Wi-Fi network and to access a shared Internet connection.

ad hoc wireless network A wireless network that doesn't use an access point.

Airplane mode An operational mode that turns off the transceivers for the phone, Wi-Fi, and Bluetooth features of an iPhone, which puts the phone in compliance with federal aviation regulations.

AirPlay A wireless technology that enables you to stream iPhone video or audio to an Apple TV device and to see or hear that media on your TV or audio receiver.

AirPrint A wireless technology that enables you to send a web page, e-mail message, or other text from your iPhone to a printer.

alert A notification message that pops up on your iPhone screen and must be dealt with before you can resume what you were doing.

app An application that is designed for and runs on a specific device (such as an iPhone) or a set of related devices (such as an iPhone, iPad, and iPod touch).

authentication See *SMTP authentication*.

Auto-Capitalization A keyboard feature that automatically activates the Shift key after you tap a sentence-ending character such as a period or question mark.

Auto-Correction A keyboard feature that automatically corrects errors as you type.

badge A small red icon that appears in the upper-right corner of an app's icon to let you know that some new activity or data awaits you on the app.

banner A notification message that appears at the top of the iPhone screen but lets you keep working.

Bluetooth A wireless networking technology that enables you to exchange data between two devices using radio frequencies when the devices are within range of each other (usually within about 33 feet/10 meters).

bookmark An Internet site saved in Safari so that you can access it quickly in future browsing sessions.

cache An area of memory where Safari stores web page text and images for faster loading when you revisit the page.

cloud The collection of networked servers that store your iCloud data and push any new data to your iPhone, Mac, or Windows PC.

crop To remove unneeded or distracting elements from a photo.

cycling Letting the iPhone battery completely discharge and then fully recharging it again.

data roaming A cell phone feature that enables you to make calls and perform other activities, such as checking for e-mail, when you're outside of your provider's normal coverage area.

digital rights management Technology that restricts the usage of content to prevent piracy.

discoverable A term to describe a device that has its Bluetooth feature turned on so that other Bluetooth devices can connect to it.

double-tap To use a fingertip to quickly press and release the iPhone screen twice.

DRM See *digital rights management.*

EDGE (Enhanced Data rates for GSM [Global System for Mobile communication] Evolution) A cellular network that's older and slower than 3G, although still supported by the iPhone.

event An appointment or meeting that you've scheduled in your iPhone Calendar.

flick To quickly and briefly drag a finger across the iPhone screen.

FM transmitter A device that sends the output of an iPhone to an FM radio frequency, which you then play through your car stereo.

geo-fence A virtual, GPS-based perimeter around a location that, when crossed by your iPhone, can be used to trigger a reminder.

GPS (Global Positioning System) A satellite-based navigation system that uses wireless signals from a GPS receiver — such as the one in the iPhone — to accurately determine the receiver's current position.

group A collection of Address Book contacts.

headset A combination of headphones for listening and a microphone for talking.

Home screen The main screen on your iPhone, which you access by pressing the Home button.

Home Sharing An iTunes feature that enables you to share the iTunes library on your Mac or PC with your iPhone.

IMAP (Internet Message Access Protocol) A type of e-mail account where incoming messages, as well as copies of messages you send, remain on the server.

Internet tethering See *tethering*.

keychain A list of saved passwords on a Mac.

location services The features and technologies that provide apps and system tools with access to location data.

magnetometer A device that measures the direction and intensity of a magnetic field.

memory effect The process where a battery loses capacity over time if you repeatedly recharge it without first fully discharging it.

mirroring Displaying your iPhone screen on your TV.

multitouch A touchscreen technology that can detect and interpret two or more simultaneous touches, such as two-finger taps, spreads, and pinches.

notification Data that an app sends to let you know that the app has had recent activity for you to check out.

pair To connect one Bluetooth device with another by entering a passkey.

pan To slide a photo or other image up, down, left, or right.

passcode A four-digit code used to secure or lock an iPhone.

personal hotspot An iPhone that is used as a kind of Internet gateway device where you share the iPhone's Internet connection with one or more other devices, either directly via a USB cable or wirelessly via Wi-Fi or Bluetooth.

pinch To move two fingers closer together on the iPhone screen. See also *spread*.

playlist A collection of songs that you create using iTunes.

POP (Post Office Protocol) A type of e-mail account where incoming messages are stored temporarily on the provider's mail server until you connect to the server. The messages are then downloaded to your iPhone and removed from the server. See also *IMAP*.

power cycle To turn a device off, wait a few seconds for its inner components to stop spinning, and then turn it on again.

preferences The options, settings, and other data that you've configured for your Mac via System Preferences.

private browsing A web-browsing mode where Safari doesn't add sites to the History list, doesn't store site data in the cache, and doesn't save searches and passwords.

push To send data immediately without being prompted.

Reader A Safari feature that removes ads and other distractions from a web page.

ringtone A sound that plays when an incoming call is received.

RSS feed A special file that contains the most recent information added to a website.

side switch The sliding switch that appears on the side of your iPhone, beside the volume rockers.

silent mode An operational state where the iPhone plays no sounds except alerts set with the Clock application.

slide To drag a finger across the iPhone screen.

smartphone A cell phone that also performs other tasks, such as accessing the Internet, and managing contacts and appointments.

SMTP (Simple Mail Transport Protocol) The set of protocols that determines how e-mail messages are addressed and sent.

SMTP authentication The requirement that you must log on to a provider's SMTP server to confirm that you're the person sending an e-mail.

SMTP server The server that an Internet service provider uses to process outgoing e-mail messages.

spread To move two fingers apart on the iPhone screen. See also *pinch.*

SSID (Service Set Identifier) The name that identifies a network to Wi-Fi devices.

synchronization A process that ensures that data on your computer (such as contacts, e-mail accounts, and events) is the same as the data on your iPhone.

tap To use a fingertip to quickly press and release the iPhone screen.

tethering On a device such as an iPad, Mac, or Windows PC, using an iPhone's Internet connection when the iPhone is configured as a *personal hotspot.*

text shortcut A short sequence of characters that represents a longer phrase.

touchscreen A screen that responds to touches, such as finger taps and finger slides.

transceiver A device that transmits and receives wireless signals.

trim To edit the start and end points of a video recording or voice memo.

two-fingered tap To use two fingertips to quickly press and release the iPhone screen.

user-installable A component that an end user can remove and replace.

vCard A file that contains a person's contact information.

wallpaper The background image you see when you unlock your iPhone.

web clip A Home screen icon that serves as a link to a web page and preserves the scroll position and zoom level on that page.

Wi-Fi A wireless networking standard that enables wireless devices to transmit data and communicate with other devices using radio frequency signals beamed from one device to another.

Index

The Genius is in.

When you go online, you take your life along with you, of course, so your online world becomes a natural extension of your real world. However, just because it's online doesn't mean the digital version of your life is any less busy, chaotic, or complex than the rest of your life. The Apple iCloud service is designed to ease some of that chaos and complexity by automatically syncing your most important data — your e-mail, contacts, calendars, and bookmarks. Although the syncing may be automatic, setting up is not, unfortunately. This chapter shows you what to do.